THE CHARLTON STANDARD CATALOGUE OF

ROYAL DOULTON BESWICK STORYBOOK FIGURINES

FIFTH EDITION

BY
JEAN DALE

INTRODUCTION
BY
LOUISE IRVINE

W. K. CROSS
PUBLISHER

The Charlton Press

TORONTO, ONTARIO BIRMINGHAM, MICHIGAN

Canadian Cataloguing In Publication Data

The Charlton price guide to Royal Doulton and Beswick storybook figurines

Annual.

1994-

Issues for 1995-   have title: Charlton price guide to Royal Doulton Beswick storybook figurines.

Cover title: Charlton standard catalogue of Royal Doulton Beswick storybook figurines, 1995-   .

ISSN 1198-1652

ISBN 0-88968-215-1 (1999)

1. Porcelain animals - Catalogs. 2. Royal Doulton figurines - Catalogs. I. Charlton Press. II. Title: Royal Doulton Beswick storybook figurines. III. Title: Charlton price guide to Royal Doulton Beswick storybook figurines. IV. Title: Royal Doulton and Beswick storybook figures. V. Title: Charlton standard catalogue of Royal Doulton Beswick storybook figurines, 1995-   .

NK4660.C5   738.820294   C94-900402-2

EDITORIAL

Editor	Jean Dale
Graphic Technician	Davina Rowan
Graphic Technician	Alan Ho
Photography	Marilyn and Peter Sweet

ACKNOWLEDGEMENTS

The Charlton Press wishes to thank those who have helped with the fifth edition of *The Charlton Standard Catalogue of Royal Doulton Beswick Storybook Figurines*.

Special Thanks

The publisher would like to thank Louise Irvine for writing the introduction to this edition. Louise is an independent writer and lecturer on Royal Doulton's history and products and is not connected with the pricing in this price guide.

We would also like to thank Carolyn Baker for all the work on the Beatrix Potter series, both for this edition and previous editions.

Our thanks also go to the staff of Royal Doulton (U.K.) Limited, who have helped with additional technical information, especially Valerie Baynton, Lisa Hale, Julie McKeown, Maria Murtagh, Gill Walters, Ian Howe of the Royal Doulton Visitor Centre, and Josie Hunt of Lawleys By Post.

Contributors to the Fifth Edition

The publisher would also like to thank the following individuals and companies who graciously supplied photographs or information or allowed us access to their collections for photographic purposes: **Chris Back**, Backstamp Collectables, Cambridgeshire, England; **George and Nora Bagnall**, Precious Memories, Charlottetown, P.E.I.; **John and Diana Callow**, England; **Frank Corley**, Alexandria, VA; **William T. Cross**, William Cross Antiques and Collectibles, Burnaby, B.C.; **Louise Fundenberg**, Newport Beach, California; **William Haight**, Sarnia, Ontario; **Suzanne Morgan**, Evesham, England; **Roland Matthews**, Surrey, England; **Ed Pascoe**, Pascoe & Company, Florida; **Jamie Pole**, Seaway China, Michigan; **Andrew Reid**, By Dollar, Scotland; **Carol Scott**, Lakefield Marketing Limited, Cumbria, England; **Leah Selig**, Merrylands, Australia; **Marilyn and Peter Sweet**, Bolton, England; **Gene Truitt**, Tru-Find Collectibles, Virgina; **Nick Tzimas**, U. K. International Ceramics, Suffolk, England; **Stan Worrey**, Colonial House, Berea, Ohio.

A SPECIAL NOTE TO COLLECTORS

We welcome and appreciate any comments or suggestions in regard to *The Charlton Standard Catalogue of Royal Doulton Beswick Storybook Figurines*. If any errors or omissions come to your attention, please write to us, or if you would like to participate in pricing or supply previously unavailable data or information, please contact Jean Dale at (416) 488-1418, or e-mail us at chpress@charltonpress.com.

Printed in Canada
in the Province of Ontario

The Charlton Press

Editorial Office
2040 Yonge Street, Suite 208, Toronto, Canada. M4S 1Z9
Telephone (416) 488-1418 Fax: (416) 488-4656
Telephone (800) 442-6042 Fax: (800) 442-1542
www.charltonpress.com e-mail: chpress@charltonpress.com

Royal Doulton

St. Tiggywinkles
THE WILDLIFE HOSPITAL TRUST

HOW TO USE THIS PRICE GUIDE

THE PURPOSE

The fifth edition of this price guide covers the complete range of children's figures issued by Royal Doulton and Beswick with the exception of the Bunnykins figurines which are included in *The Charlton Standard Catalogue of Royal Doulton Bunnykins*, First Edition. In the process we have taken liberties with the name of this catalogue, for all figures listed are certainly not derived from storybook characters. However, the great majority are, and thus we have carried the name forward.

As with the other catalogues in Charlton's Royal Doulton reference and pricing library, this publication has been designed to serve two specific purposes. First, to furnish the collector with accurate and detailed listings that provide the essential information needed to build a rewarding collection. Second, to provide collectors and dealers with current market prices for Royal Doulton and Beswick storybook figures.

STYLES AND VERSIONS

STYLES: A change in style occurs when a major element of the design is altered or modified as a result of a deliberate mould change. An example of this is *The Duchess With Flowers* (style one) and *The Duchess With a Pie* (style two).

VERSIONS: Versions are modifications in a minor style element, such as the long ears becoming short ears on *Mr. Benjamin Bunny*.

VARIATIONS: A change in colour is a variation; for example, *Mr. Jeremy Fisher's* change in colourways from spotted to striped leggings.

THE LISTINGS

The Beatrix Potter figures are arranged alphabetically. At the beginning of the Beatrix Potter listings are five pages graphically outlining backstamp variations. Backstamps are illustrated for eleven major varieties covering over fifty years of production. In the Beatrix Potter pricing charts, the reader will see Beswick and Doulton model numbers, backstamp numbers and market prices.

The Brambly Hedge figures are listed by their DBH numbers. There are no backstamp variations known.

The Snowman series is listed in numerical order by the DS numbers. There are no backstamp variations.

All of the above listings include the modeller, where known, the name of the animal figure, designer, height, colour, date of issue, varieties and series.

A WORD ON PRICING

The purpose of this catalogue is to give readers the most accurate, up-to-date retail prices for Royal Doulton and Beswick figurines in the United States, Canada, the United Kingdom and Australia.

To accomplish this, The Charlton Press continues to access an international pricing panel of experts who submit prices based on both dealer and collector retail-price activity, as well as current auction results in the U.S.A., Canada, and the U.K. These market prices are carefully averaged to reflect accurate valuations for figures in each of these markets.

The prices published herein are for figurines in mint condition. Collectors are cautioned that a repaired or restored piece may be worth as little as 25 percent of the value of the same figure in mint condition.

Current figurines are priced according to the manufacturer's suggested retail price in each of the market regions. Please be aware that price or promotional sales discounting is always possible and can result in lower prices than those listed.

One exception, however, occurs in the case of current figurines or recent limited editions issued in only one of the three markets. Since such items were priced by Doulton only in the country in which they were to be sold, prices for the other markets are not shown.

A further word on pricing. As mentioned previously, this is a catalogue giving prices for figurines in the currency of a particular market (U.S. dollars for the American market and sterling for the U.K. market). The bulk of the prices given herein are not determined by currency exchange calculations, but by actual market activity in the market concerned.

In some cases the number of models produced is so small that market activity does not exist and there is very little activity on which to base a price. An example of this is the *Mr. Toadflax* (tail in front) from Brambly Hedge. The price in this instance is purely between the buyer and the seller. We have therefore listed the last known auction price for this model. If this model was to be offered for sale at a future date the price may be higher or lower than the auction price listed depending on the demand for the model at that time.

When prices are italicized in the pricing tables, for example, for *Duchess*, this signifies that the price is only an indication. The prices are too volatile to establish a solid market price. Once again, the final price determination must be made between buyer and seller.

THE INTERNET AND PRICING

The internet is changing the way business is done in the collectable market. It links millions of collectors around the world to one another, allowing communication to flow freely between them. Chat rooms, antique and collector malls, internet auctions and producer web sites, all promote the new e-commerce.

Three major effects that e-commerce will have on the collectable market are:

1. Collectors will deal with collectors. They will also continue with their customer/dealer relationship, but the dealer's margin will come under pressure.

2. The information of new issues, new finds, and new varieties will spread faster, the bad news will spread even faster. Collectors' wants will be made known instantaneously to a wide universe of dealers and collectors.

3. Prices will be impacted on two fronts:

   a) Price differentials will disappear between global market areas as collectors and the delivery services teamup to stretch the purchasing power of the collectable dollar /pound.

   b) As margins come under pressure, overheads being low in virtual operations, prices of the common to scarce collectable itmes will adjust downward to compensate. The rare and extremely rare items will move up as a result of their increased exposure.

YEAR CYPHERS

Figurines from the 101 Dalmatians, Snow White and the Seven Dwarfs and the Winnie the Pooh series will now carry the year cypher.

The cypher for 1998 was an umbrella and the cypher for 1999 is the Top Hat as worn by Sir Henry Doulton.

A folded umbrella
the 1998 cypher

The Top Hat as worn by
Sir Henry Doulton
the 1999 cypher

CONTENTS

Benjamin, The Beswick Bear
Compton & Woodhouse

INTRODUCTION
By Louise Irvine

THE HISTORY OF STORYBOOK CHARACTERS FROM THE ROYAL DOULTON, JOHN BESWICK AND ROYAL ALBERT STUDIOS

For over a century, the Royal Doulton Studios have entertained us with storybook characters, particularly animals endowed with human personalities. In Victorian times, a group of frogs enacting a well-known fable raised a smile in much the same way as the antics of the BRAMBLY HEDGE™ mice amuse us today. The tales of BEATRIX POTTER™, with lots of different animals acting and conversing as if they were human, are as popular now as when they were first written in the early 1900s. Obviously the idea of a creature simultaneously human and animal is deep rooted in our literary culture, and it is interesting to trace when it first became apparent in the Doulton world.

A Tinworth mouse group

The Doulton factory was founded in London in 1815, but for the first 50 years production was confined to practical pottery. In the late 1860s, Sir Henry Doulton established an art studio, employing students from the Lambeth School of Art to decorate vases, jugs and plaques in fashionable Victorian styles. Some artists specialised in figurative sculpture, notably George Tinworth, who was the first to seek inspiration from well-known stories. The Bible provided him with most of his subject matter, but he also enjoyed reading the

fables of Aesop and La Fontaine. These moralistic tales feature foxes, mice, lions and other creatures exemplifying human traits, and they fascinated the Victorians, particularly after the publication of Darwin's theory of evolution. Tinworth modelled several fables groups in the 1880s, including *The Fox and the Ape, The Cat and the Cheese* and *The Ox and the Frogs*. Later he produced mice and frog subjects, based on his own observations of human nature, which reflect his perceptive sense of humour.

The potential for dressed-up animals to disguise a deeper message soon led to their widespread use in children's literature, notably *Alice's Adventures in Wonderland* and Lear's nonsense poems. In 1908, Kenneth Grahame wrote *The Wind in the Willows* to comment on the behaviour of the English aristocracy, but the exciting adventures of Mr. Toad subtly conceal the author's critical stance. The dapper toad in his pinstripes and tails was modelled shortly afterwards by Lambeth artist Francis Pope, and a companion piece shows Mr. Toad disguised as a washerwoman in order to escape from prison.

Mr. Toad disguised as a washerwoman

Figures like these probably encouraged Beatrix Potter to approach the Lambeth studio in 1908 with a view to having her own animal characters immortalised in ceramic. Miss Potter published several illustrated stories about her favourite animals after the success of *The Tale of Peter Rabbit™* in 1902, and some characters had already appeared as cuddly toys and decorative motifs on clothes, etc. Unfortunately an earlier contract with a German china firm made any arrangement with Doulton impossible, but she tried on a later occasion to have figures made of her characters at Grimwade's factory in Stoke-on-Trent. They suggested that Doulton's other factory in Burslem would be the best place to have the figures decorated, but again plans fell through. It was not until after Miss Potter's death that her dream was realised when the John Beswick factory in Longton began making little figures inspired by her books.

The John Beswick factory was founded in 1894 to produce ornamental jugs, vases and other decorative fancies. By the 1940s the Beswick artists had established a reputation for quality animal modelling, particularly portraits of famous horses by Arthur Gredington. In 1947, Gredington demonstrated his versatility when he modelled *Jemima Puddleduck* at the suggestion of Lucy Beswick, the wife of the managing director. She had been inspired by a visit to Beatrix Potter's Lake District home, where many of the tales are set. The success of this first study led to an initial collection of ten Beatrix Potter characters, including *Peter Rabbit, Benjamin Bunny* and *Mrs. Tiggy-Winkle.*

A group of Beatrix Potter books with the figures beside

Launched in 1948, the new Beatrix Potter figures were welcomed with enthusiasm, and it was not long before Gredington was at work on another collection of character animals, this time from a British animated film. The *Lion* cartoon by David Hand was released in 1948, and *Zimmy Lion* became a new star for the Rank Film Organisation. Sequel cartoons introduced *Ginger Nutt, Hazel Nutt, Dinkum Platypus, Loopy Hare, Oscar Ostrich, Dusty Mole* and *Felia Cat,* all of which were modelled in 1949 as the *DAVID HAND'S ANIMALAND*™ series. David Hand had formerly worked for the Walt Disney studios, directing Mickey Mouse shorts, as well as the major films *Snow White* and *Bambi,* and it was not long

before these cartoons also inspired a collection of Beswick figures. Arthur Gredington modelled the little figures of *Snow White and the Seven Dwarfs* whilst Jan Granoska, a trainee modeller, was given the task of portraying Mickey Mouse and friends, plus some characters from *Pinocchio* and *Peter Pan.* Although Miss Granoska was only at the Beswick studio for three years, she was responsible for some of their most desirable figures.

Music (of sorts!) is being played by the BEDTIME CHORUS™, a group of enthusiastic children accompanied by a singing cat and dog. These were amongst the first character figures to be modelled by Albert Hallam, who gradually took over responsibility for this area in the 1960s. As head mouldmaker, Hallam had made many of the production moulds for Gredington designs, so he was already familiar with the subject matter. He continued the *Beatrix Potter* collection, adding characters such as *Old Mr. Brown* and *Cecily Parsley,* and in 1968 he launched a new Disney series based on their newest cartoon hit, *Winnie the Pooh and the Blustery Day.*

The late 1960s was a time of transition for the company, as Ewart Beswick was ready to retire but he had no heir for his successful business. Fortunately the Royal Doulton group was in the midst of an expansion programme and they acquired the Beswick factory in 1969. They soon benefited from Beswick's expertise in the field of character animals.

When Albert Hallam retired in 1975, Graham Tongue became the head modeller at the Beswick Studio under Harry Sales, newly appointed as design manager. Harry Sales was primarily a graphic artist and he dreamed up many new ideas for the Beatrix Potter range, which Graham Tongue and others modelled during the 1980s. This was becoming increasingly difficult as the most popular characters had already been modelled. Favourites, such as *Peter Rabbit* and *Jemima Puddleduck,* were introduced in new poses, and he came up with the idea of double figures, for example *Mr Benjamin Bunny and Peter Rabbit* and *Tabitha Twitchet and Miss Moppet.*

As well as developing the established figure collections, Harry Sales delved into lots of other childrens books for inspiration. He reinterpreted the timeless characters from classic tales such as *Alices Adventures in Wonderland* and *The Wind in the Willows,* and he worked from contemporary picture books, notably Joan Walsh Anglund's *A Friend is Someone Who Likes You* and Norman Thelwell's *Angels on Horseback.* Whenever possible, Harry liaised closely with the originators of the characters he portrayed. He spent many happy hours of research at Thelwell's studio, studying his cartoons of shaggy ponies with comical riders, and he also worked with Alfred Bestall, the illustrator of the Rupert Bear adventures in the *Daily Express* newspaper before embarking on this series in 1980.

With their outstanding reputation for developing character animals, it is not surprising that Royal Doulton artists were invited to work on the publishing sensation of the 1980s, the Brambly Hedge stories by Jill Barklem.

Within three years of their launch the spring, summer, autumn and winter stories had been reprinted 11 times, translated into ten languages, and had sold in excess of a million copies. Readers young and old were captivated by the enchanting world of the Brambly Hedge mice, as indeed was Harry Sales, whose job it was to recreate the characters in the ceramic medium. In his own words, "The first time I read the books and studied the illustrations I felt that I was experiencing something quite unique. Over a period of many years designing for the pottery industry one develops an awareness, a feeling for that something special. Brambly Hedge had this."

Ideas flowed quickly and eight leading characters were chosen from the seasonal stories for the initial collection, which was launched in 1983. Such was the response that they were soon joined by six more subjects, making a total of 14 by 1986, when Harry left the company. Graham Tongue succeeded him as design manager and continued to add new Brambly Hedge figures from the original stories. Miss Barklem's later titles, *The Secret Staircase, The High Hills* and *The Sea Story*, provided inspiration for some of his figures; for example, *Mr and Mrs Saltapple* who supply the Brambly Hedge community with salt in *The Sea Story*.

Encouraged by the amazing success of the Brambly Hedge collection, Royal Doulton's marketing executives were soon considering other new storybook characters. Like millions of TV viewers, they were spellbound by the magical film, *The Snowman*, which was first screened in 1982. Based on the illustrated book of the same name by Raymond Briggs, the animated film about a snowman who comes to life has become traditional Christmas entertainment in many parts of the world. The absence of words gives the tale a haunting quality, and there is hardly a dry eye in the house when the little boy, James, awakes to find his Snowman friend has melted away after an exciting night exploring each other's worlds. Fortunately the SNOWMAN™ lives on in more durable form in the Royal Doulton collection. Again Harry Sales was given the challenge of transforming this amorphous character into ceramic, whilst remaining faithful to Briggs' original soft crayon drawings. He succeeded in this difficult task by adding additional curves to the contours of the figures which gives them a life-like appearance. The first four figures were ready and approved by Raymond Briggs in 1985, and the collection grew steadily until 1990, latterly under the direction of Graham Tongue.

So far, the 1990s has seen Graham Tongue and his team of artists develop the Beatrix Potter collection for the 100th birthday of *Peter Rabbit* and, in 1994, the centenary of the Beswick factory was marked with the launch of the *Pig Promenade*, featuring a special commemorative backstamp.

This series is just one of three new collections of novelty figures, and it is refreshing to see this traditional type of Beswick ware being revitalised by a new generation of artists. Amanda Hughes-Lubeck and Warren Platt created the LITTLE LOVABLES™, a series of cute clowns with special messages, such as "Good Luck" and "Congratulations," and they also worked with Martyn Alcock on the collection of ENGLISH COUNTRY FOLK™, which has been very well received.

The collecting of Beatrix Potter and Brambly Hedge figures has reached epidemic proportions in recent years, and there is now a growing awareness of the desirability of all their storybook cousins, hence the need for this much expanded price guide.

COLLECTING BEATRIX POTTER FIGURES

A number of factors have combined recently to make Beatrix Potter figures the "hottest" collectables of the 1990s. The 100th birthday of *Peter Rabbit* was celebrated amidst a storm of publicity in 1993, and the centenary of the John Beswick factory in 1994 focused a lot of collector attention on its products. 1997 saw more celebrations as Beatrix Potter figures had been in continuous production at Beswick for fifty years.

The market has been stimulated by recent withdrawals from the range — a record 19 figures were withdrawn in 1997, making more than 60 retired figures to find so far. Prices are rocketing for the early discontinued figures, and most collectors will need a bank loan to purchase *Duchess with Flowers*, the first Beatrix Potter figure to be retired, if indeed they are lucky enough to find one for sale.

Ever since the Beswick factory launched their Beatrix Potter collection in 1948, most of the figures have been bought as gifts for children. However, many young fans have grown up to find they have some very valuable figures, with early modelling and backstamp variations, and they have begun collecting in earnest to fill the gaps and find the rarities. Figures marked with a Beswick backstamp are most in demand, as this trademark was replaced with the Royal Albert backstamp in 1989. The Royal Albert factory, another famous name in the Doulton group, produces all the Beatrix Potter tableware, and the change of backstamps was made for distribution reasons. The most desirable Beswick marks are the gold varieties, which predate 1972, and these are often found on early modelling or colour variations, which also attract a premium price, for example *Mrs Rabbit* with her umbrella sticking out and *Mr Benjamin Bunny* with his pipe protruding.

As well as seeking out discontinued figures and rare variations, it is advisable to keep up to date with new models as they are introduced. A complete Beatrix Potter figure collection will encompass more than 100 of the standard-size models, around three inches tall, and ten large models, which are about twice the size. *Peter Rabbit*, the first of these large size models, was launched in 1993 with a special commemorative backstamp from the John Beswick studio, and it changed in 1994 to a Royal Albert mark. The Royal Albert mark was used on most Beatrix Potter figures between 1989 and 1998 when new John Beswick backstamps were introduced.

If owning all the Beatrix Potter figures is beyond the realms of possibility, whether for financial or display limitations, then why not focus on particular types of animals or characters from your favourite tales. There are twenty mice figures to find, a dozen cat characters and more than twenty rabbits, half of which feature *Peter Rabbit*. There are also discontinued character jugs, relief modelled plaques and a ceramic display stand to look out for, so happy hunting.

COLLECTING BRAMBLY HEDGE FIGURES

Since their introduction in 1983, the Brambly Hedge mice have overrun households in many parts of the world. They are scurrying about the shelves as Royal Doulton figures and even climbing up the walls on decorative plates. Far from being undesirable, these particular mice are considered indispensable members of the family. Children frequently receive them as gifts from doting grandparents, but adults have also been seduced by the cosy, timeless mouse world which Jill Barklem has created. The mood of rustic nostalgia has all been painstakingly researched. The interiors of the field mice homes are of the sort common in English farmhouses at the end of the 19th century, and the food served is genuine country fare, based on old recipes and tested in Jill Barklem's kitchen. The Brambly Hedge residents were all expertly drawn with the aid of her two mouse models, a keen understanding of zoology and a knowledge of historical costume.

The same attention to detail went into the Royal Doulton figures designed by Harry Sales. As he explains, "One important feature in the concept was that I chose poses which, when the figures are together, appear to be reacting to one another. I can imagine the fun children and the young at heart will have arranging the figures in conversational situations." Essentially this sums up the collectability of the Brambly Hedge mice, and as there are only 25 figures in the series, they can all be displayed effectively together on one shelf. Royal Doulton retired the entire collection in 1997 but there are plans for more figures in the future. In the meantime, there are a couple of unusual modelling variations to look out for as *Mr Toadflax's* tail was altered shortly after its introduction.

COLLECTING SNOWMAN FIGURES

Initially, the seasonal appeal of the Snowman tended to limit his collectability, as most purchases were made around Christmas time, and he was more popular in areas which regularly experience snow. Having said this, for some fans the wintry connotations were overshadowed by the inherent quality and humour of the models and there are now keen collectors in sunny Florida as well as in Australia, where beach barbecues are typical Christmas celebrations.

Between 1985 and 1990, young children regularly received the new Snowman models in their Christmas stockings, and the characters have been widely used as holiday decorations. Like the Brambly Hedge models, they were designed to interact, and the little figure of *James*, gazing up in wonder, can be positioned with various Snowman characters, whilst the band works very well as a separate display grouping. There are 19 figures and two musical boxes to collect and, as the range was withdrawn in 1994, they can now be quite difficult

to locate. In fact, prices have been snowballing, particularly for the figures that were not in production for long, notably *The Snowman Skiing*.

COLLECTING STORYBOOK CHARACTERS

The Beatrix Potter, Brambly Hedge and Snowman stories have already been discussed in some detail, as there are so many figures to collect in each of the categories. However, the Beswick artists have also sought inspiration in other children's stories, some better known than others.

The American author-illustrator, Joan Walsh Anglund, enjoyed quite a vogue in the 1960s following the publication of *A Friend is Someone Who Likes You* (1958). Three of her drawings of cute children with minimal features were modelled by Albert Hallam for the Beswick range in 1969, but they were withdrawn soon after, making them extremely hard to find today.

The bizarre cast of characters from *Alice's Adventures in Wonderland* has offered a lot more scope for collectors. First published in 1865, this classic tale has entertained generations of young readers and inspired many artistic interpretations. In the early 1900s, Doulton's Lambeth artists modelled some fantastic creatures from the tale, notably the pig-like *Rath* from the "Jabberwocky" poem. The Burslem studio designed an extensive series of nursery ware and, more recently, a collection of character jugs based on the original illustrations by Sir John Tenniel, who firmly fixed the appearance of the Wonderland characters in the public imagination. Harry Sales also consulted the Tenniel illustrations in 1973 when designing Beswick's ALICE IN WONDERLAND™.

Curiously the figures inspired by another great children's classic, *The Wind in the Willows*, did not have the same appeal. Christina Thwaites, a young book illustrator, was commissioned to produce designs for a collection of wall plates and tea wares, and her watercolours of *Mr Toad, Ratty, Mole, Badger* and others were interpreted by the Beswick modellers. Four figures were launched in 1987 and two more in 1988 as part of a co-ordinated giftware range with the Royal Albert backstamp, but they were withdrawn in 1989. Consequently *Portly* and *Weasel*, the later introductions, were only made for one year, and will no doubt prove particularly hard to find in the future.

With the WIND IN THE WILLOWS™ collection, the Royal Doulton artists have come full circle, reflecting the enthusiasm of their predecessors at Lambeth, notably Francis Pope who modelled two superb figures of *Mr Toad* shortly after the book was published. Obviously storybook characters, particularly animals in human guises, have timeless appeal.

COLLECTING CARTOON CHARACTERS

Cartoon characters, whether they be from animated films or comic book strips, are becoming a popular field for collectors. A major refernce book on the subject, together with recent introductions, such as *Tom and Jerry*, has already generated even more interest. Now is the time to start collecting, if you have not already done so.

The characters from David Hand's Animaland are virtually unknown today, but following their film debut in 1948, they were sufficiently well known to inspire Beswick's first series of cartoon figures. Modelled in 1949 and withdrawn in 1955, *Zimmy the Lion* and his seven friends now have a different kind of notoriety, stealing the show when they come up for auction.

In contrast, Mickey Mouse is the best known cartoon character in the world. Within a year of his 1928 screen debut in *Steamboat Willie*, his image was being used to endorse children's products, and by the 1950s there were more than 3,000 different Mickey Mouse items, including plates, dolls, watches and clothes. With all this merchandising activity, it is not surprising that the Beswick studio sought a license for portraying Mickey and his friends in ceramic.

A range of nursey ware was launched in 1954, along with figures of *Mickey* and his girlfriend *Minnie*, *Pluto* his dog and his crazy friends *Goofy* and *Donald Duck*. Characters from some of Walt Disney's feature-length cartoons completed the original WALT DISNEY CHARACTERS™ set of 12 figures. *Peter Pan*, the newest Disney hit in 1953, inspired four characters, *Peter* himself, *Tinkerbell*, *Smee* and *Nana*, whilst the classic *Pinocchio* (1940) provided the puppet hero and his insect conscience *Jiminy Cricket*. Surprisingly only *Thumper* was modelled from another favourite film, *Bambi* (1942), although the fawn appears on the tableware designs. The response to the initial Disney collection encouraged the Beswick factory to launch a second set the following year, featuring *Snow White and the Seven Dwarfs* from Disney's first feature symphony. All the Disney characterisations are superb, making them extremely desirable amongst collectors of Beswick and Disneyana and they are all hard to find, even though they were produced until 1967.

The 1960s saw the rise of a new Disney star, Winnie the Pooh, who became a very popular merchandising character after his cartoon debut in 1966. The Beswick factory was quick off the mark, launching an initial collection of six characters from the film in 1968, followed by two more in 1971. "The Bear of Little Brain" originated in bedtime stories about nursery toys told by A. A. Milne to his son Christopher Robin in the 1920s, and he was visualised in the resulting books by the illustrator E. H. Shepard. To celebrate the 70th anniversary of the first *Winnie the Pooh* book, Royal Doulton launched a second series of figures in 1996 and these have been a great success. Royal Doulton continue to work closely with the Walt Disney company today and they have launched two exciting figurine collections featuring Disney *Princesses* and *Villains* exclusively for sale in the Disney stores. The other new Disney collections have been distributed through specialist china shops, notably the *101 Dalmatians* series, which was inspired by the live action film, and the second series of *Snow White and the Seven Dwarfs*, which was prompted by the 60th anniversary of the film. A new Disney series featuring Mickey Mouse and his gang, was launched during 1998 so don't miss the opportunity to add these to your cartoon collection.

The massive marketing campaigns for Disney characters have made them household names all over the world. British cartoon characters, by comparison, are less well known internationally. The *Daily Express* newspaper was slow to capitalise on the success of *Rupert the Bear*, who has been the star of their children's comic strip since 1920. Originated by Mary Tourtel, the Rupert stories were enlivened by Alfred Bestall who took over the daily drawings in 1935. Rupert enjoys the most extraordinary adventures with his friends Bill the Badger, Algy Pug and Pong-Ping, always returning safely to his comfortable family home in Nutwood. Rupert Bear annuals sold in millions from the mid 1930s, and his exploits were adapted for TV in the 1970s, but his following is essentially British. No doubt it was for this reason that the five figures in the RUPERT THE BEAR™ collection, designed by Harry Sales in 1980, were relatively short lived.

A similar fate befell the NORMAN THELWELL™ figures, which were in production from 1981 to 1989. Norman Thelwell was a humorous illustrator for *Punch* magazine, who made his reputation with comical observations of young riders and their mounts. *Angels on Horseback*, published in 1957, was the first compilation of his successful cartoons, and many other popular books followed. Thelwell worked closely with Harry Sales to create the most effective figures, both in ceramic and resin, and the results are guaranteed to raise a smile without breaking the bank.

After a gap of nearly 15 years, famous British cartoon characters are back on the drawing board at the Royal Doulton studios once again. *Denis the Menace* and *Desperate Dan*, stars of the long-established children's comics, *The Beano* and *The Dandy*, have been immortalised as character jugs. This is the first time large-size character jugs have been used for portraying cartoons, although there are similarities to the set of six THUNDERBIRDS™ busts modelled by jug designer Bill Harper to celebrate the 30th anniversary of this children's TV show in 1992.

COLLECTING CHARACTER ANIMALS

In the 1880s Doulton's first artist, George Tinworth, was modelling groups of mice engaged in popular human pastimes, and nearly a century later Kitty MacBride did much the same thing with her *Happy Mice*. The appeal of these anthropomorphic creatures is timeless, and collectors have responded with enthusiasm from Victorian times to the present day. Admittedly, developing a taste for Tinworth's sense of humour will prove very expensive, with models costing several hundreds of pounds each, but the KITTY MACBRIDE™ whimsical mice are still relatively affordable.

Kitty MacBride was a writer and illustrator who began to model little clay figures of mice in 1960. Initially they were sold through a London dealer, but when she could not keep up with the demand she asked the Beswick factory to produce 11 of them commercially, which they did between 1975 and 1983.

The Beswick studio has had a considerable reputation for character animals since the launch of the Beatrix Potter collection in 1948. However, the modellers have not only interpreted illustrations from famous books, from time to time they have envisaged their own comical creatures. Albert Hallam was responsible for a succession of animals with human expressions in the late 1960s. Similar humanising traits can be found in the LITTLE LIKEABLES™ collection, which was produced briefly in the mid 1980s. Robert Tabbenor's animals play up the humour of their situation, notably the carefree frog, *Watching the World Go By*, whilst Diane Griffiths takes a more sentimental approach, using human feelings to describe her cartoon-like animals.

The fun has continued in recent years with a collection of footballer cats, produced in 1987 only, and the on-going series of *English Country Folk*, depicting appropriate animals with human manners and costumes. However, the last laugh is reserved for the *Pig Promenade*. The absurdity of nine different breeds of pigs playing musical instruments makes this one of the most hilarious series of character animals.

MAKING STORYBOOK CHARACTERS

All the current storybook characters are made at the John Beswick factory in Longton, which became part of the Royal Doulton group in 1969. They have over fifty years' experience in the production of humorous figures and character animals, and essentially the methods have not changed since the earliest days of the Beatrix Potter figures.

First of all the designer has to familiarise himself thoroughly with the character to be portrayed, reading the story and studying the illustration. Having chosen the most suitable pose for interpretation in ceramic, he will produce reference drawings for the modeller. Often he can only see one side of the character in the original illustration, so he has to improvise for his three-dimensional model.

In consultation with the designer, the modeller will create the figure in modelling clay, and if satisfactory, a set of master moulds will be made in plaster of Paris. The number of mould parts will depend on the complexity of the figure, and sometimes the head and arms have to be moulded separately. Two or three prototype figures will be cast from the master mould for colour trials and subsequent approval by the original artist or his agent.

In the case of the Beatrix Potter figures, all the models are scrutinised by the licensing agents, Copyrights, working on behalf of Miss Potter's original publishers, Frederick Warne. Raymond Briggs, who was responsible for the Snowman, is generally quite relaxed about letting experts in other media interpret his drawings. He thought Royal Doultons models were marvellous and really captured the spirit of the story, although he maintained he would "jolly well say so" if he thought

they had got it wrong! Jill Barklem, the creator of Brambly Hedge, likes to get very involved in the licensing of her characters, and design manager Harry Sales spent a lot of time working with her on the finer points of detail. Sometimes slight modifications need to be made to the model or the colour scheme before the figure is approved by all concerned.

The next stage is to produce plaster of Paris working moulds from the master, and supplies are sent to the casting department. An earthenware body is used to cast all the character figures produced at the John Beswick studio, and it is poured into the mould in liquid form, known as slip. The moisture in the slip is absorbed into the plaster of Paris moulds and a "skin" of clay forms the interior.

Once the clay has set to the required thickness, the excess clay is poured out and the mould is carefully dismantled. Any separate mould parts, such as projecting arms, will be joined on at this stage using slip as an adhesive, and the seams will be gently sponged away. The figure is then allowed to dry slowly before it goes for its first firing. The high temperature in the kiln drives out the moisture in the body and the figure shrinks by about 1/12th of its original size, forming a hard "biscuit" body.

Skilled decorators will paint the figure, using special under-glaze ceramic colours. They work from an approved colour sample and great care is taken to match the colours to the original book illustrations. A second firing hardens on the colour before the figure is coated with a solution of liquid glaze. When the figure is fired in the glost kiln, it emerges with a shiny transparent finish which enhances and permanently protects the vibrant colours underneath. After a final inspection, the figures are dispatched to china shops all over the world where they will capture the hearts of collectors young and old.

RESIN FIGURES

Several collectables manufacturers began experimenting with new sculptural materials in the 1980s and developed different types of resin bodies that allow more intricately modelled detail than conventional ceramic processes. Royal Doulton launched its new "bonded ceramic body" in 1984, and two storybook collections were included in its Beswick Studio Sculptures, as the range was known. Seven subjects were chosen from the *Tales of Beatrix Potter* and two from the Thelwell series. Production was short-lived, despite the minute detailing of the animals' fur and the tiny pebbles and grasses in their habitat, which would have been impossible to achieve in traditional earthenware. Royal Doulton ceased production of resin at the end of 1985, but designs have been commissioned from resin specialists, notably the *Paddington Bear* and *St. Tiggywinkles* series.

ROYAL DOULTON COLLECTORS CLUB AND GUILD

Royal Doulton International Collectors Club

Founded in 1980, the Royal Doulton International Collectors Club provides an information service on all aspects of the company's products, past and present. A club magazine, *Gallery*, is published four times a year with information on new products and current events that will keep the collector up-to-date on the happenings in the world of Royal Doulton. Upon joining the club, each new member will receive a free gift and invitations to special events and exclusive offers throughout the year.

To join the Royal Doulton Collectors Club, please contact your local stockist, or contact the club directly at the address or telephone numbers below:

Royal Crown Derby Collectors Guild

The Royal Crown Derby Collectors Guild was established in 1994 to establish closer contact with Royal Crown Derby Collectors. Membership entitles the collector to a yearly subscription to the quarterly *Gallery* magazine, *Royal Crown Derby News*, membership gifts and free admission to the Royal Crown Derby Visitor Centre.

To join the Royal Crown Derby Collectors Guild, please contact the guild at the address or telephone number below:

Minton House
London Road, Stoke-on-Trent
Staffordshire ST4 7QD, England

Telephone:
    U.K.: (01782) 292127
    U.S.A. and Canada: 1-800-747-3045 (toll free)
    Australia: 011-800-142624 (toll free)
Fax: U.K.: (01782) 292099
Attn.: Maria Murtagh

Caithness Glass Paperweight Collectors Society Caithness Glass International Paperweight Collectors Society

Formed in 1997, by Colin Terris, the society is the clearing house for all information on Caithness Glass Paperweights. Membership of the society entitles the collector to receive *Reflections*, the society's twice yearly magazine, plus three newsletters and a personal tour of the paperweight studios in Perth, Scotland, if you are ever in the area. An annual International Convention is held in Scotland in October.

To join the Caithness Glass Paperweight Collectors Society, please contact the society at one of the addresses or telephone numbers below:

In the U.K. and International
Caithness Glass Paperweight Collectors Scoiety
Caithness Glass Inc.
Inveralmond, Perth PH1 3TZ, Scotland
Tel.: (44) (0) 1738 637373
Fax: (44) (0) 1738 622494

In the U.S.A.
Caithness Glass Paperweight Collectors Society
Caithness Glass Inc.
141 Lanza Avenue, Building No. 12
Garfield, N.J. 07026, U.S.A.
Tel.: 973-340-3330
Fax: 973-340-9415

COLLECTOR CLUB CHAPTERS

Chapters of the RDICC have formed across North America and are worthy of consideration in those areas.

Detroit Chapter
Frank Americk, President
1771 Brody, Allen Park, MI 48101

Edmonton Chapter
Mildred's Collectibles
6813 104 Street, Edmonton, AB

New England Chapter
Charles Wood, President
Charles Briggs, Secretary
21 Walpole Street, Norwood, MA 02062
Tel.: (781) 784-8121

Northern California Chapter
Donald A. Blubaugh, President
P.O. Box 3665, Walnut Creek, CA 94598
Tel.: (925) 945-1687 Fax: (925) 938-6674
Blubaugh@usa.net

Northwest, Bob Haynes, Chapter
Alan Matthew, President
15202 93rd Place N.E., Bothell, WA 98011
Tel.: (425) 488-9604

Ohio Chapter
Reg Marvis, President
Dick Maschmeier, Treasurer
5556 White Haven Avenue,
North Olmstead, Ohio 44070
Tel.: (216) 779 5554

Rochester Chapter
Judith L. Trost President
103 Garfield Street, Rochester, N.Y. 14611
Tel.: (716) 436-3321

Western Pennsylvania Chapter
John Re, President
9589 Parkedge Drive, Allison Park, PA 15101
Tel.: (412) 366-0201 Fax: (412) 366-2558

ROYAL DOULTON VISITOR CENTRES

Royal Doulton Visitor Centre

Opened in the summer of 1996, the Royal Doulton Visitor Centre houses the largest collection of Royal Doulton figurines in the world. The centre also is home to the Minton Fine Art Studio, which specializes in hand painting and gilding. Demonstration areas offer the collector a first hand insight on how figurines are assembled and decorated. Also at the Visitor Centre is a cinema showing a 20 minute video on the history of Royal Doulton, plus a restaurant, and a retail shop offering both best quality ware and slight seconds.

Factory tours may be booked, Monday to Friday, at the Visitor Centre.

Nile Street, Burslem
Stoke-on-Trent, ST6 2AJ, England
Tel.: (01782) 292434
Fax: (01782) 292424
Attn.: Yvonne Wood

Royal Doulton John Beswick Studios

Tours of the John Beswick Factory and Museum are available Monday to Thursday by appointment only. Please book in advance.

Gold Street, Longton
Stoke-on-Trent, ST3 2JP, England
Tel.: (01782) 291213
Fax: (01782) 291279
Attn.: Joan Barker

Royal Crown Derby Visitor Centre

Opened in the spring of 1998, the Visitor Centre was created to provide an insight into the tradition, history and skills that go into making Royal Crown Derby collectables. The centre houses the largest collection of Royal Crown Derby seen anywhere in the world, a demonstration area for skilled Royal Crown Derby artists and crafts people, restaurants, and shops.

Factory tours may be booked Monday to Friday at the centre, with advance bookings suggested.

194 Osmaston Road
Derby, DE23 8JZ, England
Tel.: (01332) 712841
Fax: (01332) 712899
Attn.: Stella Birks

Caithness Glass Visitor Centre

The Visitor Centre is home to the largest public display of Caithness Glass paperweights. Over 1200 designs are on display. A special viewing gallery enables visitors to watch the complete paperweight making process.

Inveralmond
Perth, PH1 3TZ, Scotland
Tel.: (44) (0)1738 637373
Fax: (44) (0)1738 622494

Factory Shops

Royal Doulton Visitor Centre
Nile Street, Burslem
Stoke-on-Trent, England
Tel.: (01782) 292451

Royal Doulton Group Factory Shop
Lawley Street, Longton, England
Stoke-on-Trent ST3 2PH
Tel.: (01782) 291172

Royal Doulton Factory Shop
Minton House, London Road
Stoke-on-Trent, ST4 7QD, England
Tel.: (01782) 292121

Royal Doulton Factory Shop
Leek New Road, Baddeley Green,
Stoke-on-Trent ST2 7HS, England
Tel.: (01782) 291700

Royal Doulton Factory Shop
Victoria Road, Fenton,
Stoke-on-Trent ST4 2PJ, England
Tel.: (01782) 291869

Beswick Factory Shop
Barford Street, Longton,
Stoke-on-Trent. ST3 2JP, England
Tel.: (01782) 291237

Web Site and E-mail Addresses

Sites: www.royal-doulton.com
www.caithnessglass.co.uk
E-mail:
Clubs: icc@royal-doulton.com
Visitor Centre: Visitor@royal-doulton.com
Consumer Enquiries: enquiries@royal-doulton.com
Museum Curator: heritage@royal-doulton.com
Lawleys by Post: lbp@royal-doulton.com

WHERE TO BUY

Discontinued Doulton collectables can be found in Antique shops, Markets, Auctions, Shows and Fairs. Specialist dealers in Royal Doulton collectables attend many of the events listed below.

For Auction happenings it is necessary to subscribe to Auction Houses that hold 20th Century or Doulton Auctions.

UNITED KINGDOM
Auction Houses

BBR Auctions
Elsecar Heritage Centre
Nr. Barnsley,
South Yorkshire, S74 8HJ, England
Tel.: (01226) 745156
Fax: (01226) 351561
Attn: Alan Blakeman

Bonhams
65-69 Lots Road, Chelsea,
London, SW10 0RN, England
Tel.: (0171) 393-3900
Fax: (0171) 393-3906
www.bonhams.com
Attn: Neil Grenyer

Christie's South Kensington
85 Old Brompton Road
London, SW7 3LD, England
Tel.: (0171) 581 7611
Fax: (0171) 321-3321
www.christies.com
Attn: Michael Jeffrey

Potteries Specialist Auctions
271 Waterloo Road
Stoke-on-Trent
Staffordshire, ST6 3HR, England
Tel.: (01782) 286622
Fax: (01782) 213777
Attn: Steve Anderson

Louis Taylor
Britannia House
10 Town Road, Hanley,
Stoke-on-Trent, ST1 2QG
England
Tel.: (01782) 21411
Fax: (01782) 287874
Attn: Clive Hillier

Phillips
101 New Bond Street
London, W1Y 0AS, England
Tel.: (0171) 629-6602
Fax: (0171) 629-8876
www.phillips-auctions.com
Attn: Mark Oliver

Sotheby's
34-35 New Bond Street
London, W1A 2AA, England
Tel.: (0171) 293-5000
Fax: (0171) 293-5989
www.sothebys.com
Attn: Christina Donaldson

Sotheby's Sussex
Summers Place
Billingshurst, Sussex, RH14 9AF
England
Tel.: (01403) 833500
Fax: (01403) 833699

Thomson Roddick & Laurie
60 Whitesands
Dumfries, DG1 2RS
Scotland
Tel.: (01387) 255366
Fax: (01387) 266236
Attn: Sybelle Medcalf

Peter Wilson Auctioneers
Victoria Gallery, Market Street
Nantwich, Cheshire, CW5 5DG
England
Tel.: (01270) 623878
Fax: (01270) 610508
Attn: Stella Ashbrook or
    Robert Stone

Antique Fairs

Doulton and Beswick Collectors Fair
National Motorcycle Museum, Meriden, Birmingham,
Usually March and August
For information on times and dates:
Doulton and Beswick Dealers Association
(0181) 303 3316

Doulton and Beswick Collectors Fair
The Queensway Hall Civic Centre, Dunstable,
Bedfordshire. Usually in October.
For information on times and location:
UK Fairs Ltd. 10 Wilford Bridge Spur,
Melton,Woodbridge, Suffolk, IP12 1 RJ
901394) 386663

20th Century Fairs
266 Glossop Road, Sheffield S10 2HS, England
Usually the last week in May or the first week in June.
For information on times and dates:
Tel.: (0114) 275-0333
Fax: (0114) 275-4443

International Antique & Collectors Fair
Newark, Nottinghamshire
Usually six fairs annually.
For information on times and dates:
International Antique & Collectors Fair Ltd.
P.O. Box 100, Newark, Nottinghamshire, NG2 1DJ
(01636) 702326

West London Wade Beswick & Doulton Fair
Brunel University, Kingston Lane,
Uxbridge, Middlesex
For information on times and dates:
B & D Fairs, P.O. Box 273, Uxbridge,
Middlesex, UB9 4LP
(01895) 834694 or 834357

Yesterdays Doulton Fair
Usually November.
For information on times and location:
Doulton and Beswick Dealers Association
Tel.: (0181) 303-3316

London Markets

Alfie's Antique Market
13-25 Church Street, London
Tuesday - Saturday

Camden Passage Market
London
Wednesday and Saturday

New Caledonia Market
Bermondsey Square, London
Friday morning

Portobello Road Market
Portobello Road, London
Saturday

UNITED STATES
Auction Houses

Christie's East
219 East 67th Street
New York, NY 10021
(212) 606-0400
www.christies.com
Attn: Timothy Luke

Sotheby's Arcade Auctions
1334 York Avenue
New York, NY 10021
(212) 606-7000
www.sothebys.com
Attn: Andrew Cheney

Collectable Shows

Atlantique City
New Atlantic City Convention Centre
Atlantic City, NJ
Usually March and October
For information on times and dates:
Brimfield and Associates
P.O. Box 1800, Ocean City, NJ 08226
(609) 926-1800
www.atlantiquecity.com

Florida Doulton Convention & Sale
Sheraton Inn
1825 Griffin Road
Dania, Florida
Usually mid-January
For information on times and dates:
Pascoe and Company, 101 Almeria Avenue,
Coral Gables, Florida 33134. (305) 44503229
Charles Dombeck, 29720 Rich Walk Court
Davie, Florida 33328. (954) 452-9174

O'Hare National Antiques Show & Sale
Rosemont Convention Centre,
Chicago, IL.
Usually April, August and November
For information on times and dates:
Manor House Shows Inc.
P.O. Box 7320, Fort Lauderdale, Florida 33338
(954) 563-6747

Royal Doulton Convention & Sale
John S. Knight Convention Centre
77 E. Mill Street, Akron, Ohio 44308
Usually August.
For information on times and dates:
Colonial House Productions
182 Front Street, Berea, Ohio 44017
(800) 344-9299

CANADA
Auction Houses

Maynards
415 West 2nd Avenue, Vancouver, BC V5Y 1E3
Tel.: (604) 876-1311

Ritchie's
288 King Street East, Toronto, Ontario. M5A 1K4
Tel.: (416) 364-1864   Fax: (416) 364-0704
Attn: Caroline Kaiser

Collectable Shows

Canadian Art & Collectibles Show & Sale
Kitchener Memorial Auditorium, Kitchener, Ontario.
Usually early May.
For information on times and location:
George or Jackie Benninger
P.O. Box 130, Durham. Ont. N0G 1R0. (519) 369-6950

Canadian Doulton & Collectable Fair
Toronto, Ontario.
Usually early September.
For information on times and location:
George or Jackie Benninger
P.O. Box 130, Durham, Ont. N0G 1R0. (519) 369-6950

FURTHER READING

Storybook Figurines

The Charlton Standard Catalogue of Bunnykins by Jean Dale and Louise Irvine
Cartoon Classics and other Character Figures by Louise Irvine
Royal Doulton Bunnykins Figures by Louise Irvine
Bunnykins Collectors Book by Louise Irvine
Beatrix Potter Figures and Giftware edited by Louise Irvine
The Beswick Price Guide by Harvey May

Animals, Figures and Character Jugs

Royal Doulton Figures by Desmond Eyles, Louise Irvine and Valerie Baynton
The Charlton Standard Catalogue of Beswick Animals by Diane & John Callow
  and Marilyn & Peter Sweet
The Charlton Standard Catalogue of Royal Doulton Animals by Jean Dale
The Charlton Standard Catalogue of Royal Doulton Beswick Figurines by Jean Dale
The Charlton Standard Catalogue of Royal Doulton Beswick Jugs by Jean Dale
Collecting Character and Toby Jugs by Jocelyn Lukins
Collecting Doulton Animals by Jocelyn Lukins
Doulton Flambé Animals by Jocelyn Lukins
The Character Jug Collectors Handbook by Kevin Pearson
The Doulton Figure Collectors Handbook by Kevin Pearson

General

The Charlton Standard Catalogue of Beswick Pottery by Diane and John Callow
Discovering Royal Doulton by Michael Doulton
The Doulton Story by Paul Atterbury and Louise Irvine
Royal Doulton Series Ware by Louise Irvine (Vols. 1-5)
Limited Edition Loving Cups by Louise Irvine and Richard Dennis
Doulton for the Collector by Jocelyn Lukins
Doulton Kingsware Flasks by Jocelyn Lukins
Doulton Burslem Advertising Wares by Jocelyn Lukins
Doulton Lambeth Advertising Ware, by Jocelyn Lukins
The Doulton Lambeth Wares by Desmond Eyles
The Doulton Burslem Wares by Desmond Eyles
Hannah Barlow by Peter Rose
George Tinworth by Peter Rose
Sir Henry Doulton Biography by Edmund Gosse
Phillips Collectors Guide by Catherine Braithwaite
Royal Doulton by Jennifer Queree
John Beswick: A World of Imagination. Catalogue reprint (1950-1996)
Royal Doulton by Julie McKeown

Magazines and Newsletters

Rabbitting On (Bunnykins Newsletter) Contact Leah Selig: 2 Harper Street, Merrylands 2160
  New South Wales, Australia. Tel./Fax 61 2 9637 2410 (International), 02 637 2410 (Australia)

Collect It! Contact subscription department at: P.O. Box 3658, Bracknell, Berkshire RG12 7XZ
  Telephone: (1344) 868280 or e-mail: collectit@dialpipex.com

Collecting Doulton Magazine, Contact Doug Pinchin, P.O. Box 310, Richmond, Surrey TW9 1FS,
England

Doulton News, published by Thorndon Antiques & Fine China Ltd., edited by David Harcourt
  P.O. Box 12-076 (109 Molesworth Street), Wellington, New Zealand

Beswick Quarterly (Beswick Newsletter) Contact Laura J. Rock-Smith: 10 Holmes Ct., Sayville,
  N.Y. 11782-2408, U.S.A. Tel./Fax 516-589-9027

Royal Doulton
Brambly Hedge

FIGURES

1 Lord Woodmouse DBH4
2 Primrose Woodmouse DBH8
3 Lady Woodmouse DBH5
4 Wilfred Toadflax DBH7
5 Catkin DBH12
6 Flax Weaver DBH20
7 Lily Weaver DBH19
8 Clover DBH16
9 Mrs. Toadflax DBH11
10 Mr. Toadflax DBH10
11 Poppy Eyebright DBH1
12 Dusty Dogwood DBH6
13 Mrs. Apple DBH3
14 Mr. Apple DBH2
15 Mrs. Crustybread DBH15
16 Conker DBH21
17 Mr. Saltapple DBH24
18 Mrs. Saltapple DBH25
19 Old Mrs. Eyebright DBH9
20 Wilfred Entertains DBH23
21 Primrose Entertains DBH22

Advertisement for Brambly Hedge Figurines

ALICE IN WONDERLAND

BESWICK EARTHENWARE SERIES
BESWICK FINE CHINA SERIES
ROYAL DOULTON RESIN SERIES

ALICE IN WONDERLAND

EARTHENWARE SERIES 1973-1983

2476
ALICE™
Style One

Designer:	Albert Hallam and Graham Tongue
Height:	4 ¾", 12.1 cm
Colour:	Dark blue dress, white apron with red trim
Issued:	1973 - 1983

Beswick Number		Price		
	U.S. $	Can. $	U.K. £	Aust. $
2476	450.00	600.00	225.00	550.00

2477
WHITE RABBIT™
Style One

Designer:	Graham Tongue
Height:	4 ¾", 12.1 cm
Colour:	White rabbit wearing a brown coat, yellow waistcoat
Issued:	1973 - 1983

Beswick Number		Price		
	U.S. $	Can. $	U.K. £	Aust. $
2477	500.00	650.00	250.00	600.00

2478
MOCK TURTLE™

Designer:	Graham Tongue
Height:	4 ¼", 10.8 cm
Colour:	Browns and grey
Issued:	1973 - 1983

Beswick		*Price*		
Number	*U.S. $*	*Can. $*	*U.K. £*	*Aust. $*
2478	200.00	300.00	95.00	275.00

2479
MAD HATTER™
Style One

Designer:	Albert Hallam
Height:	4 ¼", 10.8 cm
Colour:	Burgundy coat, yellow and blue checked trousers, yellow and red bowtie, grey hat
Issued:	1973 - 1983

Beswick		*Price*		
Number	*U.S. $*	*Can. $*	*U.K. £*	*Aust. $*
2479	300.00	450.00	175.00	475.00

2480
CHESHIRE CAT™
Style One

Designer:	Albert Hallam and Graham Tongue
Height:	1 ½", 3.8 cm
Colour:	Tabby cat
Issued:	1973 - 1982

Beswick		*Price*		
Number	*U.S. $*	*Can. $*	*U.K. £*	*Aust. $*
2480	600.00	775.00	350.00	750.00

2485
GRYPHON™

Designer:	Albert Hallam
Height:	3 ¼", 8.3 cm
Colour:	Browns and greens
Issued:	1973 - 1983

Beswick		Price		
Number	U.S. $	Can. $	U.K. £	Aust. $
2485	175.00	250.00	100.00	225.00

2489
KING OF HEARTS™

Designer:	Graham Tongue
Height:	3 ¾", 9.5 cm
Colour:	Burgundy, yellow, white, blue and green
Issued:	1973 - 1983

Beswick		Price		
Number	U.S. $	Can. $	U.K. £	Aust. $
2489	100.00	150.00	65.00	165.00

2490
QUEEN OF HEARTS™
Style One

Designer:	Graham Tongue
Height:	4", 10.1 cm
Colour:	Blue, green, yellow, white and burgundy
Issued:	1973 - 1983

Beswick		Price		
Number	U.S. $	Can. $	U.K. £	Aust. $
2490	100.00	135.00	65.00	165.00

2545
DODO™
Style One

Designer:	David Lyttleton
Height:	4", 10.1 cm
Colour:	Browns and greens
Issued:	1975 - 1983

ALICE SERIES
"Dodo"
BESWICK
MADE IN ENGLAND
© ROYAL DOULTON TABLEWARE LTD 1976
REGISTRATION APPLIED FOR

Beswick Number	Price			
	U.S. $	Can. $	U.K. £	Aust. $
2545	250.00	375.00	150.00	325.00

2546
FISH FOOTMAN™

Designer:	David Lyttleton
Height:	4 ¾", 14.6 cm
Colour:	Blue, gold, white and brown
Issued:	1975 - 1983

ALICE SERIES
"Fish Footman"
BESWICK
MADE IN ENGLAND
© ROYAL DOULTON TABLEWARE LTD 1976
REGISTRATION APPLIED FOR

Beswick Number	Price			
	U.S. $	Can. $	U.K. £	Aust. $
2546	300.00	450.00	175.00	500.00

2547
FROG FOOTMAN™

Designer:	David Lyttleton
Height:	4 ¼", 10.8 cm
Colour:	Maroon jacket with yellow trim, blue trousers
Issued:	1975 - 1983

ALICE SERIES
"Frog Footman"
BESWICK
MADE IN ENGLAND
© ROYAL DOULTON TABLEWARE LTD 1976
REGISTRATION APPLIED FOR

Beswick Number	Price			
	U.S. $	Can. $	U.K. £	Aust. $
2547	375.00	550.00	225.00	500.00

ALICE IN WONDERLAND

FINE CHINA SERIES 1998

THE MAD HATTER'S TEA PARTY

Designer: Adrian Hughes
Modeller: Martyn Alcock
Size: 5" x 8½", 12.7 x 21.6 cm
Colour: Green, yellow, red and blue
Issued: 1998 in a limited edition of 1,998
Series: 1. Alice's Adventure
2. Tableau

Beswick	Price			
Number	U.S. $	Can. $	U.K. £	Aust. $
—	250.00	375.00	150.00	375.00

ALICE IN WONDERLAND

RESIN SERIES 1997-1997

ALICE™
Style Two

Designer:	Adrian Hughes
Height:	4", 10.1 cm
Colour:	Pale blue and white dress, red and white toadstool, green base
Issued:	1997 - 1997

Doulton Number	Price			
	U.S. $	Can. $	U.K. £	Aust. $
—	45.00	65.00	25.00	65.00
Complete Set (6 pcs.)	250.00	375.00	150.00	375.00

CHESHIRE CAT™
Style Two

Designer:	Adrian Hughes
Height:	4", 10.1 cm
Colour:	Orange striped cat, blue butterfly, red ladybird, brown tree stump, green base
Issued:	1997 - 1997

Doulton Number	Price			
	U.S. $	Can. $	U.K. £	Aust. $
—	45.00	65.00	25.00	65.00

DODO™
Style Two

Designer:	Adrian Hughes
Height:	4", 10.1 cm
Colour:	White bird with blue wing tips, yellow head and black beak
Issued:	1997 - 1997

Doulton Number	Price			
	U.S. $	Can. $	U.K. £	Aust. $
—	45.00	65.00	25.00	65.00

Note: The *Alice In Wonderland* resin series does not carry a backstamp. It was sold as a set through Lawleys By Post.

MAD HATTER™
Style Two

Designer:	Adrian Hughes
Height:	4", 10.1 cm
Colour:	Brown trousers and top hat, green jacket, blue waistcoat, green base
Issued:	1997 - 1997

Doulton Number	Price			
	U.S. $	Can. $	U.K. £	Aust. $
—	45.00	65.00	25.00	65.00

QUEEN OF HEARTS™
Style Two

Designer:	Adrian Hughes
Height:	4", 10.1 cm
Colour:	Red coat trimmed with white, white dress with red and black design, black and red crown
Issued:	1997 - 1997

Doulton Number	Price			
	U.S. $	Can. $	U.K. £	Aust. $
—	45.00	65.00	25.00	65.00

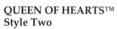

WHITE RABBIT™
Style Two

Designer:	Adrian Hughes
Height:	4", 10.1 cm
Colour:	White rabbit with brown jacket and green waistcoat, green base
Issued:	1997 - 1997

Doulton Number	Price			
	U.S. $	Can. $	U.K. £	Aust. $
—	45.00	65.00	25.00	65.00

BEATRIX POTTER FIGURINES

BEATRIX POTTER BACKSTAMPS

BP-1   BESWICK GOLD CIRCLE AND BESWICK GOLD PARALLEL LINES ISSUED 1948 TO 1954

BP-1 was the original Beswick Beatrix Potter backstamp; it was used on 21 figures plus one variation between 1948 and 1954. In addition, there are reports that it may have been used in error on *Tommy Brock*. There are two varieties of this backstamp.

BP-1a (gold circle). The first variety has the words "Beswick" and "England" forming a circle; a copyright notice may or may not appear. This variety was used on 19 figures; plus one variation and the *Tommy Brock* error.

The following is a list of the 19 figures on which the BP-1a backstamp was used:

> Benjamin Bunny, first version
> Flopsy, Mopsy and Cottontail
> Foxy Whiskered Gentleman, first version
> Hunca Munca
> Jemima Puddle-Duck, first version, first variation
> Johnny Town-Mouse
> Lady Mouse
> Little Pig Robinson, first variation
> Miss Moppet, first variation
> Mr. Jeremy Fisher, first and second variations
> Mrs. Tiggy-Winkle, first version, first variation
> Mrs. Tittlemouse
> Peter Rabbit, first version, first variation
> Ribby
> Samuel Whiskers
> Squirrel Nutkin, first version, first variation
> Timmy Tiptoes, first variation
> Timmy Willie From Johnny Town-Mouse
> Tom Kitten, first version, first variation

BP-1a Beswick Gold Circle

BP-1b (gold parallel lines). The second variety has the words "Beswick" and "England" arranged in parallel lines, "Beswick" atop "England;" the word "Copyright" appears in script. This variety, BP-1b, was used on two figures:

> Mrs. Rabbit, first version, first variation
> The Tailor of Gloucester, first version

It was also used in error on a few other figures, including *Benjamin Bunny*. An illustration of this backstamp was not available at press time.

BP-2   BESWICK GOLD OVAL ISSUED 1955 TO 1972

The gold oval was in use for 18 years, between 1955 and 1972, on 38 figures plus 4 versions/variations. *Pig-Wig*, introduced in 1972, was the last in line for the gold oval backstamp, and in some quarters they still doubt that it officially exists.

The following is a list of figures that can found with a BP-2 backstamp:

> Amiable Guinea-Pig
> Anna Maria
> Apply Dappley, first version
> Aunt Pettitoes
> Benjamin Bunny, first and second versions
> Cecily Parsley, first version
> Cousin Ribby
> Duchess (with flowers)
> Flopsy, Mopsy and Cottontail
> Foxy Whiskered Gentleman, first version
> Goody Tiptoes
> Hunca Munca
> Jemima Puddle-Duck, first version, first variation
> Johnny Town-Mouse
> Lady Mouse
> Little Pig Robinson, first variation
> Miss Moppet, first variation
> Mr. Benjamin Bunny, first version
> Mr. Jeremy Fisher, first version, first variation
> Mrs. Flopsy Bunny
> Mrs. Rabbit, first version
> Mrs. Tiggy-Winkle, first verion, first and second variations
> Mrs. Tittlemouse
> Old Mr. Brown
> Old Woman Who Lived in a Shoe, The
> Peter Rabbit, first version, first variation
> Pickles
> Pigling Bland, first variation
> Pig-Wig
> Ribby
> Samuel Whiskers
> Squirrel Nutkin, first version, first variation
> Tabitha Twitchit, first variation
> Tailor of Gloucester, first version
> Timmy Tiptoes, first and second variations
> Timmy Willie From Johnny Town-Mouse
> Tom Kitten, first version, first variation
> Tommy Brock, first version, first and second variations

BP-2 Beswick Gold Oval

Between BP-2 and BP-3 there exist transitional backstamps. These appear on a very limited number of figures. The backstamp is part gold and part brown line; usually "Beatrix Potter" and the figure's name appear in gold with the last three lines in brown.

Part gold, part brown line backstamp

BP-3   BESWICK BROWN LINE
ISSUED 1973 TO 1988

There are three varieties of this backstamp, which has the words "Beswick" and "England" in a straight line. It was used on 70 figures plus 27 versions/varieties for 16 years.

BP-3a Potter's, no date, issued 1973 to 1974
(no copyright date)
Used on 41 figures, plus 9 versions/varieties

BP-3b Potter's, date, issued 1974 to 1985
(copyright date)
Used on 63 figures, plus 16 versions/varieties

BP-3c Potter, date, issued 1985 to 1988
(no "s" on Potter)
Used on 63 figures, plus 16 versions/varieties

BP-4   BESWICK SIGNATURE
ISSUED 1988 TO 1989

This era saw the Beswick backstamp converted to the Royal Doulton backstamp. The connection with Beswick was kept by the addition of the John Beswick signature to the backstamp. In use for a year to a year and a half, this is one of the shortest time periods for a backstamp.

BP-4 Beswick Signature
Used on a total of 29 figures

BP-5   ROYAL ALBERT GOLD CROWN
ISSUED 1989

The gold backstamp was reinstituted for 1989 to mark the change from the Doulton/Beswick backstamps to Royal Albert. It was used on only the following six figures:

Benjamin Bunny, third version, first variation
Flopsy, Mopsy and Cottontail
Hunca Munca
Jemima Puddleduck, first version, first variation
Mrs. Rabbit and Bunnies
Peter Rabbit, first version, second variation

BP-5 Royal Albert Gold Crown

BP-6   ROYAL ALBERT BROWN CROWN
ISSUED 1989 TO 1998

This backstamp was issued in two sizes. A small version was used on the standard figures with a larger size for the large size figures. The small size was issued in 1989 and was used on 90 figures. The large size was issued in 1993 and was used on 10 figures.. A variation of the small size exists without the crown for small base figures.

BP-6a Small brown crown   BP-6b Large brown crown

BP-7 BESWICK BROWN OVAL
ISSUED 1993

Issued only on the large size Peter Rabbit to commemorate the 100th anniversary of Peter Rabbit 1893-1993.

BP-7 Brown Oval

BP-8 BESWICK WARE BROWN SCRIPT
ISSUED 1994 TO 1998

"Beswick Ware England" or the mark that followed, "Beswick Ware Made in England" is the earliest printed backstamp of the J. W. Beswick, Baltimore Works, Longton, and it was for the Beswick Centenary that the Beswick Ware logo was reinstated as the primary backstamp of the John Beswick Studio of Royal Doulton.

Since the first Beswick Ware stamp was used in 1894, and with the release of the new "Beswick Crest" series of backstamps in 1999, we find it now a good time put these backstamps in order.

BP-8a General Backstamp
Issued 1998

Issued as a general backstamp for a very short period of time in 1998, the brown script may turn out to be the rarest of the Beatrix Potter backstamps. It is found on only 2 figures.

Jemima and her Ducklings
Mrs. Tiggy-Winkle Washing

BP-8a Beswick Ware Brown Script

Note: BP-8b is a gold Beswick Ware backstamp which was inadvertently misplaced. The 100th anniversary stamp belongs in BP9. It will go there in the 6th edition.

BP-8b 100th Anniversary of
John Beswick Studios, Issued 1994

Issued to commemorate the 100th anniversary of the founding of the Beswick studios. This backstamp was available only on Jemima Puddle-duck.

BP-8b Beswick Centenary

BP-8c 50th Anniversary of Production of
Beatrix Potter Figures at Beswick, Issued 1997

1997 was the 50th anniversary of production of Beatrix Potter figurines at the John Beswick Studios in Longton. This backstamp was in use only during 1997.

BP-8c Beswick 50th Anniversary

BP-8d Limited Edition Backstamp

BP-8d ia a modification of BP-8b and designed for a limited edition figurines. It is found on *Hiding From the Cat* and *Mittens, Tom Kitten and Moppet*.

BP-8d Beswick Ware Brown Script
Limited Edition backstamp

BP-9   BESWICK WARE GOLD SCRIPT
ISSUED 1997 TO 1999

A gold Beswick Ware script backstamp was coupled with the issue of figurines with gold or platinum highlights. There are three varieties of this backstamp.

BP-9a   General Backstamp
1997-1998

The following small size figures issued with gold accents are coupled with gold Beswick Ware backstamps.

> Benjamin Bunny, third version, second variation
> Hunca Munca Sweeping, first version, second variation
> Jemima Puddle-Duck, first version, second variation
> Mrs. Tiggy-Winkle, first version, third variation
> Peter Rabbit, first version, third variation
> Tom Kitten, first version, third variation

BP-9a Beswick Gold Script

BP-9b   Limited Edition

This backstamp, a modification of BP-9a, appears on 12 large-size figurines issued by Lawleys By Post between 1997-1999. They were issued and sold in pairs. The pairs are listed below:

> Benjamin Bunn, fourth version, second variation
> Peter Rabbit, second version, second variation
>
> Jemima Puddle-duck, second version, second variation
> Mrs Tiggy-Winkle, second version, second variation
>
> Mr. Jeremy Fisher, second version, second variation
> Tom Kitten, second version, second variation
>
> Foxy Whiskered Gentleman, second version, second variation
> Mrs. Rabbit, third version, second variation
>
> Peter and the Red Pocket Handkerchief, second version, second variation
> Tailor of Gloucester, second version, second variation
>
> Hunca Munca Sweeping, second version
> Squirrel Nutkin, second version

BP-9b Beswick Ware Gold Script
Limited Edition

BP-9c   Peter Rabbit and Friends
Limited Editions

This backstamp is a modification of BP-9a and is found on limited edition figures with gold accents issued by Peter Rabbit and Friends.

> Ginger and Pickles
> Mrs. Tiggy-Winkle and Lucie
> Peter and the Red Pocket Handkerchief

BP-9c Peter Rabbit and Friends
Limited Editions

BP-10   BESWICK BLACK CREST
ISSUED 1998 TO DATE

In 1998 the Beswick backstamp was redesigned and the Beswick crest, first seen in 1968-1969, was re-introduced for the Beswick line of Storybook figurines. There are three varieties of this backstamp.

BP-10a   Beswick Black Crest

This backstamp, now in general use, will be found on the following Beatrix Potter figurines.:

> And This Pig Had None
> Appley Dapply, second variation
> Benjamin Ate a Lettuce Leaf
> Foxy Whiskered Gentleman, first version
> Hunca Munca Sweeping, first version first variation
> Jemima and her Ducklings
> Jemima Puddle-Duck, first version, first variation
> Jemima Puddleduck and the Foxy Whiskered Gentleman

Lady Mouse
Mr. Jeremy Fisher, first version, second variation
Mrs. Tiggy-Winkle Takes Tea
Mrs. Tiggy-Winkle Washing
Old Mr. Brown
Peter and the Red Pocket Handkerchief,
    first version, first variation
Peter in Bed
Ribby and the Patty Pan
Squirrel Nutkin, first version, second variation
The Old Woman Who Lived in a Shoe Knitting
Tom Kitten in the Rockery
Tommy Brock, second version, second variation

BP-10a Beswick Black Crest

BS-10b   **Beswick Black Arch**

This backstamp is a modification of BP-10a and can be found on the following figurines. The modification was necessary due to base restriction.

Hunca Munca
Miss Moppet, second variation
Mr. Benjamin Bunny, second variation
Mr. Drake Puddle-Duck
Mr. McGregor
Mrs. Flopsy Bunny
Mrs. Rabbit and Peter
Mrs. Rabbit Cooking
Peter Ate a Raddish
Peter Rabbit, first version, second variation
Peter Rabbit Gardening
Peter with Daffodils
Peter with Postbag
Rebeccah Puddle-Duck

BP-10b A modification of backstamp BP-10a

BP-10c   **Beswick Black Circle**

This backstamp is a modification of BP-10a. Its modification is also due to base restriction. It can be found on the following figurines.

Benjamin Bunny, third version, first variation
Little Pig Robinson, second variation
Mrs. Rabbit, second version
Mrs. Tiggy-Winkle, first version, second
    variation
Pigling Bland, second variation
Ribby
Tailor of Gloucester, first version
Tom Kitten, first version, second variation

BP-10c A modification of backstamp BP-10a

BP-11   **BESWICK GOLD CREST**
                        SPECIAL EDITIONS

At the time of publication BP-11 was found only on Sweet Peter Rabbit, a limited edition figurine commissioned by Peter Rabbit and Friends. This backstamp is a gold version of BP-10a

BP-11 Beswick Gold Crest

AMIABLE GUINEA-PIG™

Modeller: Albert Hallam
Height: 3 ½", 8.9 cm
Colour: Tan jacket, white waistcoat,
             yellow trousers
Issued: 1967 - 1983

Back Stamp	Beswick Number	Doulton Number	U.S. $	Price Can. $	U.K. £	Aust. $
BP-2	2061	P2061	750.00	900.00	400.00	950.00
BP-3a			325.00	500.00	175.00	525.00
BP-3b			300.00	475.00	175.00	500.00

Note: The colour of the coat varies from tan to brown.

AND THIS PIG HAD NONE™

Modeller: Martyn Alcock
Height: 4", 10.1 cm
Colour: Mauve dress, mottled
             burgundy and green
             shawl, brown hat
Issued: 1992 - 1998

Back Stamp	Beswick Number	Doulton Number	U.S. $	Price Can. $	U.K. £	Aust. $
BP-6a	3319	P3319	50.00	75.00	20.00	85.00
BP-10a			36.00	65.00	17.00	70.00

ANNA MARIA™

Modeller: Albert Hallam
Height: 3", 7.6 cm
Colour: Blue dress and white apron
Issued: 1963 - 1983

Back Stamp	Beswick Number	Doulton Number	U.S. $	Price Can. $	U.K. £	Aust. $
BP-2	1851	P1851	525.00	650.00	300.00	525.00
BP-3a			275.00	325.00	135.00	275.00
BP-3b			225.00	275.00	125.00	225.00

Note: Dress is bright blue in earlier versions and pale blue in later versions.

APPLEY DAPPLY™
First Version (Bottle Out)

Modeller:	Albert Hallam
Height:	3 ¼", 8.3 cm
Colour:	Brown mouse, white apron, blue trim, blue bow, yellow basket, tray of jam tarts
Issued:	1971 - 1975

Back Stamp	Beswick Number	Doulton Number	U.S. $	Price Can. $	U.K. £	Aust. $
BP-2	2333	P2333/1	400.00	600.00	300.00	600.00
BP-3a			350.00	475.00	185.00	475.00
BP-3b			325.00	425.00	175.00	450.00

APPLEY DAPPLY™
Second Version (Bottle In)

Modeller:	Albert Hallam
Height:	3 ¼", 8.3 cm
Colour:	Brown mouse, white apron, blue trim, blue bow, yellow basket, tray of jam tarts
Issued:	1975 to the present

Back Stamp	Beswick Number	Doulton Number	U.S. $	Price Can. $	U.K. £	Aust. $
BP-3b	2333	P2333/2	85.00	100.00	50.00	110.00
BP-3c			95.00	115.00	60.00	125.00
BP-6a			30.00	50.00	16.00	60.00
BP-10a			36.00	63.00	17.00	70.00

AUNT PETTITOES™

Modeller:	Albert Hallam
Height:	3 ¾", 9.5 cm
Colour:	Blue dress and white cap with blue polka dots
Issued:	1970 - 1993

Back Stamp	Beswick Number	Doulton Number	U.S. $	Price Can. $	U.K. £	Aust. $
BP-2	2276	P2276	550.00	650.00	225.00	675.00
BP-3a			95.00	135.00	60.00	150.00
BP-3b			75.00	95.00	50.00	100.00
BP-3c			85.00	125.00	55.00	125.00
BP-6a			50.00	65.00	30.00	75.00

Note: The dress is light blue in earlier versions and bright blue in later versions.

BABBITTY BUMBLE™

Modeller: Warren Platt
Height: 2 ¾", 7.0 cm
Colour: Black and gold
Issued: 1989 - 1993

Back Stamp	Beswick Number	Doulton Number	U.S. $	Price Can. $	U.K. £	Aust. $
BP-6a	2971	P2971	175.00	250.00	125.00	275.00

BENJAMIN ATE A LETTUCE LEAF™

Modeller: Martyn Alcock
Height: 4 ¾", 11.9 cm
Colour: Brown, white and yellow
Issued: 1992 - 1998

Back Stamp	Beswick Number	Doulton Number	U.S. $	Price Can. $	U.K. £	Aust. $
BP-6a	3317	P3317	30.00	60.00	18.00	75.00
BP-10a			36.00	65.00	17.00	70.00

BENJAMIN BUNNY™
First Version (Ears Out, Shoes Out)

Modeller: Arthur Gredington
Height: 4", 10.1 cm
Size: Small
Colour: Variation No. 1 pale green jacket
Variation No. 2 brown jacket
Issued: 1948 - 1974

Back Stamp	Beswick Number	Colour Variation	U.S. $	Price Can. $	U.K. £	Aust. $
BP-1a	1105/1	Pale green	550.00	650.00	325.00	700.00
BP-2		Pale green	500.00	575.00	300.00	600.00
BP-2		Brown	500.00	575.00	300.00	600.00
BP-3a		Pale green	350.00	400.00	250.00	425.00
BP-3b		Brown	300.00	375.00	225.00	400.00

BENJAMIN BUNNY™
Second Version (Ears Out, Shoes In)

Modeller:	Arthur Gredington
Height:	4", 10.1 cm
Size:	Small
Colour:	Variation No. 1 pale green jacket
	Variation No. 2 brown jacket
Issued:	1972 - c.1980

Back Stamp	Beswick Number	Colour Variation	U.S. $	Price Can. $	U.K. £	Aust. $
BP-2	1105/2	Pale green	500.00	575.00	275.00	550.00
BP-3a		Pale green	325.00	350.00	250.00	375.00
BP-3a		Brown	325.00	350.00	250.00	375.00
BP-3b		Pale green	250.00	300.00	225.00	325.00
BP-3b		Brown	250.00	300.00	225.00	325.00

BENJAMIN BUNNY™
Third Version, First Variation
(Ears In, Shoes In)

Modeller:	Arthur Gredington
Height:	4", 10.1 cm
Size:	Small
Colour:	Brown jacket, green beret
	with orange pompon
Issued:	c.1980 to the present

Back Stamp	Beswick Number	Doulton Number	U.S. $	Price Can. $	U.K. £	Aust. $
BP-3b	1105/3	P1105/3	75.00	100.00	45.00	115.00
BP-3c			95.00	115.00	60.00	125.00
BP-4			100.00	125.00	70.00	135.00
BP-5			150.00	175.00	90.00	175.00
BP-6a			30.00	60.00	16.00	70.00
BP-10c			36.00	65.00	17.00	70.00

BENJAMIN BUNNY™
Third Version, Second Variation
(Gold Shoes)

Modeller:	Arthur Gredington
Height:	4", 10.1 cm
Size:	Small
Colour:	Brown jacket, green beret
	with orange pompon, gold shoes
Issued:	1998 - 1998

Back Stamp	Beswick Number	Doulton Number	U.S. $	Price Can. $	U.K. £	Aust. $
BP-9a	—	PG1105	50.00	80.00	30.00	100.00

BENJAMIN BUNNY™
Fourth Version, First Variation

Modeller:	Martyn Alcock
Height:	6 ¼", 15.9 cm
Size:	Large
Colour:	Tan jacket, green beret with orange pompon
Issued:	1994 - 1997

Back Stamp	Beswick Number	Doulton Number	U.S. $	Price Can. $	U.K.£	Aust. $
BP-6b	3403	P3403	60.00	95.00	35.00	100.00

BENJAMIN BUNNY™
Fourth Version, Second Variation
(Gold Shoes)

Modeller:	Martyn Alcock
Height:	6 ¼", 15.9 cm
Size:	Large
Colour:	Tan jacket, green beret with orange pompon, gold shoes
Issued:	1997 in a limited edition of 1,947
Series:	Gold edition

Back Stamp	Beswick Number	Doulton Number	U.S. $	Price Can. $	U.K. £	Aust. $
BP-9b	G3403	PG3403	60.00	95.00	38.00	100.00

Note: Issued, numbered and sold as a pair with Peter Rabbit, second version, second variation.

BENJAMIN BUNNY SAT ON A BANK™
First Version (Head Looks Down)

Modeller:	David Lyttleton
Height:	3 ¾", 9.5 cm
Colour:	Brown jacket
Issued:	1983 - 1985

BEATRIX POTTER'S
"Benjamin Bunny"
"Sat on a bank"
© Frederick Warne P.L.C. 1983
BESWICK ENGLAND

Back Stamp	Beswick Number	Doulton Number	U.S. $	Price Can. $	U.K. £	Aust. $
BP-3b	2803/1	P2803/1	125.00	150.00	75.00	150.00
BP-3c			145.00	175.00	100.00	175.00

BENJAMIN BUNNY SAT ON A BANK™
Second Version (Head Looks Up)

Modeller:	David Lyttleton
Height:	3 ¾", 9.5 cm
Colour:	Golden brown jacket
Issued:	1983 - 1997

Back Stamp	Beswick Number	Doulton Number	U.S. $	Price Can. $	U.K. £	Aust. $
BP-3b	2803/2	P2803/2	125.00	165.00	90.00	165.00
BP-3c			150.00	185.00	100.00	190.00
BP-6a			40.00	60.00	25.00	65.00

BENJAMIN WAKES UP™

Modeller:	Amanda Hughes-Lubeck
Height:	2 ¼", 5.7 cm
Colour:	Green, white and orange
Issued:	1991 - 1997

Back Stamp	Beswick Number	Doulton Number	U.S. $	Price Can. $	U.K. £	Aust. $
BP-6a	3234	P3234	55.00	75.00	30.00	80.00

CECILY PARSLEY™
First Version (Blue Dress, Head Down)

Modeller:	Arthur Gredington
Height:	4", 10.1 cm
Colour:	Bright blue dress, white apron, brown pail
Issued:	1965 - 1985

Back Stamp	Beswick Number	Doulton Number	U.S. $	Price Can. $	U.K. £	Aust. $
BP-2	1941/1	P1941/1	300.00	400.00	175.00	375.00
BP-3a			115.00	135.00	65.00	150.00
BP-3b			85.00	100.00	50.00	100.00
BP-3c			100.00	135.00	60.00	125.00

Note: Cecily Parsley was issued with both a dark and a light blue dress.

CECILY PARSLEY™
Second Version (Pale Blue Dress, Head Up)

Modeller:	Arthur Gredington
Height:	4", 10.1 cm
Colour:	Pale blue dress, white apron
Issued:	1985 - 1993

BEATRIX POTTER "Cecily Parsley" © Frederick Warne & Co. 1965 Licensed by Copyrights BESWICK ENGLAND

Back Stamp	Beswick Number	Doulton Number	U.S. $	Price Can. $	U.K. £	Aust. $
BP-3c	1941/2	P1941/2	125.00	150.00	75.00	160.00
BP-6a			60.00	90.00	35.00	95.00

CHIPPY HACKEE™

Modeller:	David Lyttleton
Height:	3 ¾", 9.5 cm
Colour:	Pale green blanket, white handkerchief, green foot bath
Issued:	1979 - 1993

BEATRIX POTTER'S Chippy Hackee F. Warne & Co.Ltd. © Copyright 1979 BESWICK ENGLAND

Back Stamp	Beswick Number	Doulton Number	U.S. $	Price Can. $	U.K. £	Aust. $
BP-3b	2627	P2627	85.00	115.00	55.00	125.00
BP-3c			95.00	145.00	65.00	150.00
BP-6a			75.00	100.00	45.00	95.00

Note: The colour of the blanket may range from pale green to pale yellow.

CHRISTMAS STOCKING™

Modeller:	Martyn Alcock
Height:	3 ¼", 8.3 cm
Colour:	Brown mice, red and white striped stocking
Issued:	1991 - 1994

ROYAL ALBERT ® ENGLAND The Christmas Stocking Beatrix Potter © F. WARNE & CO. 1991 © 1991 ROYAL ALBERT LTD

Back Stamp	Beswick Number	Doulton Number	U.S. $	Price Can. $	U.K. £	Aust. $
BP-6a	3257	P3257	250.00	300.00	125.00	325.00

COTTONTAIL™

Modeller:	David Lyttleton
Height:	3 ¾", 9.5 cm
Colour:	Blue dress, brown chair
Issued:	1985 - 1996

Back Stamp	Beswick Number	Doulton Number	U.S. $	Price Can. $	U.K.£	Aust. $
BP-3b	2878	P2878	65.00	75.00	30.00	75.00
BP-3c			75.00	100.00	45.00	110.00
BP-4			85.00	110.00	60.00	125.00
BP-6a			35.00	60.00	25.00	65.00

COUSIN RIBBY™

Modeller:	Albert Hallam
Height:	3 ½", 8.9 cm
Colour:	Pink skirt and hat, green apron, blue shawl, yellow basket
Issued:	1970 - 1993

Back Stamp	Beswick Number	Doulton Number	U.S. $	Price Can. $	U.K. £	Aust. $
BP-2	2284	P2284	575.00	650.00	275.00	675.00
BP-3a			85.00	125.00	50.00	95.00
BP-3b			65.00	100.00	40.00	75.00
BP-3c			75.00	115.00	45.00	85.00
BP-6a			55.00	90.00	40.00	65.00

DIGGORY DIGGORY DELVET™

Modeller:	David Lyttleton
Height:	2 ¾", 7.0 cm
Colour:	Grey mole
Issued:	1982 - 1997

Back Stamp	Beswick Number	Doulton Number	U.S. $	Price Can. $	U.K. £	Aust. $
BP-3b	2713	P2713	75.00	100.00	45.00	125.00
BP-3c			85.00	115.00	50.00	135.00
BP-6a			45.00	70.00	25.00	75.00

DUCHESS™
Style One (Holding Flowers)

Modeller:	Graham Orwell
Height:	3 ¾", 9.5 cm
Colour:	Black dog, multi-coloured flowers
Issued:	1955 - 1967

Back Stamp	Beswick Number	Doulton Number	U.S. $	Price Can. $	U.K. £	Aust. $
BP-2	1355	P1355	3,000.00	4,500.00	1,800.00	4,500.00

Note: Italicized prices are indications only, and the actual selling price may be higher or lower, depending on market conditions.

DUCHESS™
Style Two (Holding a Pie)

Modeller:	Graham Tongue
Height:	4", 10.1 cm
Colour:	Black dog, blue bow, light brown pie
Issued:	1979 - 1982

BEATRIX POTTER'S
"Duchess"
F. Warne & Co.Ltd.
© Copyright 1979
BESWICK ENGLAND

Back Stamp	Beswick Number	Doulton Number	U.S. $	Price Can. $	U.K. £	Aust. $
BP-3b	2601	P2601	500.00	600.00	275.00	600.00

FIERCE BAD RABBIT™
First Version (Feet Out)

Modeller:	David Lyttleton
Height:	4 ¾", 12.1 cm
Colour:	Dark brown and white rabbit, red-brown carrot, green seat
Issued:	1977 - 1980

BEATRIX POTTER'S
"Fierce Bad Rabbit"
F. Warne & Co.Ltd.
© Copyright 1977
BESWICK ENGLAND

Back Stamp	Beswick Number	Doulton Number	U.S. $	Price Can. $	U.K. £	Aust. $
BP-3b	2586/1	P2586/1	200.00	325.00	150.00	325.00

FIERCE BAD RABBIT™
Second Version (Feet In)

Modeller:	David Lyttleton
Height:	4 ¾", 12.1 cm
Colour:	Light brown and white rabbit, red-brown carrot, green seat
Issued:	1980 - 1997

BEATRIX POTTER
"Fierce Bad Rabbit"
© Frederick Warne & Co. 1977
Licensed by Copyrights
BESWICK ENGLAND

Back Stamp	Beswick Number	Doulton Number	U.S. $	Price Can. $	U.K. £	Aust. $
BP-3b	2586/2	P2586/2	75.00	100.00	50.00	125.00
BP-3c			95.00	140.00	65.00	150.00
BP-4			85.00	125.00	60.00	125.00
BP-6a			40.00	60.00	25.00	70.00

FLOPSY, MOPSY AND COTTONTAIL™

Modeller:	Arthur Gredington
Height:	2 ½", 6.4 cm
Colour:	Brown and white rabbits wearing rose-pink cloaks
Issued:	1954 - 1997

BEATRIX POTTER'S
Flopsy, Mopsy
and Cotton Tail
E, WARNE & CO. LTD.
COPYRIGHT
BESWICK ENGLAND

Back Stamp	Beswick Number	Doulton Number	U.S. $	Price Can. $	U.K. £	Aust. $
BP-1a	1274	P1274	400.00	500.00	200.00	475.00
BP-2			275.00	325.00	150.00	300.00
BP-3a			100.00	135.00	60.00	100.00
BP-3b			65.00	100.00	40.00	75.00
BP-3c			75.00	115.00	45.00	85.00
BP-4			85.00	125.00	50.00	95.00
BP-5			175.00	200.00	100.00	195.00
BP-6a			40.00	60.00	25.00	60.00

Note: Colour variations of the cloaks exist. Angle of bunnies heads may vary.

FOXY READING COUNTRY NEWS™

Modeller:	Amanda Hughes-Lubeck
Height:	4 ¼", 10.8 cm
Colour:	Brown and green
Issued:	1990 - 1997

ROYAL ALBERT ®
ENGLAND
Foxy Reading
Beatrix Potter
© F. WARNE & CO. 1990
© 1990 ROYAL ALBERT LTD

Back Stamp	Beswick Number	Doulton Number	U.S. $	Price Can. $	U.K. £	Aust. $
BP-6a	3219	P3219	65.00	100.00	40.00	100.00

FOXY WHISKERED GENTLEMAN™
First Version, Small

Modeller:	Arthur Gredington
Height:	4 ¾", 12.1 cm
Colour:	Pale green jacket and trousers, pink waistcoat
Issued:	1954 - 1998

Back Stamp	Beswick Number	Doulton Number	U.S. $	Price Can. $	U.K. £	Aust. $
BP-1a	1277	P1277	400.00	475.00	200.00	500.00
BP-2			300.00	350.00	125.00	375.00
BP-3a			125.00	150.00	75.00	165.00
BP-3b			95.00	125.00	50.00	125.00
BP-3c			100.00	175.00	60.00	150.00
BP-4			100.00	175.00	60.00	150.00
BP-6a			30.00	50.00	16.00	60.00
BP-10a			36.00	65.00	17.00	70.00

Note: Variations occur with the head looking either right or left.

FOXY WHISKERED GENTLEMAN™
Second Version, First Variation

Modeller:	Arthur Gredington
Height:	6", 15 cm
Size:	Large
Colour:	Pale green jacket and trousers, pink waistcoat
Issued:	1995 - 1997

Back Stamp	Beswick Number	Doulton Number	U.S. $	Price Can. $	U.K. £	Aust. $
BP-6b	3450	P3450	65.00	95.00	30.00	90.00

FOXY WHISKERED GENTLEMAN™
Second Version, Second Variation

Modeller:	Arthur Gredington
Height:	6", 15 cm
Size:	Large
Colour:	Pale green jacket and trousers, pink waistcoat, gold buttons
Issued:	1998 in a limited edition fo 1,947
Series:	Gold edition

Back Stamp	Beswick Number	Doulton Number	U.S. $	Price Can. $	U.K. £	Aust. $
BP-9b	—	PG3450	60.00	95.00	38.00	100.00

Note: Issued, numbered and sold as a pair with Mrs. Rabbit, third version, first variation.

GENTLEMAN MOUSE MADE A BOW™

Modeller: Ted Chawner
Height: 3", 7.6 cm
Colour: Brown, blue and white
Issued: 1990 - 1996

Back Stamp	Beswick Number	Doulton Number	U.S. $	Price Can. $	U.K. £	Aust. $
BP-6a	3200	P3200	60.00	95.00	30.00	90.00

GINGER™

Modeller: David Lyttleton
Height: 3 ¾", 9.5 cm
Colour: Green, white and brown
Issued: 1976 - 1982

Back Stamp	Beswick Number	Doulton Number	U.S. $	Price Can. $	U.K. £	Aust. $
BP-3b	2559	P2559	700.00	900.00	375.00	950.00

Note: The jacket colour varies from light to dark green.

GINGER AND PICKLES™

Modeller: Graham Tongue
Height: 4 ½", 11.9 cm
Colour: Brown, green, and white, gold highlights
Issued: 1998 in a limited edition of 2,750
Series: Tableau

Back Stamp	Beswick Number	Doulton Number	U.S. $	Price Can. $	U.K. £	Aust. $
BP-9c	3790	P3790	350.00	525.00	175.00	550.00

GOODY TIPTOES™

Modeller:	Arthur Gredington
Height:	3 ½", 8.9 cm
Colour:	Grey squirrel wearing pink dress and white apron, brown sack with yellow nuts
Issued:	1961 - 1997

Back Stamp	Beswick Number	Doulton Number	U.S. $	Price Can. $	U.K. £	Aust. $
BP-2	1675	P1675	275.00	350.00	160.00	375.00
BP-3a			95.00	110.00	60.00	115.00
BP-3b			60.00	75.00	40.00	85.00
BP-3c			90.00	100.00	60.00	100.00
BP-6a			45.00	60.00	25.00	75.00

Note: This model has two different bases and the dress comes in various shades of pink.

GOODY AND TIMMY TIPTOES™

Modeller:	David Lyttleton
Height:	4", 10.1 cm
Colour:	Timmy - rose coat Goody - pink overdress with green and biege underskirt, green umbrella
Issued:	1986 - 1996

Back Stamp	Beswick Number	Doulton Number	U.S. $	Price Can. $	U.K. £	Aust. $
BP-3c	2957	P2957	300.00	425.00	185.00	400.00
BP-6a			75.00	100.00	55.00	95.00

HIDING FROM THE CAT™

Modeller:	Graham Tongue
Height:	5", 12.7 cm cm
Colour:	Brown, blue and grey
Issued:	1998 in a limited edition of 3,500
Series	Tableau of the Year

Back Stamp	Beswick Number	Doulton Number	U.S. $	Price Can. $	U.K. £	Aust. $
BP-8d	P3766	P3766	195.00	350.00	100.00	375.00

HUNCA MUNCA™

Modeller:	Arthur Gredington
Height:	2 ¾", 7 cm
Colour:	Blue dress, white apron, pink blanket and straw cradle
Issued:	1951 to the present

Back Stamp	Beswick Number	Doulton Number	U.S. $	Price Can. $	U.K. £	Aust.
BP-1a	1198	P1198	300.00	375.00	150.00	325.0
BP-2			225.00	275.00	110.00	250.0
BP-3a			90.00	125.00	60.00	100.0
BP-3b			75.00	100.00	50.00	90.0
BP-3c			85.00	115.00	55.00	95.0
BP-4			100.00	135.00	65.00	110.0
BP-5			125.00	150.00	80.00	125.0
BP-6a			30.00	50.00	16.00	60.0
BP-10b			36.00	63.00	17.00	70.0

HUNCA MUNCA SPILLS THE BEADS™
First Version

Modeller:	Martyn Alcock
Height:	3 ¼", 8.3 cm
Colour:	Brown mouse, blue and white rice jar
Issued:	1992 - 1996

Back Stamp	Beswick Number	Doulton Number	U.S. $	Price Can. $	U.K. £	Aust. $
BP-6a	3288	P3288	60.00	90.00	35.00	95.00

HUNCA MUNCA SWEEPING™
First Version, First Variation

Modeller:	David Lyttleton
Height:	3 ½", 8.9 cm
Size:	Small
Colour:	Mauve patterned dress with white apron, green broom handle
Issued:	1977 to the present

Back Stamp	Beswick Number	Doulton Number	U.S. $	Price Can. $	U.K. £	Aust.
BP-3b	2584	P2584	90.00	125.00	60.00	125.0
BP-3c			100.00	135.00	65.00	140.0
BP-4			100.00	150.00	65.00	160.0
BP-6a			30.00	50.00	16.00	65.0
BP-10a			36.00	63.00	17.00	70.0

HUNCA MUNCA SWEEPING™
First Version, Second Variation (Gold Dustpan)

Modeller:	David Lyttleton
Height:	3 ½", 8.9 cm
Size:	Small
Colour:	Mauve patterned dress, white apron, green broom handle, gold dustpan
Issued:	1998 - 1998

Back Stamp	Beswick Number	Doulton Number	U.S. $	Price Can. $	U.K. £	Aust. $
BP-9a	—	PG2584	55.00	75.00	25.00	80.00

HUNCA MUNCA SWEEPING™
Second Version (Gold Dustpan)

Modeller:	David Lyttleton
Height:	Unknown
Size:	Large
Colour:	Mauve patterned dress, white apron, green broom handle, gold dustpan
Issued:	1999 in a limited edition of 1,947
Series:	Gold edtion

Back Stamp	Beswick Number	Doulton Number	U.S. $	Price Can. $	U.K. £	Aust. $
BP-9b	—	PG	60.00	95.00	38.00	100.00

Note: Issued, numbered and sold as a pair with Squirrel Nutkin, large size.

JEMIMA AND HER DUCKLINGS™

Modeller:	Martyn Alcock
Height:	4 ¼", 10.5 cm
Colour:	Mauve shawl
Issued:	1998 to the present

Back Stamp	Beswick Number	Doulton Number	U.S. $	Price Can. $	U.K. £	Aust. $
BP-8a	—	P3786	200.00	300.00	100.00	300.00
BP-10a			50.00	110.00	28.00	95.00

Note: Very few examples of BP-8a are known.

JEMIMA PUDDLE-DUCK™
First Version, First Variation, Small

Modeller:	Arthur Gredington
Height:	4 ¾", 12.1 cm
Colour:	Mauve or pink shawl, light blue bonnet, yellow and beige scarf clip
Issued:	1948 to the present

Back Stamp	Beswick Number	Doulton Number	U.S. $	Price Can. $	U.K. £	Aust. $
BP-1a	1092	P1092	275.00	350.00	175.00	375.00
BP-2			195.00	250.00	125.00	275.00
BP-3a			85.00	120.00	50.00	125.00
BP-3b			60.00	90.00	40.00	100.00
BP-3c			75.00	100.00	45.00	110.00
BP-4			95.00	125.00	60.00	135.00
BP-5			125.00	165.00	90.00	175.00
BP-6a			30.00	50.00	16.00	65.00
BP-10a			36.00	63.00	17.00	70.00

JEMIMA PUDDLE-DUCK™
First Version, Second Variation
(Gold Scarf Clip)

Modeller:	Arthur Gredington
Height:	4 ¼", 10.75 cm
Size:	Small
Colour:	White duck, mauve or pink shawl, light blue bonnet, gold scarf clip
Issued:	1997 - 1997

Back Stamp	Beswick Number	Doulton Number	U.S. $	Price Can. $	U.K. £	Aust. $
BP-9a	—	PG1092	50.00	85.00	28.00	95.00

JEMIMA PUDDLE-DUCK™
Second Version, First Variation

Modeller:	Martyn Alcock
Height:	6", 15 cm
Size:	Large
Colour:	White duck, mauve shawl, light blue bonnet
Issued:	1993 - 1997

Back Stamp	Beswick Number	Doulton Number	U.S. $	Price Can. $	U.K. £	Aust. $
BP-6b	—	P3373	60.00	95.00	30.00	100.00
BP-8b	Beswick Centenary		60.00	95.00	30.00	100.00

JEMIMA PUDDLE-DUCK™
Second Version, Second Variation
(Gold Scarf Clip)

Modeller:	Martyn Alcock
Height:	6", 15.0 cm
Size:	Large
Colour:	White duck, mauve shawl, light blue bonnet, gold scarf clip
Issued:	1998 in a limited edition of 1,947
Series:	Gold edition

Back Stamp	Beswick Number	Doulton Number	U.S. $	Price Can. $	U.K. £	Aust. $
BP-9b	—	PG3373	60.00	95.00	38.00	100.00

Note: Issued, numbered and sold as a pair with Mrs. Tiggy-Winkle, second version, second variation.

JEMIMA PUDDLE-DUCK MADE A FEATHER NEST™

Modeller:	David Lyttleton
Height:	2 ¼", 5.7 cm
Colour:	Blue hat, mauve or pink shawl, white duck
Issued:	1983 - 1997

BEATRIX POTTER'S
Jemima Puddleduck
Made a feather nest
c/ Frederick Warne P.L.C. 1983
BESWICK
ENGLAND

Back Stamp	Beswick Number	Doulton Number	U.S. $	Price Can. $	U.K. £	Aust. $
BP-3b	2823	P2823	65.00	70.00	35.00	95.00
BP-3c			75.00	85.00	40.00	100.00
BP-4			90.00	100.00	50.00	110.00
BP-6a			35.00	60.00	25.00	65.00

Note: This model was issued with either a mauve or pink shawl.

JEMIMA PUDDLE-DUCK WITH FOXY WHISKERED GENTLEMAN™

Modeller:	Ted Chawner
Height:	4 ¾", 12.1 cm
Colour:	Brown, green, white and blue
Issued:	1990 to the present

ROYAL ALBERT ®
ENGLAND
Jemima Puddleduck with
Foxy Whiskered Gentleman
Beatrix Potter
© F WARNE & CO 1989
© 1989 ROYAL ALBERT LTD

Back Stamp	Beswick Number	Doulton Number	U.S. $	Price Can. $	U.K. £	Aust. $
BP-6a	3193	P3193	60.00	85.00	26.00	100.00
BP-10a			60.00	94.00	28.00	110.00

JOHN JOINER™

Modeller:	Graham Tongue
Height:	2 ½", 6.4 cm
Colour:	Brown dog wearing green jacket
Issued:	1990 - 1997

BEATRIX POTTER

ROYAL ALBERT ®
ENGLAND
John Joiner
Beatrix Potter
© F. WARNE & CO. 1990
© 1990 ROYAL ALBERT LTD

Back Stamp	Beswick Number	Doulton Number	U.S. $	Price Can. $	U.K. £	Aust. $
BP-6a	2965	P2965	50.00	75.00	25.00	80.00

Note: John Joiner will vary in shade from black to blue-black.

JOHNNY TOWN-MOUSE™

Modeller:	Arthur Gredington
Height:	3 ½", 8.9 cm
Colour:	Pale blue jacket, white and brown waistcoat
Issued:	1954 - 1993

Back Stamp	Beswick Number	Doulton Number	U.S. $	Price Can. $	U.K. £	Aust. $
BP-1a	1276	P1276	275.00	375.00	150.00	400.00
BP-2			195.00	250.00	100.00	275.00
BP-3a			85.00	120.00	50.00	135.00
BP-3b			60.00	90.00	40.00	120.00
BP-3c			75.00	100.00	45.00	100.00
BP-6a			55.00	75.00	30.00	85.00

Note: Jacket colouring varies from pale to deep blue.

JOHNNY TOWN-MOUSE WITH BAG™

Modeller:	Ted Chawner
Height:	3 ½", 8.9 cm
Colour:	Light brown coat and hat, yellow-cream waistcoat
Issued:	1988 - 1994

BEATRIX POTTER
"Johnny Town-Mouse with Bag"
© Frederick Warne & Co. 1988
Licensed by Copyrights
John Beswick
Studio of Royal Doulton
England

Back Stamp	Beswick Number	Doulton Number	U.S. $	Price Can. $	U.K. £	Aust. $
BP-4	3094	P3094	325.00	400.00	150.00	425.00
BP-6a			100.00	150.00	45.00	150.00

LADY MOUSE™

Modeller:	Arthur Gredington
Height:	4", 10.1 cm
Colour:	White dress with yellow trim and blue polka-dot sleeves, white hat with purple and blue highlights
Issued:	1950 to the present

Back Stamp	Beswick Number	Doulton Number	U.S. $	Price Can. $	U.K. £	Aust. $
BP-1a	1183	P1183	325.00	400.00	175.00	400.00
BP-2			225.00	325.00	125.00	350.00
BP-3a			85.00	120.00	50.00	125.00
BP-3b			65.00	95.00	40.00	100.00
BP-3c			75.00	100.00	45.00	110.00
BP-6a			30.00	50.00	16.00	65.00
BP-10a			36.00	63.00	17.00	70.00

LADY MOUSE MADE A CURTSEY™

Modeller:	Amanda Hughes-Lubeck
Height:	3 ¼", 8.3 cm
Colour:	Purple-pink and white
Issued:	1990 - 1997

Back Stamp	Beswick Number	Doulton Number	U.S. $	Price Can. $	U.K. £	Aust. $
BP-6a	3220	P3220	40.00	60.00	20.00	70.00

LITTLE BLACK RABBIT™

Modeller:	David Lyttleton
Height:	4 ½", 11.4 cm
Colour:	Black rabbit wearing green waistcoat
Issued:	1977 - 1997

Back Stamp	Beswick Number	Doulton Number	U.S. $	Price Can. $	U.K. £	Aust. $
BP-3b	2585	P2585	65.00	95.00	40.00	70.00
BP-3c			75.00	100.00	45.00	85.00
BP-4			125.00	175.00	75.00	140.00
BP-6a			40.00	60.00	35.00	75.00

Note: The jacket colouring varies from light to dark green.

LITTLE PIG ROBINSON™
First Variation (Blue Stripes)

Modeller:	Arthur Gredington
Height:	4", 10.2 cm
Colour:	White and blue striped dress, brown basket with yellow cauliflowers
Issued:	1948 - 1974

Back Stamp	Beswick Number	Doulton Number	U.S. $	Price Can. $	U.K. £	Aust. $
BP-1a	1104/1	P1104/1	475.00	675.00	275.00	650.00
BP-2			325.00	500.00	185.00	525.00
BP-3a			300.00	475.00	175.00	500.00
BP-3b			300.00	475.00	175.00	500.00

LITTLE PIG ROBINSON™
Second Variation (Blue Checked)

Modeller:	Arthur Gredington
Height:	3 ½", 8.9 cm
Colour:	Blue dress, brown basket with cream cauliflowers
Issued:	c.1974 to the present

Back Stamp	Beswick Number	Doulton Number	U.S. $	Price Can. $	U.K. £	Aust. $
BP-3b	1104/2	P1104/2	75.00	100.00	50.00	110.00
BP-3c			85.00	120.00	45.00	125.00
BP-6a			30.00	50.00	16.00	65.00
BP-10c			36.00	63.00	17.00	70.00

LITTLE PIG ROBINSON SPYING™

Modeller:	Ted Chawner
Height:	3 ½", 8.9 cm
Colour:	Blue and white striped dress, rose-pink chair
Issued:	1987 - 1993

Back Stamp	Beswick Number	Doulton Number	U.S. $	Price Can. $	U.K. £	Aust. $
BP-3c	3031	P3031	175.00	250.00	100.00	300.00
BP-6a			95.00	150.00	60.00	100.00

MISS DORMOUSE™

Modeller:	Martyn Alcock
Height:	4", 10.1 cm
Colour:	Blue, white and pink
Issued:	1991 - 1995

ROYAL ALBERT ®
ENGLAND
Miss Dormouse
Beatrix Potter
© F. WARNE & CO. 1991
© 1991 ROYAL ALBERT LTD

Back Stamp	Beswick Number	Doulton Number	U.S. $	Price Can. $	U.K. £	Aust. $
BP-6a	3251	P3251	100.00	150.00	60.00	165.00

MISS MOPPET™
First Variation (Mottled Brown Cat)

Modeller:	Arthur Gredington
Height:	3", 7.6 cm
Colour:	Dark brown cat, blue checkered kerchief
Issued:	1954 - c.1978

Back Stamp	Beswick Number	Doulton Number	U.S. $	Price Can. $	U.K. £	Aust. $
BP-1a	1275/1	P1275/1	250.00	350.00	150.00	375.00
BP-2			195.00	300.00	90.00	325.00
BP-3a			175.00	250.00	80.00	250.00
BP-3b			150.00	225.00	75.00	250.00

MISS MOPPET™
Second Variation (Brown Striped Cat)

Modeller:	Arthur Gredington
Height:	3", 7.6 cm
Colour:	Light brown cat, blue checkered kerchief
Issued:	1978 to the present

BEATRIX POTTER'S
"Miss. Moppet"
F. Warne & Co.Ltd.
© Copyright 1954
BESWICK ENGLAND

Back Stamp	Beswick Number	Doulton Number	U.S. $	Price Can. $	U.K. £	Aust. $
BP3a	1275/2	P1275/2	85.00	125.00	50.00	135.00
BP-3b			55.00	80.00	35.00	85.00
BP-3c			75.00	100.00	45.00	110.00
BP-6a			30.00	50.00	16.00	65.00
BP-10b			36.00	63.00	17.00	70.00

MITTENS AND MOPPET™

Modeller:	Ted Chawner
Height:	3 ¾", 9.5 cm
Colour:	Blue, brown and grey
Issued:	1990 - 1994

ROYAL ALBERT ®
ENGLAND
Mittens and Moppet
Beatrix Potter
© F. WARNE & CO. 1989
© 1989 ROYAL ALBERT LTD

Back Stamp	Beswick Number	Doulton Number	U.S. $	Price Can. $	U.K. £	Aust. $
BP-6a	3197	P3197	195.00	275.00	85.00	250.00

MITTENS, TOM KITTEN AND MOPPET™

Modeller:	Amanda Hughes-Lubeck
Height:	7", 17.8 cm
Colour:	Pale blue and beige
Issued:	1999 - 1999
Series:	Tableau of the Year

Back Stamp	Beswick Number	Doulton Number	U.S. $	Price Can. $	U.K. £	Aust. $
BP-8d	—	P3792	195.00	380.00	100.00	400.00

MOTHER LADYBIRD™

Modeller:	Warren Platt
Height:	2 ½", 6 .4 cm
Colour:	Red and black
Issued:	1989 - 1996

ROYAL ALBERT ®
ENGLAND
Mother Ladybird
Beatrix Potter
© F. WARNE & CO. 1989
© 1989 ROYAL ALBERT LTD

Back Stamp	Beswick Number	Doulton Number	U.S. $	Price Can. $	U.K. £	Aust. $
BP-6a	2966	P2966	75.00	100.00	45.00	100.00

MR. ALDERMAN PTOLEMY™

Modeller: Graham Tongue
Height: 3 ½", 8.9 cm
Colour: Brown, grey and green
Issued: 1973 - 1997

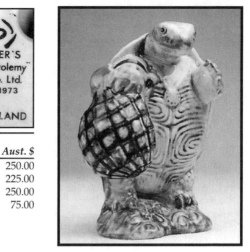

Back Stamp	Beswick Number	Doulton Number	U.S. $	Price Can. $	U.K. £	Aust. $
BP-3a	2424	P2424	200.00	275.00	125.00	250.00
BP-3b			150.00	200.00	85.00	225.00
BP-3c			175.00	250.00	100.00	250.00
BP-6a			40.00	60.00	25.00	75.00

MR. BENJAMIN BUNNY™
First Version (Pipe Out)

Modeller: Arthur Gredington
Height: 4 ¼", 10.8 cm
Colour: 1. Dark maroon jacket
           2. Lilac jacket
Issued: 1965 - 1974

Back Stamp	Beswick Number	Colour Variation	U.S. $	Price Can. $	U.K. £	Aust. $
BP-2	1940/1	Dark maroon	600.00	800.00	325.00	750.00
BP-3a		Dark maroon	525.00	625.00	250.00	625.00
BP-3a		Lilac	525.00	625.00	250.00	625.00

MR. BENJAMIN BUNNY™
Second Version (Pipe In)

Modeller: Arthur Gredington
Height: 4 ¼", 10.8 cm
Colour: 1. Dark maroon jacket
           2. Lilac jacket
Issued: 1. c.1970 - c.1974
           2. 1975 to the present

Back Stamp	Beswick Number	Colour Variation	U.S. $	Price Can. $	U.K. £	Aust. $
BP-3a	1940/2	Dark maroon	500.00	675.00	250.00	650.00
BP-3a		Lilac	85.00	120.00	50.00	125.00
BP-3b		Dark maroon	500.00	675.00	250.00	650.00
BP-3b		Lilac	60.00	90.00	35.00	100.00
BP-3c		Lilac	85.00	120.00	50.00	125.00
BP-4		Lilac	75.00	100.00	40.00	100.00
BP-6a		Lilac	30.00	50.00	16.00	65.00
BP-10b		Lilac	36.00	63.00	17.00	70.00

MR. BENJAMIN BUNNY AND PETER RABBIT™

Modeller:	Alan Maslankowski
Height:	4", 10.1 cm
Colour:	Benjamin Bunny - lilac jacket, yellow waistcoat
	Peter Rabbit - blue jacket
Issued:	1975 - 1995

BEATRIX POTTER'S
"Mr. Benjamin Bunny
& Peter Rabbit"
F. Warne & Co.Ltd.
© Copyright 1975
BESWICK ENGLAND

Back Stamp	Beswick Number	Doulton Number	U.S. $	Price Can. $	U.K. £	Aust. $
BP-3b	2509	P2509	150.00	200.00	65.00	225.00
BP-3c			175.00	225.00	95.00	250.00
BP-6a			70.00	100.00	40.00	90.00

MR. DRAKE PUDDLE-DUCK™

Modeller:	David Lyttleton
Height:	4", 10.1 cm
Colour:	White duck, blue waistcoat and trousers
Issued:	1979 to the present

BEATRIX POTTER
"Mr. Drake Puddle-Duck"
© Frederick Warne & Co. 1979
Licensed by Copyrights
BESWICK ENGLAND

Back Stamp	Beswick Number	Doulton Number	U.S. $	Price Can. $	U.K. £	Aust. $
BP-3b	2628	P2628	60.00	90.00	35.00	95.00
BP-3c			80.00	115.00	45.00	120.00
BP-4			85.00	120.00	45.00	125.00
BP-6a			30.00	50.00	16.00	65.00
BP-10b			36.00	63.00	17.00	70.00

MR JACKSON™
First Variation (Green Toad)

Modeller:	Albert Hallam
Height:	2 ¾", 7.0 cm
Colour:	Green toad wearing mauve jacket
Issued:	1974 - c.1974

BEATRIX POTTER'S
"Mr Jackson"
F. Warne & Co.Ltd.
Copyright
BESWICK ENGLAND

Back Stamp	Beswick Number	Doulton Number	U.S. $	Price Can. $	U.K. £	Aust. $
BP-3a	2453/1	P2453/1	600.00	750.00	325.00	700.00

MR JACKSON™
Second Variation (Brown Toad)

Modeller:	Albert Hallam
Height:	2 ¾", 7.0 cm
Colour:	Brown toad wearing mauve jacket
Issued:	1975 - 1997

BEATRIX POTTER'S
"Mr Jackson"
F. Warne & Co.Ltd.
© Copyright 1974
BESWICK ENGLAND

Back Stamp	Beswick Number	Doulton Number	U.S. $	Price Can. $	U.K. £	Aust. $
BP-3b	2453/2	P2453/2	85.00	110.00	60.00	125.00
BP-3c			95.00	135.00	65.00	150.00
BP-6a			40.00	50.00	25.00	60.00

MR. JEREMY FISHER™
First Version, First Variation (Spotted Legs)

Modeller:	Arthur Gredington
Height:	3", 7.6 cm
Size:	Small
Colour:	Lilac coat, green frog with small brown spots on head and legs
Issued:	1950 - c.1974

BEATRIX POTTER'S
"Mr. Jeremy Fisher"
F. Warne & Co. Ltd.
Copyright
BESWICK ENGLAND

Back Stamp	Beswick Number	Doulton Number	U.S. $	Price Can. $	U.K. £	Aust. $
BP-1	1157/1	P1157/1	400.00	525.00	250.00	550.00
BP-2			300.00	350.00	175.00	325.00
BP-3a			200.00	250.00	90.00	200.00
BP-3b			175.00	225.00	80.00	185.00

MR. JEREMY FISHER™
First Version, Second Variation (Striped Legs)

Modeller:	Arthur Gredington
Height:	3", 7.6 cm
Size:	Small
Colour:	Lilac coat, green frog with large spots on head and stripes on legs
Issued:	c.1950 to the present

BEATRIX POTTER'S
"Mr. Jeremy Fisher"
Copyright
BESWICK ENGLAND

Back Stamp	Beswick Number	Doulton Number	U.S. $	Price Can. $	U.K. £	Aust. $
BP-1	1157/2	P1157/2	400.00	525.00	250.00	550.00
BP-3b			65.00	95.00	40.00	100.00
BP-3c			85.00	120.00	50.00	125.00
BP-6a			30.00	50.00	16.00	60.00
BP-10a			36.00	63.00	17.00	70.00

Note: BP-3c backstamp name exists with and without "Mr."

MR. JEREMY FISHER™
Second Version, First Variation

Modeller:	Martyn Alcock
Height:	5", 12.7 cm
Size:	Large
Colour:	Lilac coat, green frog with stripes on legs
Issued:	1994 - 1997

BEATRIX POTTER'S
"Mr. Jeremy Fisher"
F. Warne & Co. Ltd.
© Copyright 1950
BESWICK ENGLAND

Back Stamp	Beswick Number	Doulton Number	U.S. $	Price Can. $	U.K. £	Aust. $
BP-6b	3372	P3372	65.00	95.00	30.00	100.00

MR. JEREMY FISHER™
Second Version, Second Variation (gold buttons)

Modeller:	Martyn Alcock
Height:	5", 12.7 cm
Size:	Large
Colour:	Green frog with stripes on legs, lilac coat with gold buttons
Issued:	1998 in a limited edition of 1,947
Series:	Gold edition

Back Stamp	Beswick Number	Doulton Number	U.S. $	Price Can. $	U.K. £	Aust. $
BP-9b	—	PG3372	65.00	95.00	38.00	100.00

Note: Issued, numbered and sold as a pair with Tom Kitten, second version, second variation.

MR. JEREMY FISHER DIGGING™

Modeller:	Ted Chawner
Height:	3 ¾", 9.5 cm
Colour:	Mauve coat, pink waistcoat, white cravat, green frog with brown highlights
Issued:	1988 - 1994

BEATRIX POTTER
"Mr. Jeremy Fisher Digging"
© F. Warne & Co. 1988
Licensed by Copyrights
John Beswick
Studio of Royal Doulton
England

Back Stamp	Beswick Number	Doulton Number	U.S. $	Price Can. $	U.K. £	Aust. $
BP-4	3090	P3090	325.00	450.00	200.00	475.00
BP-6a			150.00	200.00	75.00	225.00

Note: Jeremy Fisher's skin may have dark or light spots.

MR. McGREGOR™
First Version (Arm up)

Modeller: Martyn Alcock
Height: 5 ¼", 13.5 cm
Colour: Brown hat and trousers,
tan vest and pale blue shirt
Issued: 1995 to the present

ROYAL ALBERT ®
ENGLAND
Mr McGregor
Beatrix Potter
© F. WARNE & CO. 1995
© 1995 ROYAL ALBERT LTD

Back Stamp	Beswick Number	Doulton Number	U.S. $	Price Can. $	U.K. £	Aust. $
BP-6a	3506/1	P3506/1	40.00	60.00	20.00	75.00
BP-10b			48.00	75.00	19.00	90.00

MR. McGREGOR™
Second Version (Arm down)

Modeller: Martyn Alcock
Height: 5 ¼", 13.5 cm
Colour: Brown hat and trousers,
tan vest and pale blue shirt
Issued: Unknown

Back Stamp	Beswick Number	Doulton Number	U.S. $	Price Can. $	U.K. £	Aust. $
BP-6a	3506/2	P3506/2	100.00	135.00	65.00	110.00

BEATRIX POTTER
"Mr. Tod"
© F. Warne & Co. 1988
Licensed by Copyrights
John Beswick
Studio of Royal Doulton
England

MR. TOD™

Modeller: Ted Chawner
Height: 4 ¾", 12.1 cm
Colour: Green suit, red waistcoat,
dark brown walking stick
Issued: 1988 - 1993

Back Stamp	Beswick Number	Doulton Number	U.S. $	Price Can. $	U.K. £	Aust. $
BP-4	3091/1	P3091/1	275.00	375.00	150.00	425.00
BP-6a			150.00	185.00	75.00	175.00

Note: Variations occur with the head facing right or left and the base in either
green or brown.

MRS FLOPSY BUNNY™

Modeller:	Arthur Gredington
Height:	4", 10.1 cm
Colour:	1. Dark blue dress, pink bag
	2. Light blue dress, pink bag
Issued:	1965 - 1998

Back Stamp	Beswick Number	Colour Variation	U.S. $	Price Can. $	U.K. £	Aust. $
BP-2	1942	Dark blue	225.00	300.00	150.00	250.00
BP-3a		Dark blue	75.00	110.00	50.00	80.00
BP-3b		Dark blue	60.00	95.00	40.00	100.00
BP-3b		Light blue	60.00	95.00	40.00	100.00
BP-3c		Light blue	80.00	120.00	55.00	125.00
BP-4		Light blue	85.00	125.00	60.00	135.00
BP-6a		Light blue	30.00	50.00	16.00	65.00
BP-10b		Light blue	36.00	63.00	17.00	70.00

MRS RABBIT™
First Version (Umbrella Out)

Modeller:	Arthur Gredington
Height:	4 ¼", 10.8 cm
Size:	Small
Colour:	1. Pink and yellow striped dress
	2. Lilac and pale green striped dress
Issued:	1951 - c.1974

Back Stamp	Beswick Number	Colour Variation	U.S. $	Price Can. $	U.K.£	Aust. $
BP-1	1200/1	Pink	575.00	775.00	325.00	800.00
BP-2		Pink	475.00	625.00	250.00	625.00
BP-2		Lilac	475.00	625.00	250.00	625.00
BP-3a		Lilac	325.00	450.00	150.00	450.00
BP-3b		Lilac	300.00	425.00	150.00	425.00

Note: The base is too small to carry the circular Beswick England backstamp. It is flattened and the copyright date is carried in script.

MRS RABBIT™
Second Version (Umbrella Moulded to Dress)

Modeller:	Arthur Gredington
Height:	4 ¼", 10.8 cm
Size:	Small
Colour:	Lilac and yellow striped dress, red collar and cap, light straw coloured basket
Issued:	c.1975 to the present

Back Stamp	Beswick Number	Doulton Number	U.S. $	Price Can. $	U.K. £	Aust. $
BP-3b	1200/2	P1200/2	60.00	95.00	40.00	100.00
BP-3c			80.00	120.00	60.00	125.00
BP-4			85.00	125.00	65.00	125.00
BP-6a			30.00	50.00	16.00	65.00
BP-10c			36.00	63.00	17.00	70.00

MRS RABBIT™
Third Version, First Variation

Modeller:	Martyn Alcock
Height:	6 ¼", 15.9 cm
Size:	Large
Colour:	White, pink, yellow and green
Issued:	1994 - 1997

ROYAL ALBERT ®
ENGLAND
Mrs Rabbit
Beatrix Potter
© F. WARNE & CO. 1993
© 1993 ROYAL ALBERT LTD.

Back Stamp	Beswick Number	Doulton Number	U.S. $	Price Can. $	U.K. £	Aust. $
BP-6b	3398	P3398	60.00	95.00	35.00	100.00

MRS RABBIT™
Third Version, Second Variation (Gold umbrella point and handle)

Modeller:	Martyn Alcock
Height:	6 ¼", 15.9 cm
Size:	Large
Colour:	White, pink, yellow and green, gold umbrella point and handle
Issued:	1998 in a limited edition of 1,947
Series:	Gold edition

Back Stamp	Beswick Number	Doulton Number	U.S. $	Price Can. $	U.K. £	Aust. $
BP-9b	—	PG3398	60.00	95.00	38.00	100.00

Note: Issued, numbered and sold as a pair with Foxy Whiskered Gentleman, second version, second variation.

MRS. RABBIT AND BUNNIES™

Modeller:	David Lyttleton
Height:	3 ¾", 9.5 cm
Colour:	Blue dress with white apron, dark blue chair
Issued:	1976 - 1997

BEATRIX POTTER'S
Mrs. Rabbit and Bunnies
F. Warne & Co. Ltd.
© Copyright 1976
BESWICK ENGLAND

Back Stamp	Beswick Number	Doulton Number	U.S. $	Price Can. $	U.K. £	Aust. $
BP-3b	2543	P2543	85.00	125.00	50.00	90.00
BP-3c			110.00	160.00	70.00	125.00
BP-4			110.00	160.00	70.00	125.00
BP-5			135.00	175.00	85.00	150.00
BP-6a			45.00	60.00	25.00	70.00

MRS RABBIT AND THE FOUR BUNNIES™

Modeller:	Shane Ridge
Height:	4 ½", 11.9 cm
Colour:	Mrs Rabbit - light blue dress, brown basket; Bunnies - brown, rose tunic; Peter: light blue coat, yellow buttons
Issued:	1997 in a limited edition of 1,997
Series:	Tableau of the Year

Beswick Ware
MADE IN ENGLAND
MRS. RABBIT AND THE FOUR BUNNIES
1947-1997
© F. WARNE & CO. 1996
© 1996 ROYAL DOULTON
LIMITED EDITION OF 1,997
THIS IS N° 54

Back Stamp	Beswick Number	Doulton Number	U.S. $	Price Can. $	U.K. £	Aust. $
BP-8c	3672	P3672	500.00	750.00	325.00	800.00

MRS. RABBIT AND PETER™

Modeller:	Warren Platt
Height:	3 ½", 8.9 cm
Colour:	Mrs Rabbit - light blue dress Peter - light blue coat
Issued:	1997 to the present

ROYAL ALBERT ®
ENGLAND
Mrs Rabbit and Peter
Beatrix Potter
© F. WARNE & CO. 1996
© 1996 ROYAL ALBERT LTD.

Back Stamp	Beswick Number	Doulton Number	U.S. $	Price Can. $	U.K. £	Aust. $
BP-6a	3646	P3646	60.00	95.00	28.00	90.00
BP-10b			72.00	110.00	28.00	125.00

MRS RABBIT COOKING™

Modeller:	Martyn Alcock
Height:	4", 10.1 cm
Colour:	Blue dress, white apron
Issued:	1992 to the present

ROYAL ALBERT ®
ENGLAND
Mrs Rabbit cooking
Beatrix Potter
© F. WARNE & CO. 1991
© 1992 ROYAL ALBERT LTD

Back Stamp	Beswick Number	Doulton Number	U.S. $	Price Can. $	U.K. £	Aust. $
BP-6a	3278	P3278	30.00	50.00	16.00	65.00
BP-10b			36.00	63.00	17.00	70.00

MRS TIGGY-WINKLE™
First Version, First Variation (Diagonal Stripes)

Modeller:	Arthur Gredington
Height:	3 ¼", 8.3 cm
Size:	Small
Colour:	Red-brown and white dress, green and blue striped skirt, white apron
Issued:	1948 - 1974

Back Stamp	Beswick Number	Doulton Number	U.S. $	Price Can.$	U.K. £	Aust. $
BP-1	1107/1	P1107/1	300.00	425.00	175.00	450.00
BP-2			250.00	325.00	125.00	350.00
BP-3a			125.00	125.00	65.00	175.00

Note: This figurine is also recognisable by the heavily patterned bustle.

MRS TIGGY-WINKLE™
First Version, Second Variation (Plaid)

Modeller:	Arthur Gredington
Height:	3 ¼", 8.3 cm
Size:	Small
Colour:	Red-brown and white dress, green and blue striped skirt, white apron
Issued:	1972 to the present

Back Stamp	Beswick Number	Doulton Number	U.S. $	Price Can. $	U.K. £	Aust. $
BP-2	1107/2	P1107/2	225.00	300.00	125.00	250.00
BP-3a			85.00	125.00	55.00	90.00
BP-3b			65.00	95.00	40.00	75.00
BP-3c			75.00	100.00	45.00	80.00
BP-4			95.00	150.00	60.00	100.00
BP-6a			30.00	50.00	16.00	65.00
BP-12c			36.00	63.00	17.00	70.00

MRS TIGGY-WINKLE™
First Version, Third Variation (Platinum Iron)

Modeller:	Arthur Gredington
Height:	3 ¼", 8.3 cm
Size:	Small
Colour:	Red-brown and white dress, green and blue striped skirt, white apron, platinum iron
Issued:	1998 - 1998

Back Stamp	Beswick Number	Doulton Number	U.S. $	Price Can. $	U.K. £	Aust. $
BP-10a	—	PG1107	50.00	75.00	25.00	90.00

MRS. TIGGY-WINKLE™
Second Version, First Variation

Modeller:	Amanda Hughes-Lubeck
Height:	4 ½", 11.9 cm
Size:	Large
Colour:	Brown, white and brown striped skirt, white apron
Issued:	1996 - 1997

Back Stamp	Beswick Number	Doulton Number	U.S. $	Price Can. $	U.K. £	Aust. $
BP-6b	3437	P3437	65.00	95.00	35.00	100.00

MRS. TIGGY-WINKLE™
Second Version, Second Variation
(Platinum Iron)

Modeller:	Amanda Hughes-Lubeck
Height:	4 ½", 11.9 cm
Size:	Large
Colour:	Brown, white and brown striped skirt, white apron, platinum iron
Issued:	1998 in a limited edition of 1,947
Series	Gold edition

Back Stamp	Beswick Number	Doulton Number	U.S. $	Price Can. $	U.K. £	Aust. $
BP-9b	—	PG3437	60.00	95.00	38.00	100.00

Note: Issued, numbered and sold as a pair with Jemima Puddle-Duck, second version, second variation.

MRS. TIGGY-WINKLE AND LUCIE™

Modeller:	Martyn Alcock
Height:	4", 10.1 cm
Colour:	Mrs. Tiggy-Winkle - Brown, pink and cream dress, yellow and blue striped skirt, white apron, red handkerchief, platinum iron and horseshoe; Lucie - pink dress, white pinafore, blonde hair
Issued:	1999 in a limited edition of 2,950
Series:	Tableau

Back Stamp	Beswick Number	Doulton Number	U.S. $	Price Can. $	U.K. £	Aust. $
BP-9c	3867	P3867	225.00	325.00	125.00	350.00

MRS. TIGGY WINKLE TAKES TEA™

Modeller: David Lyttleton
Height: 3 ¼", 8.3 cm
Colour: Pink and white dress, white and brown mob cap
Issued: 1985 to the present

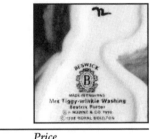

Back Stamp	Beswick Number	Doulton Number	U.S. $	Price Can. $	U.K. £	Aust. $
BP-3b	2877	P2877	100.00	130.00	75.00	100.00
BP-3c			125.00	150.00	75.00	125.00
BP-4			150.00	200.00	90.00	160.00
BP-6a			30.00	50.00	16.00	65.00
BP-10a			36.00	63.00	17.00	70.00

MRS. TIGGY WINKLE WASHING™

Modeller: David Lyttleton
Height: 2 ½", 6.4 cm
Colour: Brown and white
Issued: 1998 to the present

Back Stamp	Beswick Number	Doulton Number	U.S. $	Price Can. $	U.K. £	Aust. $
BP-8a	—	P3789	200.00	300.00	100.00	300.00
BP-10a			36.00	60.00	16.00	70.00

Note: Approximately 1,800 pieces were issued with the BP-8a backstamp.

MRS TITTLEMOUSE™

Modeller: Arthur Gredington
Height: 3 ½", 8.9 cm
Colour: White and red striped blouse, blue and white striped skirt
Issued: 1948 - 1993

Back Stamp	Beswick Number	Doulton Number	U.S. $	Price Can. $	U.K. £	Aust. $
BP-1	1103	P1103	300.00	450.00	175.00	475.00
BP-2			195.00	300.00	100.00	200.00
BP-3a			75.00	100.00	50.00	110.00
BP-3b			55.00	80.00	40.00	90.00
BP-3c			75.00	100.00	50.00	110.00
BP-6a			45.00	65.00	30.00	65.00

NO MORE TWIST™

Modeller:	Martyn Alcock
Height:	3 ½", 9.2 cm
Colour:	Brown and white mouse
Issued:	1992 - 1997

ROYAL ALBERT ®
ENGLAND
No more Twist
Beatrix Potter
© F. WARNE & CO. 1992
© 1992 ROYAL ALBERT LTD

Back Stamp	Beswick Number	Doulton Number	U.S. $	Price Can. $	U.K. £	Aust. $
BP-6a	3325	P3325	45.00	75.00	25.00	85.00

OLD MR. BOUNCER™

Modeller:	David Lyttleton
Height:	3", 7.6 cm
Colour:	Brown jacket and trousers, blue scarf
Issued:	1986 - 1995

BEATRIX POTTER
"Old Mr. Bouncer"
© Frederick Warne & Co. 1986
Licensed by Copyrights
BESWICK ENGLAND

Back Stamp	Beswick Number	Doulton Number	U.S. $	Price Can. $	U.K.£	Aust. $
BP-3c	2956	P2956	85.00	150.00	60.00	165.00
BP-6a			55.00	85.00	30.00	90.00

OLD MR BROWN™

Modeller:	Albert Hallam
Height:	3 ¼", 8.3 cm
Colour:	1. Brown owl, red squirrel
	2. Orange owl, red squirrel
Issued:	1963 to the present

BEATRIX POTTER'S
Old. Mr. Brown
F, WARNE & CO. LTD
COPYRIGHT
BESWICK
ENGLAND

Back Stamp	Beswick Number	Colour Variation	U.S. $	Price Can. $	U.K. £	Aust. $
BP-2	1796	Brown	200.00	300.00	125.00	325.00
BP-3a		Brown	85.00	125.00	55.00	135.00
BP-3b		Brown	60.00	90.00	40.00	95.00
BP-3b		Orange	70.00	100.00	45.00	110.00
BP-3c		Orange	75.00	100.00	50.00	110.00
BP-6a		Orange	30.00	50.00	16.00	65.00
BP-10a		Orange	36.00	63.00	17.00	70.00

OLD MR PRICKLEPIN™

Modeller:	David Lyttleton
Height:	2 ½", 6.4 cm
Colour:	Brown
Issued:	1983 - 1989

BEATRIX POTTER'S
"Old Mr Pricklepin"
© Frederick Warne P.L.C. 1983
BESWICK ENGLAND

Back Stamp	Beswick Number	Doulton Number	U.S. $	Price Can. $	U.K. £	Aust. $
BP-3b	2767	P2767	100.00	125.00	60.00	110.00
BP-3c			125.00	150.00	70.00	125.00
BP-6a			135.00	175.00	85.00	175.00

PETER AND THE RED POCKET HANDKERCHIEF™
First Version, First Variation

Modeller:	Martyn Alcock
Height:	4 ¾", 12.3 cm
Size:	Small
Colour:	Light blue jacket, red handkerchief
Issued:	1991 to the present

ROYAL ALBERT ®
ENGLAND
Peter and the
Red Pocket Handkerchief
Beatrix Potter
© F. WARNE & CO. 1990
© 1990 ROYAL ALBERT LTD

Back Stamp	Beswick Number	Doulton Number	U.S. $	Price Can. $	U.K. £	Aust. $
BP-6a	3242	P3242	45.00	80.00	20.00	80.00
BP-10a			48.00	85.00	18.00	90.00

PETER AND THE RED POCKET HANDKERCHIEF™
First Version, Second Variation (Gold Buttons)

Modeller:	Martyn Alcock
Height:	4 ¾", 12.3 cm
Size:	Small
Colour:	Dark blue jacket with gold buttons, red handkerchief
Issued:	1997 - 1997

Back Stamp	Beswick Number	Doulton Number	U.S. $	Price Can. $	U.K. £	Aust. $
BP-9c	—	PG5190	75.00	125.00	50.00	135.00

PETER AND THE RED POCKET HANDKERCHIEF™
Second Version, First Variation

Modeller:	Amanda Hughes-Lubeck
Height:	7 ¼", 18.4 cm
Size:	Large
Colour:	Light blue coat, red handkerchief
Issued:	1996 - 1997

ROYAL ALBERT ®
ENGLAND
Peter with Red Pocket Handkerchief
Beatrix Potter
© F. WARNE & CO. 1996
© 1996 ROYAL ALBERT LTD.

Back Stamp	Beswick Number	Doulton Number	U.S. $	Price Can. $	U.K. £	Aust. $
BP-6b	3592	P3592	65.00	95.00	35.00	100.00

Note: The backstamp on this version reads Peter "with" the Red Pocket Handkerchief.

PETER AND THE RED POCKET HANDKERCHIEF™
Second Version, Second Variation
(gold buttons)

Modeller:	Amanda Hughes-Lubeck
Height:	7 ¼", 18.4 cm
Size:	Large
Colour:	Light blue coat, red hankerchief, gold buttons
Issued:	1998 in a limited edition of 1,947
Series:	Gold edition

Beswick Ware
MADE IN ENGLAND
PETER AND THE RED POCKET HANDKERCHIEF
Beatrix Potter
© F. WARNE & CO. 1998
© 1998 ROYAL DOULTON
LIMITED EDITION OF 1,947
THIS IS N° 1276
CH

Back Stamp	Beswick Number	Doulton Number	U.S. $	Price Can. $	U.K. £	Aust. $
BP-9b	—	PG3592	60.00	95.00	38.00	100.00

Note: Issued, numbered and sold as a pair with The Tailor of Gloucester, second version, second variation.

PETER ATE A RADISH™

Modeller:	Warren Platt
Height:	4", 10.1 cm
Colour:	Blue jacket, brown and white rabbit, red radishes
Issued:	1995 - 1998

BESWICK
MADE IN ENGLAND
Peter ate a Radish
Beatrix Potter
© F. WARNE & CO. 1995
© 1995 ROYAL DOULTON

Back Stamp	Beswick Number	Doulton Number	U.S. $	Price Can. $	U.K. £	Aust. $
BP-6a	3533	P3533	40.00	65.00	25.00	75.00
BP-10b			48.00	85.00	19.00	95.00

PETER IN BED™

Modeller:	Martyn Alcock
Height:	2 ¾", 7.0 cm
Colour:	Blue, white, pink and green
Issued:	1995 to the present

Back Stamp	Beswick Number	Doulton Number	U.S. $	Price Can. $	U.K. £	Aust. $
BP-6a	3473	P3473	40.00	65.00	20.00	75.00
BP-10a			48.00	85.00	21.00	90.00

PETER IN THE GOOSEBERRY NET™

Modeller:	David Lyttleton
Height:	2", 4.6 cm
Colour:	Brown and white rabbit wearing blue jacket, green netting
Issued:	1989 - 1995

Back Stamp	Beswick Number	Doulton Number	U.S. $	Price Can. $	U.K. £	Aust. $
BP-6a	3157	P3157	70.00	100.00	50.00	105.00

PETER RABBIT™
First Version, First Variation (Deep Blue Jacket)

Modeller:	Arthur Gredington
Height:	4 ½", 11.4 cm
Size:	Small
Colour:	Brown and white rabbit wearing dark blue jacket
Issued:	1948 - c.1980

Back Stamp	Beswick Number	Doulton Number	U.S. $	Price Can. $	U.K. £	Aust. $
BP-1	1098/1	P1098/1	225.00	300.00	135.00	250.00
BP-2			200.00	275.00	125.00	225.00
BP-3a			125.00	175.00	85.00	135.00
BP-3b			100.00	150.00	65.00	125.00

PETER RABBIT™
First Version, Second Variation
(Light Blue Jacket)

Modeller:	Arthur Gredington
Height:	4 ½", 11.4 cm
Size:	Small
Colour:	Brown and white rabbit wearing light blue jacket
Issued:	c.1980 to the present

BEATRIX POTTER
"Peter Rabbit"
© F. Warne & Co. 1948
Licensed by Copyrights
John Beswick
Studio of Royal Doulton
England

Back Stamp	Beswick Number	Base Variation	U.S. $	Price Can. $	U.K. £	Aust. $
BP-3b	1098/2	Short base	65.00	90.00	40.00	100.00
BP-3b		Long base	65.00	90.00	40.00	100.00
BP-3c		Long base	75.00	100.00	45.00	110.00
BP-4		Long base	85.00	125.00	50.00	135.00
BP-5		Long base	125.00	175.00	75.00	175.00
BP-6a		Long base	30.00	50.00	16.00	65.00
BP-10b		Long base	36.00	63.00	17.00	70.00

PETER RABBIT™
First Version, Third Variation
(Light Blue Jacket, Gold Buttons)

Modeller:	Arthur Gredington
Height:	4 ½", 11.9 cm
Size:	Small
Colour:	Brown and white rabbit wearing light blue jacket with gold buttons
Issued:	1997 - 1997

Beswick Ware
MADE IN ENGLAND
Peter Rabbit
Beatrix Potter
© F. WARNE & CO. 1997
© 1997 ROYAL DOULTON

Back Stamp	Beswick Number	Doulton Number	U.S. $	Price Can. $	U.K. £	Aust. $
BP-9a	—	PG1098	50.00	75.00	25.00	80.00

PETER RABBIT™
Second Version, First Variation

Modeller:	Martyn Alcock
Height:	6 ¾", 17.1 cm
Size:	Large
Colour:	Brown rabbit wearing a light blue jacket
Issued:	1993 - 1997

BEATRIX POTTER'S
Peter Rabbit
© F. WARNE & CO. 1992
© 1992 ROYAL DOULTON
PETER RABBIT
1893 1993
F. WARNE & CO.
100
BESWICK
ENGLAND

Back Stamp	Beswick Number	Doulton Number	U.S. $	Price Can. $	U.K. £	Aust. $
BP-6b	3356	P3356	50.00	90.00	30.00	100.00
BP-7	100th Anniversary		75.00	100.00	50.00	115.00

PETER RABBIT™
**Second Version, Second Variation
(Gold Buttons)**

Modeller:	Martyn Alcock
Height:	6 ¾", 17.1 cm
Size:	Large
Colour:	Blue jacket with gold buttons
Issued:	1997 in a limited edtion of 1,947
Series:	Gold edition

Back Stamp	Beswick Number	Doulton Number	U.S. $	Price Can. $	U.K. £	Aust. $
BP-9b	—	PG3356	60.00	95.00	38.00	100.00

Note: Issued, numbered and sold as a pair with Benjamin Bunny, fourth version, fourth variation.

PETER RABBIT GARDENING™

Modeller:	Warren Platt
Height:	5", 12.7 cm
Colour:	Blue jacket, brown shovel, basket of carrots
Issued:	1998 to the present

Back Stamp	Beswick Number	Doulton Number	U.S. $	Price Can. $	U.K. £	Aust. $
BP-10b	3739	P3739	48.00	90.00	20.00	100.00

PETER WITH DAFFODILS™

Modeller:	Warren Platt
Height:	4 ¾", 12.1 cm
Colour:	Light blue coat, yellow daffodils
Issued:	1996 to the present

Back Stamp	Beswick Number	Doulton Number	U.S. $	Price Can. $	U.K. £	Aust. $
BP-6a	3597	P3597	45.00	75.00	20.00	85.00
BP-10b			48.00	92.00	19.00	100.00

PETER WITH POSTBAG

Modeller:	Amanda Hughes-Lubeck	
Height:	4 ¾", 12.1 cm	
Colour:	Light brown rabbit and postbag, lilac jacket trimmed in red	
Issued:	1996 to the present	

Back Stamp	Beswick Number	Doulton Number	U.S. $	Price Can. $	U.K. £	Aust. $
BP-6a	3591	P3591	45.00	75.00	20.00	85.00
BP-10b			48.00	92.00	19.00	100.00

PICKLES™

Modeller:	Albert Hallam
Height:	4 ½", 11.4 cm
Colour:	Black face dog with brown jacket and white apron, pink book
Issued:	1971 - 1982

Back Stamp	Beswick Number	Doulton Number	U.S. $	Price Can. $	U.K. £	Aust. $
BP-2	2334	P2334	850.00	1,200.00	500.00	1,250.00
BP-3a			525.00	800.00	325.00	750.00
BP-3b			450.00	675.00	300.00	650.00

PIGLING BLAND™
First Variation (Deep Maroon Jacket)

Modeller:	Graham Orwell
Height:	4 ¼", 10.8 cm
Colour:	Purple jacket, blue waistcoat, yellow trousers
Issued:	1955 - 1974

Back Stamp	Beswick Number	Doulton Number	U.S. $	Price Can. $	U.K. £	Aust. $
BP-2	1365/1	P1365/1	500.00	725.00	275.00	800.00
BP-3a			275.00	375.00	160.00	400.00
BP-3b			250.00	350.00	145.00	375.00

PIGLING BLAND™
Second Variation (Lilac Jacket)

Modeller: Graham Orwell
Height: 4 ¼", 10.8 cm
Colour: Lilac jacket, blue waistcoat, yellow trousers
Issued: c.1975 - 1998

Back Stamp	Beswick Number	Doulton Number	U.S. $	Price Can. $	U.K. £	Aust. $
BP-3b	1365/2	P1365/2	60.00	90.00	40.00	100.00
BP-3c			75.00	100.00	45.00	100.00
BP-6a			30.00	50.00	16.00	65.00
BP-10c			36.00	63.00	17.00	70.00

PIGLING EATS HIS PORRIDGE™

Modeller: Martyn Alcock
Height: 4", 10.1 cm
Colour: Brown coat, blue waistcoat and yellow trousers
Issued: 1991 - 1994

Back Stamp	Beswick Number	Doulton Number	U.S. $	Price Can. $	U.K. £	Aust. $
BP-6a	3252	P3252	175.00	225.00	125.00	250.00

PIG-WIG™

Modeller: Albert Hallam
Height: 4", 10.1 cm
Colour: 1. Grey pig, pale blue dress
2. Black pig, deep blue dress
Issued: 1972 - 1982

Back Stamp	Beswick Number	Colour Variation	U.S. $	Price Can. $	U.K. £	Aust. $
BP-2	2381	Grey pig		Rare		
BP-3a		Black pig	625.00	875.00	375.00	900.00
BP-3b		Black pig	600.00	825.00	350.00	850.00

POORLY PETER RABBIT™

Modeller:	David Lyttleton
Height:	3 ¾", 9.5 cm
Colour:	Brown-red and white blanket
Issued:	1976 - 1997

BEATRIX POTTER
"Poorly Peter Rabbit"
© Frederick Warne & Co. 1976
Licensed by Copyrights
BESWICK ENGLAND

Back Stamp	Beswick Number	Doulton Number	Price			
			U.S. $	Can. $	U.K. £	Aust. $
BP-3b	2560	P2560	65.00	85.00	40.00	90.00
BP-3c			75.00	95.00	50.00	100.00
BP-4			85.00	110.00	55.00	115.00
BP-6a			40.00	60.00	20.00	70.00

Note: Later models have a lighter brown blanket.

BEATRIX POTTER'S
Rebeccah Puddle-Duck
F. Warne & Co Ltd.
© Copyright 1981
BESWICK ENGLAND

REBECCAH PUDDLE-DUCK™

Modeller:	David Lyttleton
Height:	3 ¼", 8.3 cm
Colour:	White goose, pale blue coat and hat
Issued:	1981 to the present

Back Stamp	Beswick Number	Doulton Number	Price			
			U.S. $	Can. $	U.K. £	Aust. $
BP-3b	2647	P2647	65.00	85.00	40.00	90.00
BP-3c			80.00	100.00	50.00	110.00
BP-4			85.00	110.00	55.00	125.00
BP-6a			30.00	50.00	16.00	65.00
BP-10b			36.00	63.00	17.00	70.00

RIBBY™

Modeller:	Arthur Gredington
Height:	3 ¼", 8.3 cm
Colour:	White dress with blue rings, white apron, pink and white striped shawl
Issued:	1951 to the present

BESWICK ENGLAND
BEATRIX POTTER'S
"RIBBY"
F. WARNE & CO. LTD.
COPYRIGHT

Back Stamp	Beswick Number	Doulton Number	Price			
			U.S. $	Can. $	U.K. £	Aust. $
BP-1	1199	P1199	325.00	450.00	200.00	425.00
BP-2			200.00	275.00	120.00	275.00
BP-3a			90.00	125.00	55.00	125.00
BP-3b			65.00	85.00	40.00	90.00
BP-3c			80.00	100.00	50.00	125.00
BP-6a			30.00	50.00	16.00	65.00
BP-10c			36.00	63.00	17.00	70.00

Note: The name shown on BP-6a and BP-10c is Mrs Ribby.

RIBBY AND THE PATTY PAN™

Modeller:	Martyn Alcock
Height:	3 ½", 8.9 cm
Colour:	Blue dress, white apron
Issued:	1992 - 1998

Back Stamp	Beswick Number	Doulton Number	U.S. $	Price Can. $	U.K. £	Aust. $
BP-6a	3280	P3280	30.00	50.00	16.00	65.00
BP-10a			36.00	63.00	17.00	70.00

SALLY HENNY PENNY™

Modeller:	Albert Hallam
Height:	4", 10.1 cm
Colour:	Brown and gold chicken, black hat and cloak, two yellow chicks
Issued:	1974 - 1993

Back Stamp	Beswick Number	Doulton Number	U.S. $	Price Can. $	U.K. £	Aust. $
BP-3a	2452	P2452	65.00	90.00	40.00	95.00
BP-3b			55.00	80.00	35.00	90.00
BP-3c			65.00	90.00	40.00	95.00
BP-6a			55.00	80.00	35.00	90.00

SAMUEL WHISKERS™

Modeller:	Arthur Gredington
Height:	3 ¼", 8.3 cm
Colour:	Light green coat, yellow waistcoat and trousers
Issued:	1948 - 1995

Back Stamp	Beswick Number	Doulton Number	U.S. $	Price Can. $	U.K. £	Aust. $
BP-1	1106	P1106	275.00	425.00	165.00	425.00
BP-2			225.00	325.00	140.00	325.00
BP-3a			85.00	120.00	50.00	125.00
BP-3b			55.00	85.00	35.00	90.00
BP-3c			75.00	100.00	45.00	110.00
BP-4			75.00	100.00	45.00	100.00
BP-6a			35.00	55.00	25.00	60.00

SIMPKIN™

Modeller:	Alan Maslankowski
Height:	4", 10.1 cm
Colour:	Green coat
Issued:	1975 - 1983

BEATRIX POTTER'S
"Simpkin"
F. Warne & Co.Ltd.
© Copyright 1975
BESWICK ENGLAND

Back Stamp	Beswick Number	Doulton Number	U.S. $	Price Can. $	U.K. £	Aust. $
BP-3b	2508	P2508	700.00	1,000.00	425.00	950.00

SIR ISAAC NEWTON™

Modeller:	Graham Tongue
Height:	3 ¾", 9.5 cm
Colour:	Pale green jacket, yellow waistcoat with tan markings
Issued:	1973 - 1984

BEATRIX POTTER'S
"Sir Isaac Newton"
F. Warne & Co. Ltd.
© Copyright 1973
BESWICK
MADE IN ENGLAND

Back Stamp	Beswick Number	Doulton Number	U.S. $	Price Can. $	U.K. £	Aust. $
BP-3a	2425	P2425	525.00	750.00	275.00	775.00
BP-3b			500.00	700.00	225.00	725.00

Note: The colour and size of Sir Isaac Newton may vary.

SQUIRREL NUTKIN™
First Version, First Variation (Red-brown Squirrel)

Modeller:	Arthur Gredington
Height:	3 ¾", 9.5 cm
Size:	Small
Colour:	Red-brown squirrel, green-brown nut
Issued:	1948 - c.1980

BEATRIX POTTER'S
Squirrel Nutkin
Copyright
BESWICK. ENGLAND

Back Stamp	Beswick Number	Doulton Number	U.S. $	Price Can. $	U.K. £	Aust. $
BP-1	1102/1	P1102/1	250.00	350.00	150.00	375.00
BP-2			200.00	275.00	125.00	300.00
BP-3a			150.00	200.00	90.00	225.00
BP-3b			100.00	150.00	60.00	175.00

SQUIRREL NUTKIN™
First Version, Second Variation
(Golden Brown Squirrel)

Modeller:	Arthur Gredington
Height:	3 ¾", 9.5 cm
Size:	Small
Colour:	Golden brown squirrel, green nut
Issued:	c.1980 to the present

Back Stamp	Beswick Number	Doulton Number	U.S. $	Price Can. $	U.K. £	Aust. $
BP-3b	1102/2	P1102/2	65.00	90.00	40.00	95.00
BP-3c			95.00	135.00	60.00	150.00
BP-6a			30.00	50.00	16.00	65.00
BP-10a			36.00	63.00	17.00	70.00

SQUIRREL NUTKIN™
Second Version (Gold Nut)

Modeller:	Arthur Gredington
Height:	Unknown
Size:	Large
Colour:	Golden brown squirrel, gold nut
Issued:	1999 in a limited edition of 1,947
Series:	Gold edition

Back Stamp	Beswick Number	Doulton Number	U.S. $	Price Can. $	U.K. £	Aust. $
BP-9b			60.00	95.00	38.00	100.00

Note: Issued, numbered and sold as a pair with Hunca Munca Sweeping, second version.

SUSAN™

Modeller:	David Lyttleton
Height:	4", 10.1 cm
Colour:	Blue dress, green, pink and black shawl and hat
Issued:	1983 - 1989

Back Stamp	Beswick Number	Doulton Number	U.S. $	Price Can. $	U.K. £	Aust. $
BP-3b	2716	P2716	275.00	400.00	150.00	375.00
BP-3c			300.00	425.00	175.00	400.00
BP-6a			275.00	400.00	150.00	375.00

Note: The colour and size of Susan may vary.

SWEET PETER RABBIT™

Modeller: Shane Ridge
Height: 4 ¾", 12.1 cm
Colour: Beige and cream rabbit, blue jacket, green and beige base
Issued: 1999 in a special edition of 2,950

Back Stamp	Beswick Number	Doulton Number	U.S. $	Price Can. $	U.K. £	Aust. $
BP-13	388	P3888	90.00	140.00	55.00	150.00

Note: This figure was commissioned by Peter Rabbit and Friends to commemorate the Year of the Rabbit, 1999.

TABITHA TWITCHIT™
First Variation (Blue Striped Top)

Modeller: Arthur Gredington
Height: 3 ½", 8.9 cm
Colour: Blue and white striped dress, white apron
Issued: 1961 - 1974

Back Stamp	Beswick Number	Doulton Number	U.S. $	Price Can. $	U.K. £	Aust. $
BP-2	1676/1	P1676/1	325.00	450.00	175.00	425.00
BP-3a			250.00	300.00	150.00	325.00
BP-3b			200.00	250.00	125.00	250.00

TABITHA TWITCHETT™
Second Variation (White Top)

Modeller: Arthur Gredington
Height: 3 ½", 8.9 cm
Colour: Blue and white striped dress, white apron
Issued: c.1975 - 1995

Back Stamp	Beswick Number	Doulton Number	U.S. $	Price Can. $	U.K. £	Aust. $
BP-3b	1676/2	P1676/2	65.00	95.00	40.00	100.00
BP-3c			75.00	100.00	45.00	110.00
BP-6a			50.00	65.00	30.00	75.00

Note: BP-3b and forward has Twitchit spelled "Twitchett."

TABITHA TWITCHIT AND MISS MOPPET™

BEATRIX POTTER'S
Tabitha Twitchit and Miss Moppet
F. Warne & Co.Ltd.
© Copyright 1976
BESWICK ENGLAND

Modeller: David Lyttleton
Height: 3 ½", 8.9 cm
Colour: Lilac dress, white apron,
yellow sponge and hassock
Issued: 1976 - 1993

Back Stamp	Beswick Number	Doulton Number	U.S. $	Price Can. $	U.K. £	Aust. $
BP-3b	2544	P2544	200.00	250.00	125.00	275.00
BP-3c			200.00	250.00	125.00	275.00
BP-4			250.00	300.00	150.00	300.00
BP-6a			100.00	150.00	60.00	150.00

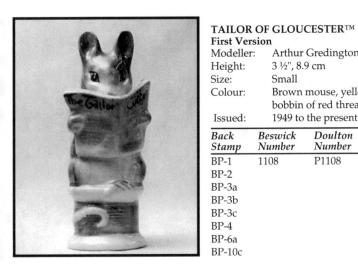

TAILOR OF GLOUCESTER™
First Version

Modeller: Arthur Gredington
Height: 3 ½", 8.9 cm
Size: Small
Colour: Brown mouse, yellow
bobbin of red thread
Issued: 1949 to the present

Back Stamp	Beswick Number	Doulton Number	U.S. $	Price Can. $	U.K. £	Aust. $
BP-1	1108	P1108	300.00	425.00	175.00	425.00
BP-2			200.00	300.00	125.00	300.00
BP-3a			65.00	90.00	40.00	95.00
BP-3b			55.00	80.00	35.00	85.00
BP-3c			65.00	90.00	40.00	95.00
BP-4			75.00	100.00	45.00	110.00
BP-6a			30.00	50.00	16.00	65.00
BP-10c			36.00	63.00	17.00	70.00

TAILOR OF GLOUCESTER™
Second Version, First Variation

Modeller: Arthur Gredington
Height: 6", 15.0 cm
Size: Large
Colour: Brown mouse, yellow
bobbin of red thread
Issued: 1995 - 1997

Back Stamp	Beswick Number	Doulton Number	U.S. $	Price Can. $	U.K. £	Aust. $
BP-6b	3449	P3449	60.00	95.00	30.00	100.00

TAILOR OF GLOUCESTER™
Second Version, Second Variation (Gold Accents)

Modeller:	Arthur Gredington
Height:	6", 15.0 cm
Size:	Large
Colour:	Brown mouse, yellow bobbin of red thread, gold accents
Issued:	1998 in a limited edition of 1,947
Series:	Gold edition

Back Stamp	Beswick Number	Doulton Number	U.S. $	Price Can. $	U.K. £	Aust. $
BP-9b	G3449	PG3449	60.00	95.00	38.00	100.00

Note: Issued, numbered and sold as a pair with Peter Rabbit and the Red Pocket Handkerchief, second version, second variation.

THE OLD WOMAN WHO LIVED IN A SHOE™

Modeller:	Colin Melbourne
Size:	2 ¾" x 3 ¾", 7.0 cm x 9.5 cm
Colour:	Blue shoe
Issued:	1959 - 1998

Back Stamp	Beswick Number	Doulton Number	U.S. $	Price Can. $	U.K. £	Aust. $
BP-2	1545	P1545	200.00	300.00	125.00	325.00
BP-3a			85.00	120.00	50.00	125.00
BP-3b			60.00	85.00	35.00	90.00
BP-3c			85.00	120.00	50.00	125.00
BP-6a			30.00	50.00	20.00	70.00

THE OLD WOMAN WHO LIVED IN A SHOE KNITTING™

Modeller:	David Lyttleton
Height:	3", 7.5 cm
Colour:	Purple dress, white apron, pale blue shawl and mob cap, yellow chair
Issued:	1983 to the present

Back Stamp	Beswick Number	Doulton Number	U.S. $	Price Can. $	U.K.£	Aust. $
BP-3b	2804	P2804	175.00	275.00	125.00	300.00
BP-3c			225.00	325.00	150.00	325.00
BP-6a			30.00	50.00	16.00	65.00
BP-10a			36.00	63.00	17.00	70.00

THOMASINA TITTLEMOUSE™

Modeller: David Lyttleton
Height: 3 ¼", 8.3 cm
Colour: Brown and pink
highlights
Issued: 1981 - 1989

BEATRIX POTTER'S
"Thomasina Tittlemouse"
F. Warne & Co Ltd.
© Copyright 1981
BESWICK ENGLAND

Correct

BEATRIX POTTER
"Tomasina Tittlemouse"
© Frederick Warne & Co. 1981
Licensed by Copyrights
BESWICK ENGLAND

Error

Backstamp Variations

Back Stamp	Beswick Number	Doulton Number	U.S. $	Price Can. $	U.K. £	Aust. $
BP-3b	2668	P2668	125.00	175.00	75.00	200.00
BP-3c	Error		150.00	200.00	85.00	225.00
BP-6a			75.00	95.00	40.00	100.00

TIMMY TIPTOES™
First Variation (Red Jacket)
Modeller: Arthur Gredington
Height: 3 ¾", 9.5 cm
Colour: 1. Brown-grey squirrel, red jacket
2. Grey squirrel, red jacket
Issued: 1948 - c.1980

BEATRIX POTTER'S
"Timmy Tiptoes"
F. Warne & Co.Ltd.
© Copyright 1948
BESWICK ENGLAND

Back Stamp	Beswick Number	Colour Variation	U.S. $	Price Can. $	U.K. £	Aust. $
BP-1	1101/1	Brown-grey	250.00	350.00	150.00	375.00
BP-1		Grey	250.00	350.00	150.00	375.00
BP-2		Brown-grey	200.00	300.00	120.00	325.00
BP-2		Grey	200.00	300.00	120.00	325.00
BP-3a		Brown-grey	150.00	200.00	85.00	225.00
BP-3a		Grey	150.00	200.00	85.00	225.00
BP-3b		Brown-grey	125.00	175.00	75.00	200.00
BP-3b		Grey	125.00	175.00	75.00	200.00

TIMMY TIPTOES™
Second Variation (Light Pink Jacket)

Modeller: Arthur Gredington
Height: 3 ½", 8.9 cm
Colour: Grey squirrel, pink jacket
Issued: c.1970 - 1997

BEATRIX POTTER'S
Timmy Tiptoes
F. WARNE & CO. LTD.
COPYRIGHT
BESWICK ENGLAND

Back Stamp	Beswick Number	Doulton Number	U.S. $	Price Can. $	U.K. £	Aust. $
BP-2	1101/2	P1101/2	250.00	350.00	150.00	375.00
BP-3b			55.00	80.00	35.00	85.00
BP-3c			75.00	100.00	45.00	110.00
BP-6a			40.00	60.00	20.00	65.00

Note: Second variations will vary in colour in a similar manner as the first.

TIMMY WILLIE FROM JOHNNY TOWN-MOUSE™

Modeller:	Arthur Gredington
Height:	2 ½", 6.4 cm
Colour:	Brown and white mouse, green or multicoloured base
Issued:	1949 - 1993

Back Stamp	Beswick Number	Doulton Number	U.S. $	Price Can. $	U.K. £	Aust. $
BP-1	1109	P1109	250.00	350.00	150.00	375.00
BP-2			175.00	275.00	125.00	300.00
BP-3a			75.00	100.00	45.00	105.00
BP-3b			55.00	80.00	35.00	85.00
BP-3c			65.00	90.00	40.00	95.00
BP-4			75.00	100.00	45.00	110.00
BP-6a			40.00	60.00	30.00	65.00

TIMMY WILLIE SLEEPING™

Modeller:	Graham Tongue
Size:	1 ¼" x 3 ¾", 3.2 cm x 9.5 cm
Colour:	Green, white and brown
Issued:	1986 - 1996

Back Stamp	Beswick Number	Doulton Number	U.S. $	Price Can. $	U.K. £	Aust. $
BP-3c	2996	P2996	225.00	300.00	150.00	300.00
BP-6a			65.00	85.00	30.00	95.00

TOM KITTEN™
First Version, First Variation
(Deep Blue Outfit)

Modeller:	Arthur Gredington
Height:	3 ½", 8.9 cm
Size:	Small
Colour:	Tabby kitten wearing blue trousers and jacket, dark green base
Issued:	1948 - c.1980

Back Stamp	Beswick Number	Doulton Number	U.S. $	Price Can. $	U.K. £	Aust. $
BP-1	1100/1	P1100/1	275.00	400.00	150.00	425.00
BP-2			175.00	275.00	125.00	300.00
BP-3a			90.00	130.00	55.00	135.00
BP-3b			75.00	100.00	45.00	110.00

TOM KITTEN™
First Version, Second Variation
(Light Blue Outfit)

Modeller: Arthur Gredington
Height: 3 ½", 8.9 cm
Size: Small
Colour: Tabby kitten wearing light
blue trousers and jacket,
light green base
Issued: c.1980 to the present

Back Stamp	Beswick Number	Doulton Number	U.S. $	Price Can. $	U.K. £	Aust. $
BP-3b	1100/2	P1100/2	70.00	90.00	40.00	95.00
BP-3c			75.00	100.00	45.00	100.00
BP-4			80.00	110.00	50.00	115.00
BP-6a			30.00	50.00	16.00	65.00
BP-10c			36.00	63.00	17.00	70.00

Note: Tom Kitten was issued with two different style bases.

TOM KITTEN™
First Version, Third Variation
(Gold Buttons)

Modeller: Arthur Gredington
Height: 3 ½", 8.9 cm
Size: Small
Colour: Tabby kitten wearing light
blue trousers and jacket with
gold buttons
Issued: 1997 - 1997

Back Stamp	Beswick Number	Doulton Number	U.S. $	Price Can. $	U.K. £	Aust. $
BP-9a	—	PG1100	50.00	80.00	30.00	90.00

TOM KITTEN™
Second Version, First Variation

Modeller: Martyn Alcock
Height: 5 ¼", 13.3 cm
Size: Large
Colour: Tabby kitten wearing light blue
trousers and jacket, light green base
Issued: 1994 - 1997

Back Stamp	Beswick Number	Doulton Number	U.S. $	Price Can. $	U.K. £	Aust. $
BP-7	3405	P3405	65.00	95.00	30.00	100.00

TOM KITTEN™
**Second Version, Second Variation
(Gold Buttons)**

Modeller:	Martyn Alcock
Height:	5 ¼", 13.3 cm
Size:	Large
Colour:	Light blue jacket and trousers, gold buttons
Issued:	1994 - 1997
Series:	Gold edition

Back Stamp	Beswick Number	Doulton Number	U.S. $	Price Can. $	U.K. £	Aust. $
BP-9b	G3405	PG3405	60.00	95.00	38.00	100.00

Note: Issued, numbered and sold as a pair with Mr. Jeremy Fisher, second version, second variation.

TOM KITTEN AND BUTTERFLY™

Modeller:	Ted Chawner
Height:	3 ½", 8.9 cm
Colour:	Blue outfit, yellow hat
Issued:	1987 - 1994

Back Stamp	Beswick Number	Doulton Number	U.S. $	Price Can. $	U.K. £	Aust. $
BP-3c	3030	P3030	325.00	425.00	175.00	425.00
BP-6a			150.00	200.00	100.00	225.00

TOM KITTEN IN THE ROCKERY™

Modeller:	Warren Platt
Height:	3 ½", 8.9 cm
Colour:	Pale blue jacket and trousers, yellow hat
Issued:	1998 to the present

Back Stamp	Beswick Number	Doulton Number	U.S. $	Price Can. $	U.K. £	Aust. $
BP-10a	3719	P3719	36.00	60.00	18.00	65.00

TOM THUMB™

Modeller:	Warren Platt
Height:	3 ¼", 8.3 cm
Colour:	Rose-pink and yellow chimney
Issued:	1987 - 1997

BEATRIX POTTER
"Tom Thumb"
© F. Warne & Co. 1987
Licensed by Copyrights
BESWICK ENGLAND

Back Stamp	Beswick Number	Doulton Number	U.S. $	Price Can. $	U.K. £	Aust. $
BP-3c	2989	P2989	150.00	225.00	100.00	200.00
BP-6a			40.00	60.00	20.00	65.00

TOMMY BROCK™
First Version, First Variation
(Handle Out, Small Eye Patch)

Modeller:	Graham Orwell
Height:	3 ½", 8.9 cm
Colour:	Blue jacket, pink waistcoat, yellow-green trousers
Issued:	1955 - 1974

BEATRIX POTTER'S
TOMMY BROCK
F. Warne & Co. Ltd.
COPYRIGHT
BESWICK
ENGLAND
45

Back Stamp	Beswick Number	Doulton Number	U.S. $	Price Can. $	U.K. £	Aust. $
BP-2	1348/1	P1348/1	500.00	700.00	275.00	675.00
BP-3a			450.00	650.00	225.00	650.00

TOMMY BROCK™
First Version, Second Variation
(Handle Out, Large Eye Patch)

Modeller:	Graham Orwell
Height:	3 ½", 8.9 cm
Colour:	Blue jacket, pink waistcoat, yellow trousers
Issued:	c.1970 - c.1974

BEATRIX POTTER'S
TOMMY BROCK
F. Warne & Co. Ltd.
COPYRIGHT
BESWICK
ENGLAND
49

Back Stamp	Beswick Number	Doulton Number	U.S. $	Price Can. $	U.K. £	Aust. $
BP-2	1348/2	P1348/2	500.00	700.00	275.00	675.00
BP-3a			450.00	650.00	225.00	650.00

TOMMY BROCK™
Second Version, First Variation
(Handle In, Small Eye Patch)

Modeller:	Graham Orwell
Height:	3 ½", 8.9 cm
Colour:	Blue-grey jacket, pink waistcoat, yellow trousers
Issued:	c.1974 - 1976

Back Stamp	Beswick Number	Doulton Number	U.S. $	Price Can. $	U.K. £	Aust. $
BP-3a	1348/3	P1348/3	150.00	225.00	85.00	250.00
BP-3b			125.00	200.00	75.00	225.00

TOMMY BROCK™
Second Version, Second Variation
(Handle In, Large Eye Patch)

Modeller:	Graham Orwell
Height:	3 ½", 8.9 cm
Colour:	Blue-grey jacket, red waistcoat, yellow trousers
Issued:	c.1975 to the present

Back Stamp	Beswick Number	Doulton Number	U.S. $	Price Can. $	U.K. £	Aust. $
BP-3b	1348/4	P1348/4	65.00	95.00	40.00	100.00
BP-3c			80.00	115.00	50.00	120.00
BP-4			85.00	125.00	50.00	125.00
BP-6a			30.00	50.00	16.00	65.00
BP-10a			36.00	63.00	17.00	70.00

Note: The jacket colour varies from pale to dark blue in BP-3b.

BEATRIX POTTER MISCELLANEOUS

CHARACTER JUGS

PLAQUES

STANDS

CHARACTER JUGS

JEMIMA PUDDLE-DUCK CHARACTER JUG™

Modeller:	Ted Chawner
Height:	4", 10.1 cm
Colour:	Blue, pink and white
Issued:	1989 - 1992

BEATRIX POTTER
'Jemima Puddle-Duck'
© F. Warne & Co. 1988
Licensed by Copyrights
John Beswick
Studio of Royal Doulton
England

Back Stamp	Beswick Number	Doulton Number	U.S. $	Price Can. $	U.K. £	Aust. $
BP-4	3088	P3088	225.00	275.00	75.00	250.00
BP-6a			195.00	250.00	85.00	225.00

MR. JEREMY FISHER CHARACTER JUG™

Modeller:	Graham Tongue
Height:	3", 7.6 cm
Colour:	Mauve
Issued:	1987 - 1992

John Beswick
ENGLAND
BEATRIX POTTER
"Jeremy Fisher"
© 1987 Frederick Warne & Co.
Licensed by Copyrights

Back Stamp	Beswick Number	Doulton Number	U.S. $	Price Can. $	U.K. £	Aust. $
BP-4	2960	P2960	225.00	275.00	75.00	250.00
BP-6a			195.00	250.00	85.00	225.00

MRS. TIGGY-WINKLE CHARACTER JUG™

Modeller:	Ted Chawner
Height:	3", 7.6 cm
Colour:	White dress with brown stripes
Issued:	1988 - 1992

BEATRIX POTTER
"Mrs.Tiggy-Winkle"
© F. Warne & Co. 1988
Licensed by Copyrights
John Beswick
Studio of Royal Doulton
England

Back Stamp	Beswick Number	Doulton Number	U.S. $	Price Can. $	U.K. £	Aust.$
BP-4	3102	P3102	225.00	275.00	75.00	250.00
BP-6a			195.00	250.00	85.00	225.00

OLD MR. BROWN
CHARACTER JUG™

Modeller:	Graham Tongue
Height:	3", 7.6 cm
Colour:	Brown and cream
Issued:	1987 - 1992

Back Stamp	Beswick Number	Doulton Number	U.S. $	Price Can. $	U.K.	Aust. $
BP-4	2959	P2959	225.00	275.00	75.00	250.00
BP-6a			195.00	250.00	85.00	225.00

PETER RABBIT
CHARACTER JUG™

Modeller:	Graham Tongue
Height:	3", 7.6 cm
Colour:	Brown, blue and white
Issued:	1987 - 1992

Back Stamp	Beswick Number	Doulton Number	U.S. $	Price Can. $	U.K. £	Aust. $
BP-4	3006	P3006	225.00	275.00	75.00	250.00
BP-6a			195.00	250.00	85.00	225.00

TOM KITTEN
CHARACTER JUG™

Modeller:	Ted Chawner
Height:	3", 7.6 cm
Colour:	Brown, blue and white
Issued:	1989 - 1992

Back Stamp	Beswick Number	Doulton Number	U.S. $	Price Can. $	U.K. £	Aust. $
BP-4	3103	P3103	225.00	275.00	75.00	250.00
BP-6a			195.00	250.00	85.00	225.00

PLAQUES

JEMIMA PUDDLE-DUCK PLAQUE™

Modeller:	Albert Hallam
Height:	6", 15.2 cm
Colour:	White duck, mauve shawl, pale blue bonnet
Issued:	1967 - 1969

Back Stamp	Beswick Number	Doulton Number	U.S. $	Price Can. $	U.K. £	Aust. $
BP-2	2082	P2082		Extremely rare		

JEMIMA PUDDLE-DUCK WITH FOXY WHISKERED GENTLEMAN PLAQUE™

Modeller:	Harry Sales and David Lyttleton
Size:	7 ½" x 7 ½", 19.1 cm x 19.1 cm
Colour:	Brown, green, white and blue
Issued:	1977 - 1982

Back Stamp	Beswick Number	Doulton Number	U.S. $	Price Can. $	U.K. £	Aust. $
BP-3	2594	P2594	200.00	275.00	100.00	300.00

MRS. TITTLEMOUSE PLAQUE™

Modeller:	Harry Sales
Height:	7 ½" x 7 ½", 19.1 cm x 19.1 cm
Colour:	Blue, pink and green
Issued:	1982 - 1984

Back Stamp	Beswick Number	Doulton Number	U.S. $	Price Can. $	U.K. £	Aust. $
BP-3	2685	P2685	200.00	275.00	100.00	300.00

PETER RABBIT PLAQUE™
First Version

Modeller:	Graham Tongue
Height:	6", 15.2 cm
Colour:	Brown rabbit wearing a blue coat
Issued:	1967 - 1969

Back Stamp	Beswick Number	Doulton Number	U.S. $	Price Can. $	U.K. £	Aust. $
BP-2	2083	P2083		Extremely rare		

PETER RABBIT PLAQUE™
Second Version

Modeller:	Harry Sales and David Lyttleton
Size:	7 ½" x 7 ½", 19.1 cm x 19.1 cm
Colour:	Blue, green, brown and orange
Issued:	1979 - 1983

Back Stamp	Beswick Number	Doulton Number	U.S. $	Price Can. $	U.K. £	Aust. $
BP-3	2650	P2650	200.00	275.00	100.00	300.00

TOM KITTEN PLAQUE™

Modeller:	Graham Tongue
Height:	6", 15.2 cm
Colour:	Unknown
Issued:	1967 - 1969

Back Stamp	Beswick Number	Doulton Number	U.S. $	Price Can. $	U.K.	Aust. $
BP-2	2085	P2085	1,200.00	2,000.00	750.00	2,000.00

STANDS

DISPLAY STAND

Modeller:	Andrew Brindley
Size:	12 ½" x 12 ½",
	31.7 cm x 31.7 cm
Colour:	Brown, light brown
Issued:	1970 - 1997

Back Stamp	Beswick Number	Doulton Number	U.S. $	Price Can. $	U.K. £	Aust. $
Beswick	2295	P2295	150.00	125.00	75.00	125.00
Doulton			75.00	65.00	25.00	75.00

TREE LAMP BASE™

Modeller:	Albert Hallam and
	James Hayward
Height:	7", 17.8 cm
Colour:	Brown and green
Issued:	1958 - 1982

Back Stamp	Beswick Number	Doulton Number	U.S. $	Price Can. $	U.K. £	Aust. $
BP-2	1531	P1531	450.00	425.00	200.00	400.00
BP-3			375.00	350.00	150.00	325.00

Note: The price of this lamp will vary in accordance with the figurine found attached to the base.

BEATRIX POTTER

RESIN STUDIO SCULPTURES

SS1
TIMMY WILLIE™

Designer: Harry Sales
Modeller: Graham Tongue
Height: 4 ¼", 10.8 cm
Colour: Green and brown
Issued: 1985 - 1985

Beswick Number	Price U.S. $	Can. $	U.K. £	Aust. $
SS1	125.00	175.00	75.00	200.00

SS2
FLOPSY BUNNIES™

Designer: Harry Sales
Modeller: Graham Tongue
Height: 5", 12.7 cm
Colour: Browns and green
Issued: 1985 - 1985

Beswick Number	Price U.S. $	Can. $	U.K. £	Aust. $
SS2	135.00	185.00	85.00	200.00

SS3
MR. JEREMY FISHER™

Designer: Harry Sales
Modeller: David Lyttleton
Height: 4", 10.1 cm
Colour: Beige, green and cream
Issued: 1985 - 1985

Beswick Number	Price U.S. $	Can. $	U.K. £	Aust. $
SS3	150.00	225.00	90.00	250.00

SS4
PETER RABBIT™

Designer:	Harry Sales
Modeller:	Graham Tongue
Height:	7", 17.8 cm
Colour:	Browns, blue and green
Issued:	1985 - 1985

Beswick Number	U.S. $	Price Can. $	U.K. £	Aust. $
SS4	150.00	225.00	90.00	250.00

SS11
MRS. TIGGY WINKLE™

Designer:	Harry Sales
Modeller:	Graham Tongue
Height:	5", 12.7 cm
Colour:	Browns, green, white and blue
Issued:	1985 - 1985

Beswick Number	U.S. $	Price Can. $	U.K. £	Aust. $
SS11	150.00	225.00	90.00	250.00

SS26
YOCK YOCK™
(In The Tub)

Designer:	Harry Sales
Modeller:	David Lyttleton
Height:	1 7/8", 5.0 cm
Colour:	Pink and brown
Issued:	1986 - 1986

Beswick Number	U.S. $	Price Can. $	U.K. £	Aust. $
SS26	350.00	475.00	225.00	450.00

SS27
PETER RABBIT™
(In The Watering Can)

Designer:	Harry Sales
Modeller:	David Lyttleton
Height:	3 ¼", 8.3 cm
Colour:	Browns and blue
Issued:	1986 - 1986

Beswick Number	U.S. $	Price Can. $	U.K. £	Aust. $
SS27	450.00	500.00	300.00	450.00

BEDTIME CHORUS

1801
PIANIST™

Designer:	Albert Hallam
Height:	3", 7.6 cm
Colour:	Pale blue and yellow
Issued:	1962 - 1969

Beswick Number	Price U.S. $	Can. $	U.K. £	Aust. $
1801	150.00	200.00	90.00	195.00

1802
PIANO™

Designer:	Albert Hallam
Height:	3", 7.6 cm
Colour:	Brown and white
Issued:	1962 - 1969

Beswick Number	Price U.S. $	Can. $	U.K. £	Aust. $
1802	85.00	125.00	50.00	125.00

1803
CAT - SINGING™

Designer:	Albert Hallam
Height:	1 ¼", 3.2 cm
Colour:	Ginger stripe
Issued:	1962 - 1971

Beswick Number	Price U.S. $	Can. $	U.K. £	Aust. $
1803	85.00	125.00	50.00	125.00

1804
BOY WITHOUT SPECTACLES™

Designer:	Albert Hallam
Height:	3 ½", 8.9 cm
Colour:	Yellow, white and blue
Issued:	1962 - 1969

Beswick Number		Price		
	U.S. $	Can. $	U.K. £	Aust. $
1804	200.00	300.00	125.00	300.00

1805
BOY WITH SPECTACLES™

Designer:	Albert Hallam
Height:	3", 7.6 cm
Colour:	Green, white and blue
Issued:	1962 - 1969

Beswick Number		Price		
	U.S. $	Can. $	U.K. £	Aust. $
1805	250.00	375.00	150.00	350.00

1824
DOG - SINGING™

Designer:	Albert Hallam
Height:	1 ½", 3.8 cm
Colour:	Tan
Issued:	1962 - 1971

Beswick Number		Price		
	U.S. $	Can. $	U.K. £	Aust. $
1824	85.00	125.00	50.00	125.00

1825
BOY WITH GUITAR™

Designer:	Albert Hallam
Height:	3", 7.6 cm
Colour:	Blue-grey, brown and blue
Issued:	1962 - 1969

Beswick Number		Price		
	U.S. $	Can. $	U.K. £	Aust. $
1825	200.00	300.00	125.00	300.00

1826
GIRL WITH HARP™

Designer:	Albert Hallam
Height:	3 ½", 8.9 cm
Colour:	Purple, red and brown
Issued:	1962 - 1969

Beswick Number		Price		
	U.S. $	Can. $	U.K. £	Aust. $
1826	200.00	300.00	125.00	300.00

BESWICK BEARS

BB001
WILLIAM™

Designer:	Unknown
Height:	2 ¼", 5.7 cm
Colour:	Brown bear, blue apron, white and rose book
Issued:	1993 - 1993

Beswick Bears
WILLIAM
BB001

Beswick Number	Price			
	U.S. $	Can. $	U.K. £	Aust.
BB001	125.00	175.00	75.00	175.0

BB002
BILLY™

Designer:	Unknown
Height:	4", 10.1 cm
Colour:	Brown bear, green waistcoat, blue hat, yellow, red and blue ball
Issued:	1993 - 1993

BILLY
kicked his ball up high
and it landed "SPLAT"
in the apple pie.
Beswick Bears
BB002

Beswick Number	Price			
	U.S. $	Can. $	U.K. £	Aust. $
BB002	85.00	125.00	50.00	125.00

BB003
HARRY™

Designer:	Unknown
Height:	3 ¼", 8.3 cm
Colour:	Brown bear, blue waistcoat, brown hat, white plates
Issued:	1993 - 1993

HARRY
slipped – he'd made a mistake.
He dropped the plates,
but saved his cake.
Beswick Bears
BB003

Beswick Number	Price			
	U.S. $	Can. $	U.K. £	Aust.
BB003	85.00	125.00	50.00	125.

BB004
BOBBY™

Designer:	Unknown
Height:	4", 10.1 cm
Colour:	Brown bear, blue waistcoat, brown hat, yellow ball, black and red bat
Issued:	1993 - 1993

BOBBY
hits his ball in the air,
It comes to land,
he knows not where.
Beswick Bears
BB004

Beswick Number	Price			
	U.S. $	Can. $	U.K. £	Aust. $
BB004	85.00	125.00	50.00	125.00

BB005
JAMES™

Designer:	Unknown
Height:	3 ¾", 9.5 cm
Colour:	Brown bear, yellow waistcoat, blue hat, blue parcel with pink ribbon
Issued:	1993 - 1993

JAMES
has a gift wrapped up in a bow –
It's a nice little "thank you",
un petit cadeau.
Beswick Bears
BB005

Beswick Number	Price			
	U.S. $	Can. $	U.K. £	Aust. $
BB005	85.00	125.00	50.00	125.00

BB006
SUSIE™

Designer:	Unknown
Height:	3 ½", 8.9 cm
Colour:	Brown bear, blue dress, brown recorder
Issued:	1993 - 1993

SUSIE
is playing her new recorder
Any time she'll play to order.
Beswick Bears
BB006

Beswick Number	Price			
	U.S. $	Can. $	U.K. £	Aust. $
BB006	85.00	125.00	50.00	125.00

BB007
ANGELA™

Designer:	Unknown
Height:	3 ¼", 8.3 cm
Colour:	Brown bear, yellow dress, white flowers
Issued:	1993 - 1993

ANGELA
kneels to pick some flowers
Happily dreaming for
hours and hours.
Beswick Bears
BB007

Beswick Number	Price			
	U.S. $	Can. $	U.K. £	Aust. $
BB007	85.00	125.00	50.00	125.00

BB008
CHARLOTTE™

Designer:	Unknown
Height:	4", 10.1 cm
Colour:	Brown bear, pink dress, blue and yellow parasol
Issued:	1993 - 1993

CHARLOTTE
tries to keep in the shade,
Twirling her parasol,
a pretty young maid.
Beswick Bears
BB008

Beswick Number	Price			
	U.S. $	Can. $	U.K. £	Aust. $
BB008	85.00	125.00	50.00	125.00

BB009
SAM™

Designer:	Unknown
Height:	3 ½", 8.9 cm
Colour:	Brown bear, rose waistcoat, yellow banjo
Issued:	1993 - 1993

SAM
plays his banjo all day long,
Amusing friends
with a tune and a song.
Beswick Bears
BB009

Beswick Number	Price			
	U.S. $	Can. $	U.K. £	Aust. $
BB009	85.00	125.00	50.00	125.00

BB010
LIZZY™

Designer:	Unknown
Height:	2 ¼", 5.7 cm
Colour:	Brown bear, pink dress, paint box
Issued:	1993 - 1993

Beswick Number	Price U.S. $	Can. $	U.K. £	Aust. $
BB010	85.00	125.00	50.00	125.00

BB011
EMILY™

Designer:	Unknown
Height:	3 ½", 8.9 cm
Colour:	Brown bear, pale blue dress, brown picnic hamper
Issued:	1993 - 1993

Beswick Number	Price U.S. $	Can. $	U.K. £	Aust. $
BB011	85.00	125.00	50.00	125.00

BB012
SARAH™

Designer:	Unknown
Height:	3 ¼", 8.3 cm
Colour:	Brown bear, green dress, white cup and saucer
Issued:	1993 - 1993

Beswick Number	Price U.S. $	Can. $	U.K. £	Aust. $
BB012	85.00	125.00	50.00	125.00

BRAMBLY HEDGE

DBH1
POPPY EYEBRIGHT™

Designer:	Harry Sales
Modeller:	David Lyttleton
Height:	3 ¼", 8.3 cm
Colour:	Grey-white and pink dress, white apron trimmed with blue flowers
Issued:	1983 - 1997

Doulton Number	Price			
	U.S. $	Can. $	U.K. £	Aust.
DBH1	90.00	125.00	30.00	125.0

DBH2
MR APPLE™

Designer:	Harry Sales
Modeller:	David Lyttleton
Height:	3 ¼", 8.3 cm
Colour:	Black trousers, white and blue striped shirt, white apron
Issued:	1983 - 1997

Doulton Number	Price			
	U.S. $	Can. $	U.K. £	Aust. $
DBH2	95.00	135.00	30.00	125.00

DBH3
MRS. APPLE™

Designer:	Harry Sales
Modeller:	David Lyttleton
Height:	3 ¼", 8.3 cm
Colour:	White and blue striped dress, white apron
Issued:	1983 - 1997

Doulton Number	Price			
	U.S. $	Can. $	U.K. £	Aust.
DBH3	100.00	135.00	50.00	125.0

DBH4
LORD WOODMOUSE™

Designer:	Harry Sales
Modeller:	David Lyttleton
Height:	3 ¼", 8.3 cm
Colour:	Green trousers, brown coat and burgundy waistcoat
Issued:	1983 - 1997

Doulton Number	Price			
	U.S. $	Can. $	U.K. £	Aust. $
DBH4	75.00	100.00	30.00	95.00

DBH5
LADY WOODMOUSE™

Designer:	Harry Sales
Modeller:	David Lyttleton
Height:	3 ¼", 8.3 cm
Colour:	Red and white striped dress, white apron
Issued:	1983 - 1997

Doulton Number	Price			
	U.S. $	Can. $	U.K. £	Aust. $
DBH5	75.00	100.00	30.00	95.00

DBH6
DUSTY DOGWOOD™

Designer:	Harry Sales
Modeller:	David Lyttleton
Height:	3 ¼", 8.3 cm
Colour:	Dark grey suit, red waistcoat
Issued:	1984 - 1995

Doulton Number	Price			
	U.S. $	Can. $	U.K. £	Aust. $
DBH6	100.00	135.00	35.00	125.00

DBH7
WILFRED TOADFLAX™

Designer:	Harry Sales
Modeller:	David Lyttleton
Height:	3 ¼", 8.3 cm
Colour:	Grey trousers, red and white striped shirt
Issued:	1983 - 1997

Royal Doulton
WILFRED TOADFLAX
D BH 7
FROM THE BRAMBLY HEDGE
© GIFT COLLECTION
JILL BARKLEM 1982

Doulton Number	Price			
	U.S. $	Can. $	U.K. £	Aust. $
DBH7	75.00	100.00	30.00	95.00

DBH8
PRIMROSE WOODMOUSE™

Designer:	Harry Sales
Modeller:	David Lyttleton
Height:	3 ¼", 8.3 cm
Colour:	Yellow dress with white apron
Issued:	1983 - 1997

Royal Doulton
PRIMROSE WOODMOUSE
D BH 8.
FROM THE BRAMBLY HEDGE
© GIFT COLLECTION
JILL BARKLEM 1982

Doulton Number	Price			
	U.S. $	Can. $	U.K. £	Aust. $
DBH8	75.00	100.00	30.00	95.00

DBH9
OLD MRS EYEBRIGHT™

Designer:	Harry Sales
Modeller:	David Lyttleton
Height:	3 ¼", 8.3 cm
Colour:	Mauve skirt, white and pink striped shawl, white apron
Issued:	1984 - 1995

Royal Doulton
OLD MRS EYE BRIGHT
D BH 9
FROM THE BRAMBLY HEDGE
© GIFT COLLECTION
JILL BARKLEM 1983

Doulton Number	Price			
	U.S. $	Can. $	U.K. £	Aust. $
DBH9	150.00	200.00	75.00	175.00

DBH10A
MR. TOADFLAX™
First Version (Tail at front, with cushion)

Designer: Harry Sales
Modeller: David Lyttleton
Height: 3 ¼", 8.3 cm
Colour: Blue and white striped shirt,
           pink trousers, burgundy braces
Issued: 1984 - Unknown

Doulton Number	U.S. $	Price Can. $	U.K. £	Aust. $
DBH10A	2,500.00	3,000.00	1,500.00	3,000.00

DBH10B
MR. TOADFLAX™
Second Version (Tail at back, with cushion)

Designer: Harry Sales
Modeller: David Lyttleton
Height: 3 ¼", 8.3 cm
Colour: Blue and white striped shirt,
           lilac trousers, burgundy braces,
           multi-coloured patchwork cushion
Issued: Unknown

Doulton Number	U.S. $	Price Can. $	U.K. £	Aust. $
DBH10B	450.00	600.00	250.00	600.00

DBH10C
MR. TOADFLAX™
Third Version (Tail at back, without cushion)

Designer: Harry Sales
Modeller: David Lyttleton
Height: 3 ¼", 8.3 cm
Colour: Blue and white striped shirt,
           pink trousers, burgundy braces
Issued: Unknown - 1997

Doulton Number	U.S. $	Price Can. $	U.K. £	Aust. $
DBH10C	85.00	125.00	30.00	125.00

Note: For further illustrations see page 100.

DBH11
MRS. TOADFLAX™

Designer:	Harry Sales
Modeller:	David Lyttleton
Height:	3 ¼", 8.3 cm
Colour:	Green and white striped dress, white apron
Issued:	1985 - 1995

Doulton Number	Price U.S. $	Can. $	U.K. £	Aust. $
DBH11	95.00	125.00	35.00	125.00

DBH12
CATKIN™

Designer:	Harry Sales
Modeller:	David Lyttleton
Height:	3 ¼", 8.3 cm
Colour:	Yellow dress and white apron
Issued:	1985 - 1994

Doulton Number	Price U.S. $	Can. $	U.K. £	Aust. $
DBH12	195.00	250.00	125.00	250.00

DBH13
OLD VOLE™

Designer:	Harry Sales
Modeller:	David Lyttleton
Height:	3 ¼", 8.3 cm
Colour:	Green jacket, blue trousers, yellow waistcoat
Issued:	1985 - 1992

Doulton Number	Price U.S. $	Can. $	U.K. £	Aust. $
DBH13	325.00	425.00	175.00	400.00

DBH14
BASIL™

Designer:	Harry Sales
Modeller:	David Lyttleton
Height:	3 ¼", 8.3 cm
Colour:	Brown waistcoat, green and white striped trousers
Issued:	1985 - 1992

Doulton	Price			
Number	U.S. $	Can. $	U.K. £	Aust. $
DBH14	325.00	425.00	175.00	400.00

DBH15
MRS. CRUSTYBREAD™

Designer:	Graham Tongue
Modeller:	Ted Chawner
Height:	3 ¼", 8.3 cm
Colour:	Yellow dress, white apron and cap
Issued:	1987 - 1994

Doulton	Price			
Number	U.S. $	Can. $	U.K. £	Aust. $
DBH15	250.00	350.00	150.00	325.00

DBH16
CLOVER™

Designer:	Graham Tongue
Modeller:	Graham Tongue
Height:	3 ¼", 8.3 cm
Colour:	Burgundy dress, white apron
Issued:	1987 - 1997

Doulton	Price			
Number	U.S. $	Can. $	U.K. £	Aust. $
DBH16	75.00	100.00	30.00	100.00

DBH17
TEASEL™

Designer:	Graham Tongue
Modeller:	Ted Chawner
Height:	3 ¼", 8.3 cm
Colour:	Blue-grey dungarees, blue and white striped shirt
Issued:	1987 - 1992

Royal Doulton®
TEASEL
D B H 17
FROM THE BRAMBLY HEDGE
© GIFT COLLECTION
1987 JILL BARKLEM

Doulton Number	Price U.S. $	Can. $	U.K. £	Aust. $
DBH17	450.00	600.00	250.00	625.00

Royal Doulton®
STORE STUMP MONEY BOX
D B H 18
FROM THE BRAMBLY HEDGE
© GIFT COLLECTION
1987 JILL BARKLEM

DBH18
STORE STUMP MONEY BOX™

Designer:	Martyn Alcock
Height:	3 ¼", 8.3 cm
Colour:	Browns
Issued:	1987 - 1989

Doulton Number	Price U.S. $	Can. $	U.K. £	Aust. $
DBH18	200.00	300.00	125.00	275.00

DBH19
LILY WEAVER™

Designer:	Graham Tongue
Modeller:	Ted Chawner
Height:	3 ¼", 8.3 cm
Colour:	White dress with green and mauve, white cap
Issued:	1988 - 1993

Royal Doulton®
LILY WEAVER
D B H 19
FROM THE BRAMBLY HEDGE
GIFT COLLECTION
1988 JILL BARKLEM

Doulton Number	Price U.S. $	Can. $	U.K. £	Aust. $
DBH19	325.00	450.00	200.00	425.00

DBH20
FLAX WEAVER™

Designer:	Graham Tongue
Modeller:	Ted Chawner
Height:	3 ¼", 8.3 cm
Colour:	Grey trousers, grey and white striped shirt
Issued:	1988 - 1993

Doulton Number	Price			
	U.S. $	Can. $	U.K. £	Aust. $
DBH20	275.00	400.00	175.00	425.00

DBH21
CONKER™

Designer:	Graham Tongue
Modeller:	Ted Chawner
Height:	3 ¼", 8.3 cm
Colour:	Green jacket, yellow waistcoat, green striped trousers
Issued:	1988 - 1994

Doulton Number	Price			
	U.S. $	Can. $	U.K. £	Aust. $
DBH21	275.00	400.00	175.00	425.00

DBH22
PRIMROSE ENTERTAINS™

Designer:	Graham Tongue
Modeller:	Alan Maslankowski
Height:	3 ¼", 8.3 cm
Colour:	Green and yellow dress
Issued:	1990 - 1995

Doulton Number	Price			
	U.S. $	Can. $	U.K. £	Aust. $
DBH22	125.00	175.00	75.00	150.00

DBH23
WILFRED ENTERTAINS™

Designer:	Graham Tongue
Modeller:	Alan Maslankowski
Height:	3 ¼", 8.3 cm
Colour:	Burgundy and yellow outfit, black hat
Issued:	1990 - 1995

Doulton Number	Price U.S. $	Can. $	U.K. £	Aust $
DBH23	125.00	175.00	75.00	165.00

DBH24
MR. SALTAPPLE™

Designer:	Graham Tongue
Modeller:	Warren Platt
Height:	3 ¼", 8.3 cm
Colour:	Blue and white striped outfit, beige base
Issued:	1993 - 1997

Doulton Number	Price U.S. $	Can. $	U.K. £	Aust. $
DBH24	80.00	100.00	40.00	95.00

DBH25
MRS. SALTAPPLE™

Designer:	Graham Tongue
Modeller:	Warren Platt
Height:	3 ¼", 8.3 cm
Colour:	Rose and cream dress, beige hat and base
Issued:	1993 - 1997

Doultom Number	Price U.S. $	Can. $	U.K. £	Aust. $
DBH25	80.00	100.00	40.00	95.00

DBH26
DUSTY AND BABY™

Designer:	Graham Tongue
Modeller:	Martyn Alcock
Height:	3 ¾", 9.5 cm
Colour:	Dusty - blue striped shirt with beige dungarees
	Baby - white gown
Issued:	1995 - 1997

Doulton Number	U.S. $	Price Can. $	U.K. £	Aust. $
DBH26	85.00	125.00	45.00	125.00

Mr. Toadflax
front view

Second Version —Tail at the Back   First Version — Tail at the Front   Third Version — Tail at the Back

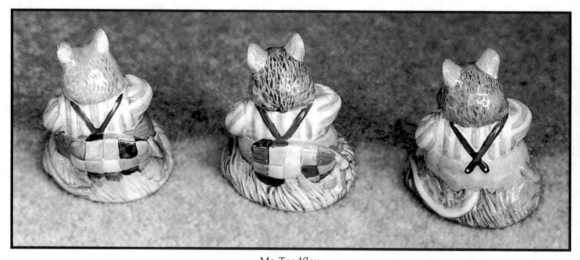

Mr. Toadflax
back view

Second Version —With Cushion   First Version — With Cushion   Third Version — Without Cushion

THE CAT'S CHORUS

CC1
PURRFECT PITCH™

Designer:	Shane Ridge
Height:	4", 10.1 cm
Colour:	White cat, black dress, red gloves and shoes, black hair
Issued:	1998 to the present

Beswick Number	Price U.S. $	Can. $	U.K. £	Aust. $
CC1	45.00	65.00	26.00	65.00

CC2
CALYPSO KITTEN™

Designer:	Shane Ridge
Height:	4", 10.1 cm
Colour:	Black cat, patterned yellow shirt, beige trousers, red and yellow drum
Issued:	1998 to the present

Beswick Number	Price U.S. $	Can. $	U.K. £	Aust. $
CC2	45.00	65.00	26.00	65.00

CC3
ONE COOL CAT™

Designer:	Shane Ridge
Height:	4", 10.1 cm
Colour:	Ginger cat, blue suit with black lapels, cuffs and pockets, white shirt, black shoes, yellow saxaphone
Issued:	1998 to the present

Beswick Number	Price U.S. $	Can. $	U.K. £	Aust. $
CC3	45.00	65.00	26.00	65.00

CC4
RATCATCHER BILK

Designer:	Shane Ridge			
Height:	4", 10.1 cm			
Colour:	White cat, blue shirt and hat, yellow			
	waistcoat, black trousers and clarinet			
Issued:	1998 to the present			

Beswick		Price		
Number	U.S. $	Can. $	U.K. £	Aust. $
CC4	45.00	65.00	26.00	65.00

CC5
TRAD JAZZ TOM™

Designer:	Shane Ridge
Height:	4", 10.1 cm
Colour:	Grey cat, trousers and waistcoat,
	lemon shirt, black hat, yellow trumpet
Issued:	1998 to the present

Beswick		Price		
Number	U.S. $	Can. $	U.K. £	Aust. $
CC5	45.00	65.00	26.00	65.00

CC6
CATWALKING BASS™

Designer:	Shane Ridge
Height:	4", 10.1 cm
Colour:	White cat, yellow jacket, green shirt,
	red trousers, black hat, tan bass
Issued:	1998 to the present

Beswick		Price		
Number	U.S. $	Can. $	U.K. £	Aust. $
CC6	45.00	65.00	26.00	65.00

CC7
FELINE FLAMENCO™

Designer:	Shane Ridge
Height:	4", 10.1 cm
Colour:	Ginger cat, lemon shirt, black waistcoat and trousers, red and white cumberbund, tan guitar
Issued:	1998 to the present

Beswick		Price		
Number	U.S. $	Can. $	U.K. £	Aust. $
CC7	45.00	65.00	26.00	65.00

CC8
BRAVURA BRASS

Designer:	Shane Ridge
Height:	4", 10.1 cm
Colour:	Ginger cat, black suit and shoes, shite shirt, yellow french horn
Issued:	1998 to the present

Beswick		Price		
Number	U.S. $	Can. $	U.K. £	Aust. $
CC8	45.00	65.00	26.00	65.00

CC9
FAT CAT™

Designer:	Shane Ridge
Height:	3 ¾", 9.5 cm
Colour:	Brown, yellow and blue
Issued:	1999 to the present

Beswick		Price		
Number	U.S. $	Can. $	U.K. £	Aust. $
CC9	45.00	65.00	26.00	65.00

CC10
GLAM GUITAR™

Designer:	Shane Ridge	
Height:	4 ¼", 10.8 cm	
Colour:	Red, yellow and white	
Issued:	1999 to the present	

Beswick Number	Price U.S. $	Can. $	U.K. £	Aust. $
CC10	45.00	65.00	26.00	65.00

COMPTON & WOODHOUSE

ARCHIE

Designer:	Unknown
Height:	4 ½", 11.9 cm
Colour:	Brown bear with light blue waistcoat and red and white spotted handkerchief
Issued:	1997 to the present
Series:	The Beswick Bears Collection

CW
ARCHIE
by *John Beswick*
Compton & Woodhouse
— 1997 —

Beswick Number	Price			
	U.S. $	Can. $	U.K. £	Aust. $
—	85.00	125.00	50.00	125.00

BENJAMIN

Designer:	Unknown
Height:	4 ½", 11.9 cm
Colour:	Brown bear wearing a bright yellow scarf
Issued:	1996 to the present
Series:	The Beswick Bears Collection

CW
BENJAMIN
by *John Beswick*
Compton & Woodhouse
— 1996 —

Beswick Number		Price			
		U.S. $	Can. $	U.K. £	Aust. $
—		85.00	125.00	50.00	125.00

BERTIE

Designer:	Unknown
Height:	4 ½", 11.9 cm
Colour:	Dark brown bear, light brown straw hat with red and purple band, yellow cane
Issued:	1997 to the present
Series:	The Beswick Bears Collection

Beswick Number		Price		
	U.S. $	Can. $	U.K. £	Aust. $
—	85.00	125.00	50.00	125.00

HENRY

Designer:	Unknown
Height:	4 ½", 11.9 cm
Colour:	Dark brown bear, purple tie, brown briefcase
Issued:	1998 to the present
Series:	The Beswick Bears Collection

Beswick Number		Price		
	U.S. $	Can. $	U.K. £	Aust. $
—	85.00	125.00	50.00	125.00

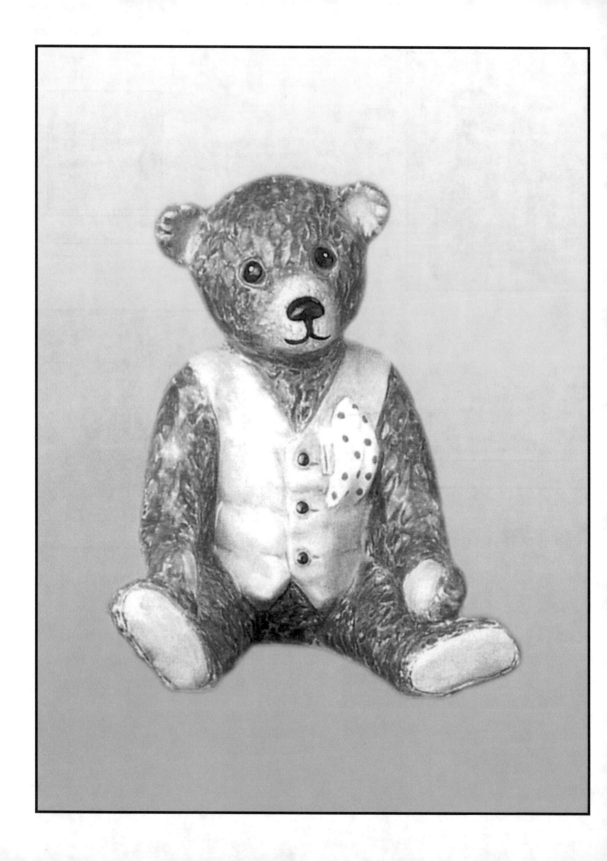

COUNTRY COUSINS

PM 2101
SWEET SUZIE
Thank You

Designer:	Unknown
Height:	2 ¾", 7.0 cm
Colour:	Brown rabbit wearing a brown and yellow pinafore
Issued:	1994 - 1994

Back Stamp	Beswick Number	Price U.S. $	Can. $	U.K. £	Aust. $
BK-1	PM2101	35.00	50.00	20.00	55.00

PM 2102
PETER
Once Upon A Time

Designer:	Unknown
Height:	2 ½", 5.6 cm
Colour:	Brown hedgehog wearing a blue suit and a white bowtie
Issued:	1994 - 1994

Back Stamp	Beswick Number	Price U.S. $	Can. $	U.K. £	Aust. $
BK-1	PM2102	35.00	50.00	20.00	55.00

PM 2103
HARRY
A New Home for Fred

Designer:	Unknown
Height:	2", 5.0 cm
Colour:	Brown hedgehog wearing a blue and white jumper and brown trousers
Issued:	1994 - 1994

Back Stamp	Beswick Number	Price U.S. $	Can. $	U.K. £	Aust. $
BK-1	PM2103	35.00	50.00	20.00	55.00

PM 2104
MICHAEL
Happily Ever After

Designer:	Unknown
Height:	2 ½", 6.4 cm
Colour:	Brown rabbit wearing a green jacket
Issued:	1994 - 1994

Back Stamp	Beswick Number	U.S. $	Price Can. $	U.K. £	Aust. $
BK-1	PM2104	35.00	50.00	20.00	55.00

PM 2105
BERTRAM
Ten Out of Ten

Designer:	Unknown
Height:	3", 7.6 cm
Colour:	Brown owl wearing a green and blue striped waistcoat, a red bow tie and blue mortar board with red tassel
Issued:	1994 - 1994

Back Stamp	Beswick Number	U.S. $	Price Can. $	U.K. £	Aust. $
BK-1	PM2105	35.00	50.00	20.00	55.00

PM 2106
LEONARDO
Practice Makes Perfect

Designer:	Unknown
Height:	2 ¾", 7.0 cm
Colour:	Brown owl wearing a brown hat; white palette and blue paintbrush
Issued:	1994 - 1994

Back Stamp	Beswick Number	U.S. $	Price Can. $	U.K. £	Aust. $
BK-1	PM2106	35.00	50.00	20.00	55.00

PM 2107
LILY
Flowers Picked Just for You

Designer:	Unknown
Height:	3", 7.6 cm
Colour:	Brown hedgehog wearing a pink dress with matching bonnet with white ribbon, yellow pinafore with white collar,
Issued:	1994 - 1994

Back Stamp	Beswick Number	U.S. $	Price Can. $	U.K. £	Aust. $
BK-1	PM2107	35.00	50.00	20.00	55.00

PM 2108
PATRICK
This Way's Best

Designer:	Unknown
Height:	3", 7.6 cm
Colour:	Brown owl wearing a blue and yellow checked waistcoat, white collar and blue bow tie, yellow hat with red band
Issued:	1994 - 1994

Back Stamp	Beswick Number	U.S. $	Price Can. $	U.K. £	Aust. $
BK-1	PM2108	35.00	50.00	20.00	55.00

PM 2109
JAMIE
Hurrying Home

Designer:	Unknown
Height:	3", 7.6 cm
Colour:	Brown hedgehog wearing apink sailor top with white stripes, blue trousers
Issued:	1994 - 1994

Back Stamp	Beswick Number	U.S. $	Price Can. $	U.K. £	Aust. $
BK-1	PM2109	35.00	50.00	20.00	55.00

PM 2111
MUM AND LIZZIE
Let's Get Busy

Designer:	Unknown
Height:	3 ¼", 8.3 cm
Colour:	Large brown rabbit wearing a blue dress and white pinafore; Small brown rabbit wearing a white pinafore
Issued:	1994 - 1994

Back Stamp	Beswick Number	Price			
		U.S. $	Can. $	U.K. £	Aust. $
BK-1	PM2111	50.00	75.00	30.00	65.00

PM 2112
MOLLY AND TIMMY
Picnic Time

Designer:	Unknown
Height:	2 ¾", 7 cm
Colour:	Large brown mouse wearing a pink dress, blue pinafore, yellow bonnet; Small brown mouse wearing yellow dungarees, white top, blue hat, carrying a brown teddy bear
Issued:	1994 - 1994

Back Stamp	Beswick Number	Price			
		U.S. $	Can. $	U.K. £	Aust. $
BK-1	PM2112	50.00	75.00	30.00	65.00

PM 2113
POLLY AND SARAH
Good News!

Designer:	Unknown
Height:	3 ¼", 8.3 cm
Colour:	Brown rabbit wearing a blue dress and a pink apron; Brown hedgehog wearing a blue dress and scarf, green jacket and a white pinafore
Issued:	1994 - 1994

Back Stamp	Beswick Number	Price			
		U.S. $	Can. $	U.K. £	Aust. $
BK-1	PM2113	50.00	75.00	30.00	65.00

PM 2114
BILL AND TED
Working Together

Designer:	Unknown
Height:	3 ¼", 8.3 cm
Colour:	Brown mouse in blue dungarees
	Brown hedgehog in green dungarees
Issued:	1994 - 1994

Back Stamp	Beswick Number	Price U.S. $	Can. $	U.K. £	Aust. $
BK-1	PM2114	50.00	75.00	30.00	60.00

PM 2115
JACK AND DAISY
How Does Your Garden Grow

Designer:	Unknown
Height:	2 ¾", 7 cm
Colour:	Male - brown mouse, white shirt, blue dungarees
	Female - brown mouse, pink and white striped dress, white pinafore
Issued:	1994 - 1994

Back Stamp	Beswick Number	Price U.S. $	Can. $	U.K. £	Aust. $
BK-1	PM2115	50.00	75.00	30.00	60.00

PM 2116
ALISON AND DEBBIE
Friendship is Fun

Designer:	Unknown
Height:	2 ¾", 7 cm
Colour:	Rabbit - brown, pink dress, white pinafore
	Squirrel - brown, blue dress, pink apron
Issued:	1994 - 1994

Back Stamp	Beswick Number	Price U.S. $	Can. $	U.K. £	Aust. $
BK-1	PM2116	50.00	75.00	30.00	60.00

PM 2119
ROBERT AND ROSIE
Perfect Partners

Designer:	Unknown
Height:	3 ¼", 8.3 cm
Colour:	Male - brown squirrel, blue dungarees, blue hat with red band Female - brown squirrel, pink dress with white collar, yellow hat
Issued:	1994 - 1994

Back Stamp	Beswick Number	U.S. $	Price Can. $	U.K. £	Aust. $
BK-1	PM2119	50.00	75.00	30.00	60.00

PM 2120
SAMMY
Treasure Hunting

Designer:	Unknown
Height:	2 ¼", 5.7 cm
Colour:	Brown squirrel wearing a green shirt; blue sack
Issued:	1994 - 1994

Back Stamp	Beswick Number	U.S. $	Price Can. $	U.K. £	Aust. $
BK-1	PM2120	35.00	50.00	20.00	55.00

DAVID HAND'S ANIMALAND

1148
DINKUM PLATYPUS™

Designer:	Arthur Gredington
Height:	4 ¼", 10.8 cm
Colour:	Brown and beige platypus, green base
Issued:	1949 - 1955

Beswick Number		Price		
	U.S. $	Can. $	U.K. £	Aust. $
1148	200.00	300.00	135.00	275.00

1150
ZIMMY LION™

Designer:	Arthur Gredington
Height:	3 ¾", 9.5 cm
Colour:	Brown lion with white face
Issued:	1949 - 1955

Beswick Number		Price		
	U.S. $	Can. $	U.K. £	Aust. $
1150	500.00	700.00	325.00	725.00

1151
FELIA™

Designer:	Arthur Gredington
Height:	4", 10.1 cm
Colour:	Green cat
Issued:	1949 - 1955

Beswick Number		Price		
	U.S. $	Can. $	U.K. £	Aust. $
1151	750.00	1,100.00	400.00	1,000.00

1152
GINGER NUTT™

Designer:	Arthur Gredington
Height:	4", 10.1 cm
Colour:	Brown and beige squirrel, green base
Issued:	1949 - 1955

Beswick Number	Price			
	U.S. $	Can. $	U.K. £	Aust. $
1152	700.00	1,000.00	450.00	1,100.00

1153
HAZEL NUTT™

Designer:	Arthur Gredington
Height:	3 ¾", 9.5 cm
Colour:	Brown and beige squirrel, green base
Issued:	1949 - 1955

Beswick Number	Price			
	U.S. $	Can. $	U.K. £	Aust. $
1153	700.00	1,100.00	450.00	1,100.00

1154
OSCAR OSTRICH™

Designer:	Arthur Gredington
Height:	3 ¾", 9.5 cm
Colour:	Beige and mauve ostrich, brown base
Issued:	1949 - 1955

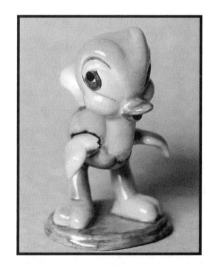

Beswick Number	Price			
	U.S. $	Can. $	U.K. £	Aust. $
1154	700.00	1,000.00	450.00	1,000.00

1155
DUSTY MOLE™

Designer:	Arthur Gredington
Height:	3 ½", 8.9 cm
Colour:	Blue mole, white face
Issued:	1949 - 1955

Beswick	Price			
Number	U.S. $	Can. $	U.K. £	Aust. $
1155	375.00	500.00	225.00	475.00

1156
LOOPY HARE™

Designer:	Arthur Gredington
Height:	4 ¼", 10.8 cm
Colour:	Brown and beige hare
Issued:	1949 - 1955

Beswick	Price			
Number	U.S. $	Can. $	U.K. £	Aust. $
1156	650.00	1,000.00	350.00	975.00

ENGLISH COUNTRY FOLK

ECF 1
HUNTSMAN FOX™

Designer:	Amanda Hughes-Lubeck
Height:	5 ¾", 14.6 cm
Colour:	Dark green jacket and cap, blue-grey trousers, green wellingtons
Issued:	1993 - 1998

BESWICK
B
IRELAND
ECF 1
HUNTSMAN FOX

Back Stamp	Beswick Number		Price		
		U.S. $	Can. $	U.K. £	Aust. $
ECF 1	9150	70.00	100.00	35.00	100.00

ECF 2
FISHERMAN OTTER™

Designer:	Warren Platt
Height:	5 ¾", 14.6 cm
Colour:	Yellow shirt and hat, dark green waistcoat, blue-grey trousers, green wellingtons
Issued:	1993 - 1998

BESWICK
B
IRELAND
ECF 2
FISHERMAN OTTER

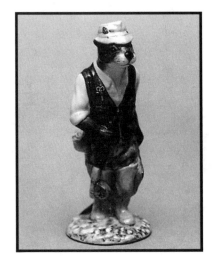

Back Stamp	Beswick Number		Price		
		U.S.$	Can. $	U.K. £	Aust. $
ECF 2	9152	70.00	100.00	35.00	100.00

ECF 3
GARDENER RABBIT™
First Variation

Designer:	Warren Platt
Height:	6", 15.0 cm
Colour:	White shirt, red pullover, blue trousers, grey hat, black wellingtons
Issued:	1993 to the present
Varieties:	ECF 12

BESWICK
B
IRELAND
ECF 3
GARDENER RABBIT

Back Stamp	Beswick Number		Price		
		U.S. $	Can. $	U.K. £	Aust. $
ECF 3	9155	70.00	100.00	35.00	100.00

ECF 4
GENTLEMAN PIG™
First Variation

Designer:	Amanda Hughes-Lubeck
Height:	5 ¾", 14.6 cm
Colour:	Dark brown suit, yellow waistcoat
Issued:	1993 to the present
Varieties:	ECF 10

BESWICK
ECF 4
GENTLEMAN PIG

Back Stamp	Beswick Number	U.S. $	Price Can. $	U.K. £	Aust. $
ECF 4	9149	70.00	100.00	35.00	110.00

ECF 5
SHEPHERD SHEEPDOG™

Designer:	Warren Platt
Height:	6 ¾", 17.2 cm
Colour:	Yellow smock
Issued:	1993 to the present

BESWICK
ECF 5
SHEPHERD SHEEPDOG

Back Stamp	Beswick Number	U.S. $	Price Can. $	U.K. £	Aust. $
ECF 5	9156	70.00	100.00	35.00	110.00

ECF 6
HIKER BADGER™
First Variation

Designer:	Warren Platt
Height:	5 ¼", 13.3 cm
Colour:	Yellow shirt, blue waistcoat, red cap and socks
Issued:	1993 to the present
Varieties:	ECF 9

BESWICK
ECF 6
HIKER BADGER

Back Stamp	Beswick Number	U.S. $	Price Can. $	U.K. £	Aust. $
ECF 6	9157	70.00	100.00	35.00	110.00

ECF 7
MRS RABBIT BAKING™
First Variation

Designer: Martyn Alcock
Height: 5 ½", 14.0 cm
Colour: Mauve dress, white apron and cap
Issued: 1994 to the present
Varieties: ECF 13

ECF 7
MRS RABBIT BAKING

Back Stamp	Beswick Number	Price			
		U.S. $	Can. $	U.K. £	Aust. $
ECF 7	—	75.00	110.00	35.00	110.00

ECF 8
THE LADY PIG™
First Variation

Designer: Amanda Hughes-Lubeck
Height: 5 ½", 14.0 cm
Colour: Green jacket, skirt and hat, brown umbrella
Issued: 1995 to the present
Varieties: ECF 11

ECF 8
THE LADY PIG

Back Stamp	Beswick Number	Price			
		U.S. $	Can. $	U.K. £	Aust. $
ECF 8	—	75.00	110.00	35.00	110.00

ECF 9
HIKER BADGER™
Second Variation

Designer: Warren Platt
Height: 5 ¼", 13.3 cm
Colour: Green shirt and trousers, red jumper, hat and socks, black walking stick
Issued: 1997 in a special edition of 1,000
Varieties: ECF 6

ECF 9
HIKER BADGER
Sinclairs
China, Crystal & Luxuries
NEW COLOURWAY 1997
PRODUCED EXCLUSIVELY FOR
20th CENTURY FAIRS JUNE 1997
IN A SPECIAL EDITION OF 1,000

85

Back Stamp	Beswick Number	Price			
		U.S. $	Can. $	U.K. £	Aust. $
ECF 9	9157	125.00	150.00	65.00	160.00

ECF 10
GENTLEMAN PIG™
Second Variation

Designer:	Amanda Hughes-Lubeck
Height:	5 ¾", 14.6 cm
Colour:	Light brown suit and waistcoat
Issued:	1998 in a limited edition of 2,000
Varieties:	ECF 4

Back Stamp	Beswick Number	U.S. $	Price Can. $	U.K. £	Aust. $
ECF 10	—	50.00	75.00	30.00	80.00

ECF 11
THE LADY PIG™
Second Variation

Designer:	Amanda Hughes-Lubeck
Height:	5 ½", 14.0 cm
Colour:	Brown skirt, jacket and hat, light brown umbrella
Issued:	1998 in a limited edition of 2,000
Varieties:	ECF 8

Back Stamp	Beswick Number	U.S. $	Price Can. $	U.K. £	Aust. $
ECF 11	—	50.00	75.00	30.00	80.00

ECF 12
GARDENER RABBIT™
Second Variation

Designer:	Warren Platt
Height:	6", 15.0 cm
Colour:	Black hat, slate pullover
Issued:	1998 in a limited edition of 2,000
Varieties:	ECF 3

Back Stamp	Beswick Number	U.S. $	Price Can. $	U.K. £	Aust. $
ECF 12	9155	75.00	115.00	45.00	125.00

ECF 13
MRS RABBIT BAKING™
Second Variation

Designer:	Martyn Alcock
Height:	5 ½", 14.0 cm
Colour:	Grey dress, yellow trimmed apron, rust cap
Issued:	1998 in a limited edition of 2,000
Varieties:	ECF 7

Back Stamp	Beswick Number	U.S. $	Price Can. $	U.K. £	Aust. $
ECF 13	—	75.00	115.00	45.00	125.00

ENID BLYTON
NODDY™ COLLECTION

3676
BIG EARS™

Designer:	Enid Bliyton
Modeller:	Andy Moss
Height:	5", 12.7 cm
Colour:	Red and white striped shirt, dark blue jacket, yellow buttons and trousers, red hat
Issued:	1997 in a special edition of 1,500

Doulton		Price		
Number	U.S. $	Can. $	U.K. £	Aust. $
3676	100.00	150.00	60.00	150.00

3678
NODDY™

Designer:	Enid Bliyton
Modeller	Andy Moss
Height:	5", 12.7 cm
Colour:	Red shirt and shoes, light blue trousers, dark blue hat with light brown bell
Issued:	1997 in a special edition of 1,500

Doulton		Price		
Number	U.S. $	Can. $	U.K. £	Aust. $
3678	100.00	150.00	60.00	150.00

3769
MR. PLOD™

Designer:	Enid Bliyton
Modeller:	Andy Moss
Height:	5", 12.7 cm
Colour:	Dark blue uniform, yellow buttons, white stripes on cuffs and shoulders; blue helmet with yellow
Issued:	1998 each in a special edition of 1,500

Doulton		Price		
Number	U.S. $	Can. $	U.K. £	Aust.
3679	100.00	150.00	60.00	150.00

3770
TESSIE BEAR™

Designer:	Enid Blyton
Modeller:	Andy Moss
Height:	5", 12.7 cm
Colour:	Yellow bear wearing a pink and green skirt and a pink hat with a white bow
Issued:	1998 each in a special edition of 1,500

Doulton Number	Price			
	U.S. $	Can. $	U.K. £	Aust.
3770	100.00	150.00	60.00	150.00

EXPRESS NEWSPAPERS PLC
RUPERT BEAR

2694
RUPERT BEAR™
Style One

Designer:	Harry Sales
Height:	4 ¼", 10.8 cm
Colour:	Red sweater, yellow check trousers and scarf
Issued:	1980 - 1986

Beswick		*Price*		
Number	*U.S. $*	*Can. $*	*U.K. £*	*Aust. $*
2694	450.00	600.00	250.00	625.00

2710
ALGY PUG™

Designer:	Harry Sales
Height:	4", 10.1 cm
Colour:	Grey jacket, yellow waistcoat, brown trousers
Issued:	1981 - 1986

Beswick		*Price*		
Number	*U.S. $*	*Can. $*	*U.K. £*	*Aust. $*
2710	350.00	475.00	200.00	500.00

2711
PONG PING™

Designer:	Harry Sales
Height:	4 ¼", 10.8
Colour:	Dark green jacket, gold trousers
Issued:	1981 - 1986

Beswick		*Price*		
Number	*U.S. $*	*Can. $*	*U.K. £*	*Aust. $*
2711	325.00	450.00	180.00	475.00

2720
BILL BADGER™

Designer:	Harry Sales	
Height:	2 ¾", 7.0 cm	
Colour:	Dark grey jacket, light grey trousers and red bowtie	
Issued:	1981 - 1986	

Beswick Number	U.S. $	Price Can. $	U.K. £	Aust. $
2720	450.00	600.00	250.00	625.00

2779
RUPERT BEAR SNOWBALLING™

Designer:	Harry Sales
Height:	4 ¼", 10.8 cm
Colour:	Red coat, yellow with brown striped trousers and scarf
Issued:	1982 - 1986

Beswick Number	U.S. $	Price Can. $	U.K. £	Aust. $
2779	575.00	750.00	375.00	675.00

RUPERT BEAR™
Style Two

Designer:	Martyn Alcock
Height:	5 ¾", 14.6 cm
Colour:	Red sweater, yellow check trousers and scarf
Issued:	1998 in a limited edition of 1,920

Beswick Number	U.S. $	Price Can. $	U.K. £	Aust. $
—	—	—	40.00	—

Note: Issued as one of a pair with Podgy Pig.

PODGY PIG™

Designer:	Martyn Alcock
Height:	5 ¾", 14.6 cm
Colour:	Beige, red and pink
Issued:	1998 in a limited edition of 1,920

Beswick Number		Price U.S. $	Can. $	U.K. £	Aust. $
—		—	—	40.00	—

Note: Issued as one of a pair with Rupert Bear, Style Two.

HANNA-BARBERA

THE FLINTSTONES
TOP CAT

THE FLINTSTONES

1996-1997

3577
PEBBLES FLINTSTONE™

Designer:	Simon Ward
Height:	3 ½", 8.9 cm
Colour:	Green dress, blue pants, red hair, light brown base
Issued:	1997 in a limited edition of 2,000

Beswick		Price		
Number	U.S. $	Can. $	U.K. £	Aust. $
3577	100.00	150.00	60.00	150.00
Set of 7 figures	700.00	1,000.00	450.00	1,100.00

3579
BAMM BAMM™

Designer:	Simon Ward
Height:	3", 7.6 cm
Colour:	Light and dark brown pants, white hair, yellow club, light brown base
Issued:	1997 in a limited edition of 2,000

Beswick		Price		
Number	U.S. $	Can. $	U.K. £	Aust. $
3579	100.00	150.00	60.00	150.00

3583
WILMA FLINTSTONE™

Designer:	Simon Ward
Height:	4 ¾", 12.1 cm
Colour:	White dress, red hair, light brown base
Issued:	1996 in a limited edition of 2,000

Beswick Number	Price U.S. $	Can. $	U.K. £	Aust. $
3583	125.00	175.00	75.00	185.00

3584
BETTY RUBBLE™

Designer:	Simon Ward
Height:	4", 10.1 cm
Colour:	Blue dress, black hair, light brown base
Issued:	1996 in a limited edition of 2,000

Beswick Number	Price U.S. $	Can. $	U.K. £	Aust. $
3584	125.00	175.00	75.00	185.00

3587
BARNEY RUBBLE™

Designer:	Simon Ward
Height:	3 ½", 8.9 cm
Colour:	Reddish brown shirt, yellow hair, light brown base
Issued:	1996 in a limited edition of 2,000

Beswick Number	Price U.S. $	Can. $	U.K. £	Aust. $
3587	125.00	175.00	75.00	185.00

3588
FRED FLINTSTONE™

Designer: Simon Ward
Height: 4 ¾", 12.1 cm
Colour: Light brown shirt with dark
patches, black hair, blue tie,
light brown base
Issued: 1996 in a limited edition of 2,000

Beswick Number	Price			
	U.S. $	Can. $	U.K. £	Aust. $
3588	125.00	175.00	75.00	185.00

3590
DINO™

Designer: Simon Ward
Height: 4 ¾", 12.1 cm
Colour: Purple, white and black
Issued: 1997 in a limited edition of 2,000

Beswick Number	Price			
	U.S. $	Can. $	U.K. £	Aust. $
3590	100.00	150.00	60.00	165.00

FIERCE BAD RABBIT™
First Version   Second Version

BENJAMIN BUNNY SAT ON A SUNNY BANK™
First Version   Second Version

MR. JEREMY FISHER™
First Version   Second Version

MR. JACKSON™
First Version   Second Version

BENJAMIN BUNNY™

First Version   Second Version   Third Version

MRS. RABBIT™   **CECILY PARSLEY™**

First Version   Second Version   First Version   Second Version

TOM KITTEN™

Character Jug   Large Size   First Version   Second Version

PETER RABBIT™

Large Size   First Version   Second Version   Character Jug

MISS MOPPET™

First Verson   Second Version

TABITHA TWITCHIT™

First Version   Second Version

LITTLE PIG ROBINSON

FIrst Version   Second Version

PIGLING BLAND

First Version   Second Version

TIMMY TIPTOES™
First Version   Second Version

SQUIRREL NUTKIN™
First Version   Second Verison

TOM KITTEN™
First Version   Second Version

PETER RABBIT™
First Version   Second Verison

TOMMY BROCK™

First Version   Second Version   Third Version   Fourth Version

DUCHESS™

Style One   Style Two

APPLEY DAPPLY™

First Version   Second Version

MRS. TIGGY-WINKLE™

First Version   Second Version on a Tree Lamp Base

TOMMY BROCK

Spade Out   Spade In

MR. BENJAMIN BUNNY™

First Version   Second Version

JEMIMA PUDDLE-DUCK™

Large Size   Wall Plaque   Gold Backstamp   Character Jug

DISPLAY STAND

Pig-Wig™   Simkpin™   Duchess™   Ginger™   Amiable Guinea Pig™

TOP CAT

1996-1998

3581
TOP CAT™

Designer:	Andy Moss
Height:	4 ½", 11.9 cm
Colour:	Yellow cat wearing a mauve waistcoat and hat
Issued:	1996 in a limited edition of 2,000
Series:	Top Cat

John Beswick
TOP CAT ™
© 1996 H-B PROD., INC.
LICENSED BY CPL
© 1996 ROYAL DOULTON
EXCLUSIVE EDITION OF 2,000
FOR THE DOULTON &
BESWICK FAIRS IN ENGLAND

Beswick Number		Price		
	U.S.	Can. $	U.K. £	Aust. $
3581	75.00	100.00	40.00	100.00

3586
CHOO-CHOO™

Designer:	Andy Moss
Height:	4 ½", 11.9 cm
Colour:	Pink cat wearing a white shirt
Issued:	1996 in a limited edition of 2,000
Series:	Top Cat

John Beswick
CHOO-CHOO ™
© 1996 H-B PROD., INC.
LICENSED BY CPL
© 1996 ROYAL DOULTON
EXCLUSIVE EDITION OF 2,000
FOR THE DOULTON &
BESWICK FAIRS IN ENGLAND

Beswick Number		Price		
	U.S. $	Can. $	U.K. £	Aust. $
3586	75.00	100.00	40.00	100.00

3624
FANCY FANCY™

Designer:	Andy Moss
Height:	4 ½", 11.9 cm
Colour:	Pink cat with black tip on tail, white scarf
Issued:	1997 in a limited edition of 2,000
Series:	Top Cat

John Beswick
FANCY FANCY ™
© 1997 H-B PROD., INC.
LICENSED BY CPL
© 1997 ROYAL DOULTON
EXCLUSIVE EDITION OF 2,000
FOR THE DOULTON &
BESWICK FAIRS IN ENGLAND

Beswick Number		Price		
	U.S. $	Can. $	U.K. £	Aust. $
3624	60.00	90.00	35.00	100.00

3627
BENNY™

Designer:	Andy Moss
Height:	3 ¾", 8.5 cm
Colour:	Lilac cat wearing a white jacket
Issued:	1997 in a limited edition of 2,000
Series:	Top Cat

John Beswick
BENNY ™
© 1997 H-B PROD., INC.
LICENSED BY CPL
© 1997 ROYAL DOULTON
EXCLUSIVE EDITION OF 2,000
FOR THE DOULTON &
BESWICK FAIRS IN ENGLAND

Beswick Number		Price		
	U.S. $	Can. $	U.K. £	Aust. $
3627	60.00	90.00	35.00	100.00

3671
OFFICER DIBBLE™

Designer:	Andy Moss
Height:	6 ¾", 17.5 cm
Colour:	Dark blue police uniform
Issued:	1998 in a limited edition of 2,000
Series:	Top Cat

Beswick Number		Price		
	U.S. $	Can. $	U.K. £	Aust. $
3671	125.00	175.00	70.00	185.00

3673
SPOOK

Designer:	Andy Moss
Height:	4 ½", 11.9 cm
Colour:	Beige cat with black tie
Issued:	1998 in a limited edition of 2,000
Series:	Top Cat

Beswick Number		Price		
	U.S. $	Can. $	U.K. £	Aust. $
3673	85.00	125.00	50.00	135.00

3674
BRAIN™

Designer:	Andy Moss
Height:	4", 10.1 cm
Colour:	Yellow cat wearing a purple shirt
Issued:	1998 in a limited edition of 2,000
Series:	Top Cat

Beswick Number		Price		
	U.S. $	Can. $	U.K. £	Aust. $
3674	85.00	125.00	50.00	135.00

JANE HISSEY
OLD BEAR

OB4601
OLD BEAR™

Designer:	Jane Hissey
Modeller:	Paul Gurney
Height:	4", 10.1 cm
Colour:	Light brown bear
Issued:	1997 to the present

Beswick		Price		
Number	U.S. $	Can. $	U.K. £	Aust. $
OB4601	15.00	25.00	10.00	25.00

OB4602
TIME FOR BED™

Designer:	Jane Hissey
Modeller:	Paul Gurney
Height:	4", 10.1 cm
Colour:	Golden brown giraffe; light brown bear wearing blue and white striped pyjamas; yellow toothbrush
Issued:	1997 to the present

Beswick		Price		
Number	U.S. $	Can. $	U.K. £	Aust. $
OB4602	25.00	38.00	15.00	38.00

OB4603
BRAMWELL BROWN HAS A GOOD IDEA™

Designer:	Jane Hissey
Modeller:	Paul Gurney
Height:	4", 10.1 cm
Colour:	Brown bear; beige teddy bear wearing red trousers; green and white base
Issued:	1997 - 1998

Beswick		Price		
Number	U.S. $	Can. $	U.K. £	Aust. $
OB4603	25.00	35.00	14.00	35.00

OB4604
DON'T WORRY RABBIT™

Designer:	Jane Hissey
Modeller:	Paul Gurney
Height:	4", 10.1 cm
Colour:	Light brown bear; beige rabbit; yellow and red block; green base
Issued:	1997 to the present

Beswick Number		Price		
	U.S. $	Can. $	U.K. £	Aust. $
OB4604	20.00	35.00	14.00	35.00

OB4605
THE LONG RED SCARF™

Designer:	Jane Hissey
Modeller:	Paul Gurney
Height:	4", 10.1 cm
Colour:	Golden brown giraffe wearing long red scarf, dark brown bear
Issued:	1997 - 1999

Beswick Number		Price		
	U.S. $	Can. $	U.K. £	Aust. $
OB4605	29.00	50.00	20.00	50.00

OB4606
WAITING FOR SNOW™

Designer:	Jane Hissey
Modeller:	Paul Gurney
Height:	4", 10.1 cm
Colour:	Golden brown giraffe, light brown bear, white duck with brown beak
Issued:	1997 to the present

Beswick Number		Price		
	U.S. $	Can. $	U.K. £	Aust. $
OB4606	25.00	45.00	17.00	45.00

OB4607
THE SNOWFLAKE BISCUITS™

Designer:	Jane Hissey
Modeller:	Paul Gurney
Height:	4", 10.1 cm
Colour:	Golden brown giraffe wearing red scarf, light brown bear wearing red dungarees, white donkey with black stripes, brown biscuits
Issued:	1997 to the present

Beswick Number		Price		
	U.S. $	*Can. $*	*U.K. £*	*Aust. $*
OB4607	29.00	50.00	20.00	50.00

OB4608
WELCOME HOME, OLD BEAR™

Designer:	Jane Hissey
Modeller:	Paul Gurney
Height:	4", 10.1 cm
Colour:	Brown bear with two light brown bears and a white duck
Issued:	1997 to the present

Beswick Number		Price		
	U.S. $	*Can. $*	*U.K. £*	*Aust. $*
OB4608	22.00	35.00	14.00	35.00

OB4609
RUFF'S PRIZE™

Designer:	Jane Hissey
Modeller:	Paul Gurney
Height:	2 ½", 6.5 cm
Colour:	Light brown dog wearing a dark brown coat, light brown bear wearing red dungarees
Issued:	1997 - 1999

Beswick Number		Price		
	U.S. $	*Can. $*	*U.K. £*	*Aust. $*
OB4609	22.00	35.00	14.00	35.00

OB4610
TIME FOR A CUDDLE, HUG ME TIGHT™

Designer:	Jane Hissey
Modeller:	Paul Gurney
Height:	3 ½", 8.9 cm
Colour:	Golden brown bear; light brown bear wearing blue and white striped pyjamas
Issued:	1997 to the present

Beswick Number	Price U.S. $	Can. $	U.K. £	Aust. $
OB4610	20.00	35.00	14.00	35.00

OB4611
DON'T FORGET OLD BEAR™

Designer:	Jane Hissey
Modeller:	Paul Gurney
Height:	3", 7.6 cm
Colour:	Brown bear in brown box; red book covers
Issued:	1998 to the present

Beswick Number	Price U.S. $	Can. $	U.K. £	Aust. $
OB4611	25.00	38.00	15.00	38.00

OB4612
HOLD ON TIGHT™

Designer:	Jane Hissey
Modeller:	Paul Gurney
Height:	3", 7.6 cm
Colour:	White owl wearing blue apron; light brown bear wearing blue and white striped pyjamas
Issued:	1998 to the present

Beswick Number	Price U.S. $	Can. $	U.K. £	Aust. $
OB4612	20.00	30.00	11.00	30.00

OB4613
RESTING WITH CAT™

Designer:	Jane Hissey
Modeller:	Paul Gurney
Height:	2 ½", 6.4 cm
Colour:	Black cat with red inner ears and necktie; light brown bear wearing red trousers
Issued:	1998 to the present

Beswick Number	Price			
	U.S. $	Can. $	U.K. £	Aust. $
OB4613	25.00	35.00	14.00	35.00

JOAN WALSH ANGLUND

2272
ANGLUND BOY™

Designer: Albert Hallam
Height: 4 ½", 11.9 cm
Colour: Green dungarees, brown hat
Issued: 1970 - 1971

Beswick Number	Price U.S. $	Can. $	U.K. £	Aust. $
2272	200.00	275.00	135.00	300.00

2293
ANGLUND GIRL WITH DOLL™

Designer: Albert Hallam
Height: 4 ½", 11.9 cm
Colour: Green dress and bow, white apron
Issued: 1970 - 1971

Beswick Number	Price U.S. $	Can. $	U.K. £	Aust. $
2293	200.00	275.00	135.00	300.00

2317
ANGLUND GIRL WITH FLOWERS™

Designer: Albert Hallam
Height: 4 ¾", 12.1 cm
Colour: White dress, blue leggings, straw hat with blue ribbon
Issued: 1971 - 1971

Beswick Number	Price U.S. $	Can. $	U.K. £	Aust. $
2317	200.00	275.00	135.00	300.00

KITTY MACBRIDE

2526
A FAMILY MOUSE™

Designer:	Graham Tongue
Height:	3 ½", 8.9 cm
Colour:	Brown, mauve and turquoise, light and dark green base
Issued:	1975 - 1983

Beswick Number	Price			
	U.S. $	Can. $	U.K. £	Aust. $
2526	150.00	225.00	85.00	200.00

2527
A DOUBLE ACT™

Designer:	Graham Tongue
Height:	3 ½", 8.9 cm
Colour:	Yellow, orange, brown, green and blue
Issued:	1975 - 1983

Beswick Number	Price			
	U.S. $	Can. $	U.K. £	Aust. $
2527	150.00	225.00	85.00	200.00

2528
THE RACEGOER™

Designer:	David Lyttleton
Height:	3 ½", 8.9 cm
Colour:	Brown and yellow, light and dark green base
Issued:	1975 - 1983

Beswick Number	Price			
	U.S. $	Can. $	U.K. £	Aust. $
2528	125.00	175.00	75.00	175.00

2529
A GOOD READ™

Designer:	David Lyttleton
Height:	2 ½", 6.4 cm
Colour:	Yellow, blue, brown and white
Issued:	1975 - 1983

Beswick Number	Price			
	U.S. $	Can. $	U.K. £	Aust. $
2529	300.00	450.00	165.00	425.00

2530
LAZYBONES™

Designer:	David Lyttleton
Height:	1 ½", 3.8 cm
Colour:	Blue, black and brown, green and white base
Issued:	1975 - 1983

Beswick Number	Price			
	U.S. $	Can. $	U.K. £	Aust. $
2530	150.00	225.00	85.00	200.00

2531
A SNACK™

Designer:	David Lyttleton
Height:	3 ¼", 8.3 cm
Colour:	Brown, blue and yellow, green base
Issued:	1975 - 1983

Beswick Number	Price			
	U.S. $	Can. $	U.K. £	Aust. $
2531	100.00	150.00	65.00	150.00

2532
STRAINED RELATIONS™

Designer:	David Lyttleton
Height:	3", 7.6 cm
Colour:	Brown, blue and green
Issued:	1975 - 1983

Beswick	Price			
Number	U.S. $	Can. $	U.K. £	Aust. $
2532	125.00	175.00	75.00	175.00

2533
JUST GOOD FRIENDS™

Designer:	David Lyttleton
Height:	3", 7.6 cm
Colour:	Brown, yellow, blue, red and green
Issued:	1975 - 1983

Beswick	Price			
Number	U.S. $	Can. $	U.K. £	Aust. $
2533	175.00	250.00	100.00	225.00

2565
THE RING™

Designer:	David Lyttleton
Height:	3 ¼", 8.3 cm
Colour:	Brown, white, purple and yellow
Issued:	1976 - 1983

Beswick	Price			
Number	U.S. $	Can. $	U.K. £	Aust. $
2565	200.00	300.00	125.00	275.00

2566
GUILTY SWEETHEARTS™

Designer:	David Lyttleton
Height:	2 ¼", 5.7 cm
Colour:	Brown, yellow, green and white
Issued:	1976 - 1983

Beswick Number	Price U.S. $	Can. $	U.K. £	Aust. $
2566	175.00	250.00	90.00	225.00

2589
ALL I DO IS THINK OF YOU™

Designer:	David Lyttleton
Height:	2 ½", 6.4 cm
Colour:	Brown, yellow and white
Issued:	1976 - 1983

Beswick Number	Price U.S. $	Can. $	U.K. £	Aust. $
2589	500.00	600.00	325.00	625.00

LITTLE LIKEABLES

LL1
FAMILY GATHERING™
(Hen and Two Chicks)

Designer:	Diane Griffiths
Height:	4 ½", 11.9 cm
Colour:	White hen and chicks with yellow beaks and gold comb on hen
Issued:	1985 - 1987

Beswick Number	Price U.S. $	Can. $	U.K. £	Aust. $
LL1	70.00	95.00	40.00	95.00

LL2
WATCHING THE WORLD GO BY™
(Frog)

Designer:	Robert Tabbenor
Height:	3 ¾", 9.5 cm
Colour:	White frog, black and green eyes
Issued:	1985 - 1987

Beswick Number	Price U.S. $	Can. $	U.K. £	Aust. $
LL2	110.00	155.00	65.00	160.00

LL3
HIDE AND SLEEP™
(Pig and Two Piglets)

Designer:	Robert Tabbenor
Height:	3 ¼", 8.3 cm
Colour:	White pigs with pink noses, ears and tails
Issued:	1985 - 1987

Beswick Number	Price U.S. $	Can. $	U.K. £	Aust. $
LL3	70.00	95.00	40.00	85.00

LL4
MY PONY™
(Pony)

Designer:	Diane Griffiths
Height:	7 ¼", 18.4 cm
Colour:	White pony with blue
	highlights in mane and tail
Issued:	1985 - 1987

Beswick		Price		
Number	U.S. $	Can. $	U.K. £	Aust. $
LL4	95.00	130.00	55.00	125.00

LL5
ON TOP OF THE WORLD™
(Elephant)

Designer:	Diane Griffiths
Height:	3 ¾", 9.5 cm
Colour:	White elephant with
	black eyes and gold nails
Issued:	1985 - 1987

Beswick		Price		
Number	U.S. $	Can. $	U.K. £	Aust. $
LL5	70.00	95.00	40.00	90.00

LL6
TREAT ME GENTLY™
(Fawn)

Designer:	Diane Griffiths
Height:	4 ½", 11.9 cm
Colour:	White fawn with black
	and brown eyes, black
	nose and gold hoof
Issued:	1985 - 1987

Beswick		Price		
Number	U.S. $	Can. $	U.K. £	Aust. $
LL6	70.00	95.00	40.00	85.00

LL7
OUT AT LAST™
(Duckling)

Designer:	Robert Tabbenor
Height:	3 ¼", 8.3 cm
Colour:	White duck with black and brown eyes and gold beak
Issued:	1985 - 1987

Beswick Number		Price		
	U.S. $	Can. $	U.K. £	Aust. $
LL7	70.00	95.00	40.00	85.00

LL8
CATS CHORUS™
(Cats)

Designer:	Robert Tabbenor
Height:	4 ¾", 12.1 cm
Colour:	Two white cats with black and green eyes, black nose, pink ears and mouth
Issued:	1985 - 1987

Beswick Number		Price		
	U.S. $	Can. $	U.K. £	Aust. $
LL8	70.00	95.00	40.00	95.00

LITTLE LOVABLES

LL1
HAPPY BIRTHDAY™

Designer:	Amanda Hughes-Lubeck
Height:	4 ½", 11.9 cm
Colour:	White, pink and orange (gloss)
Issued:	1992 - 1994
Varieties:	LL8; LL15; also unnamed LL22

Model		Price		
No.	U.S. $	Can. $	U.K. £	Aust. $
3328	40.00	50.00	25.00	55.00

LL2
I LOVE YOU™

Designer:	Amanda Hughes-Lubeck
Height:	4 ½", 11.9 cm
Colour:	White, green and pink (gloss)
Issued:	1992 - 1994
Varieties:	LL9, LL16; also unnamed LL23

Model		Price		
No.	U.S. $	Can. $	U.K. £	Aust. $
3320	40.00	50.00	25.00	55.00

LL3
GOD LOVES ME™

Designer:	Amanda Hughes-Lubeck
Height:	3 ¾", 9.5 cm
Colour:	White, green and turquoise (gloss)
Issued:	1992 - 1993
Varieties:	LL10, LL17; also called Please, LL33, LL34; also unnamed LL24

Model		Price		
No.	U.S. $	Can. $	U.K. £	Aust. $
3336	125.00	200.00	100.00	200.00

LL4
JUST FOR YOU™

Designer:	Warren Platt
Height:	4 ½", 11.9 cm
Colour:	White, pink and blue (gloss)
Issued:	1992 - 1994
Varieties:	LL11, LL18; also unnamed LL25

Model No.	Price			
	U.S. $	Can. $	U.K. £	Aust. $
3361	40.00	60.00	25.00	60.00

LL5
TO MOTHER™

Designer:	Amanda Hughes-Lubeck
Height:	4 ½", 11.9 cm
Colour:	White, blue and purple (gloss)
Issued:	1992 - 1994
Varieties:	LL12, LL19; also called To Daddy, also unnamed LL26

Model No.	Price			
	U.S. $	Can. $	U.K. £	Aust. $
3331	40.00	50.00	25.00	60.00

LL6
CONGRATULATIONS™

Designer:	Warren Platt
Height:	4 ½", 11.9 cm
Colour:	White, green and pink (gloss)
Issued:	1992 - 1994
Varieties:	LL13, LL20; also unnamed LL27

Model No.	Price			
	U.S. $	Can. $	U.K. £	Aust. $
3340	40.00	50.00	25.00	60.00

LL7
PASSED™

Designer: Amanda Hughes-Lubeck
Height: 3", 7.6 cm
Colour: White, lilac and pink (gloss)
Issued: 1992 - 1994
Varieties: LL14, LL21; also unnamed LL28

Model No.	Price			
	U.S. $	Can. $	U.K. £	Aust. $
3334	50.00	70.00	35.00	70.00

LL8
HAPPY BIRTHDAY™

Designer: Amanda Hughes-Lubeck
Height: 4 ½", 11.9 cm
Colour: White, yellow and green (gloss)
Issued: 1992 - 1994
Varieties: LL1, LL15; also unnamed LL22

Model No.	Price			
	U.S. $	Can. $	U.K. £	Aust. $
3328	40.00	50.00	25.00	60.00

LL9
I LOVE YOU™

Designer: Amanda Hughes-Lubeck
Height: 4 ½", 11.9 cm
Colour: White, blue and orange (gloss)
Issued: 1992 - 1994
Varieties: LL2, LL16; also unnamed LL23

Model No.	Price			
	U.S. $	Can. $	U.K. £	Aust. $
3320	40.00	50.00	25.00	60.00

LL10
GOD LOVES ME™

Designer:	Amanda Hughes-Lubeck
Height:	3 ¾", 9.5 cm
Colour:	White, gold and blue (gloss)
Issued:	1992 - 1993
Varieties:	LL3, LL17; also called Please, LL33, LL34; also unnamed LL24

Model No.	U.S. $	Price Can. $	U.K. £	Aust. $
3336	125.00	200.00	75.00	200.00

LL11
JUST FOR YOU™

Designer:	Warren Platt
Height:	4 ½", 11.9 cm
Colour:	White, yellow and pale green (gloss)
Issued:	1992 - 1994
Varieties:	LL4, LL18; also unnamed LL25

Model No.	U.S. $	Price Can. $	U.K. £	Aust. $
3361	40.00	50.00	25.00	60.00

LL12
TO MOTHER™

Designer:	Amanda Hughes-Lubeck
Height:	4 ½", 11.9 cm
Colour:	White, yellow and pink (gloss)
Issued:	1992 - 1994
Varieties:	LL5, LL19; also called To Daddy, LL29; also unnamed LL26

Model No.	U.S. $	Price Can. $	U.K. £	Aust. $
3331	40.00	50.00	25.00	60.00

LL13
CONGRATULATIONS™

Designer:	Warren Platt
Height:	4 ½", 11.9 cm
Colour:	White, pale blue and yellow (gloss)
Issued:	1992 - 1994
Varieties:	LL6, LL20; also unnamed LL27

Model No.	Price			
	U.S. $	Can. $	U.K. £	Aust. $
3340	40.00	50.00	25.00	60.00

LL14
PASSED™

Designer:	Amanda Hughes-Lubeck
Height:	3", 7.6 cm
Colour:	White, light blue and orange (gloss)
Issued:	1992 - 1994
Varieties:	LL7, LL21; also unnamed LL28

Model No.	Price			
	U.S. $	Can. $	U.K. £	Aust. $
3334	50.00	75.00	35.00	60.00

LL15
HAPPY BIRTHDAY™

Designer:	Amanda Hughes-Lubeck
Height:	4 ½", 11.9cm
Colour:	White, salmon and green (matt)
Issued:	1992 - 1993
Varieties:	LL8, LL15; also unnamed LL22

Model No.	Price			
	U.S. $	Can. $	U.K. £	Aust. $
3407	150.00	200.00	85.00	200.00

LL16
I LOVE YOU™

Designer:	Amanda Hughes-Lubeck
Height:	4 ½", 11.9 cm
Colour:	White, green and yellow (matt)
Issued:	1992 - 1993
Varieties:	LL2, LL9; also unnamed LL23

Model		Price			
No.		U.S. $	Can. $	U.K. £	Aust. $
3406		150.00	200.00	95.00	200.00

LL17
GOD LOVES ME™

Designer:	Amanda Hughes-Lubeck
Height:	3 ¾", 9.5 cm
Colour:	White, purple and yellow (matt)
Issued:	1992 - 1993
Varieties:	LL3, LL10; also called Please, LL33, LL34; also unnamed LL24

Model		Price			
No.		U.S. $	Can. $	U.K. £	Aust.
3410		150.00	200.00	95.00	200.00

LL18
JUST FOR YOU™

Designer:	Warren Platt
Height:	4 ½", 11.9 cm
Colour:	White, yellow and dark blue (matt)
Issued:	1992 - 1993
Varieties:	LL4, LL11; also unnamed LL25

Model		Price			
No.		U.S. $	Can. $	U.K. £	Aust. $
3412		150.00	200.00	85.00	200.00

LL19
TO MOTHER™

Designer:	Amanda Hughes-Lubeck
Height:	4 ½", 11.9 cm
Colour:	White, green and orange (matt)
Issued:	1992 - 1993
Varieties:	LL5, LL12; also called To Daddy, LL29; also unnamed LL26

Model No.		Price		
	U.S. $	Can. $	U.K. £	Aust. $
3408	150.00	200.00	95.00	200.00

LL20
CONGRATULATIONS™

Designer:	Warren Platt
Height:	4 ½", 11.9 cm
Colour:	White, blue and red (matt)
Issued:	1992 - 1993
Varieties:	LL6, LL13; also unnamed LL27

Model No.		Price		
	U.S. $	Can. $	U.K. £	Aust. $
3411	150.00	200.00	95.00	200.00

LL21
PASSED™

Designer:	Amanda Hughes-Lubeck
Height:	3", 7.6 cm
Colour:	White, blue and orange (matt)
Issued:	1992 - 1993
Varieties:	LL7, LL14; also unnamed LL28

Model No.		Price		
	U.S. $	Can. $	U.K. £	Aust. $
3409	150.00	200.00	95.00	200.00

LL22
(No Name)

Designer: Unknown
Height: 4 ½", 11.9 cm
Colour: White, pink and orange (gloss)
Issued: 1993 - 1993
Varieties: Also called Happy Birthday, LL1, LL8, LL15

Model No.	U.S. $	Price Can. $	U.K. £	Aust. $
3329	95.00	125.00	65.00	100.00

LL23
(No Name)

Designer: Amanda Hughes-Lubeck
Height: 4 ½", 11.9 cm
Colour: White, green and pink (gloss)
Issued: 1993 - 1993
Varieties: Also called I Love You, LL2, LL9, LL16

Model No.	U.S. $	Price Can. $	U.K. £	Aust. $
3320	95.00	125.00	65.00	100.00

LL24
(No Name)

Designer: Amanda Hughes-Lubeck
Height: 3 ¾", 9.5 cm
Colour: White, green and turquoise (gloss)
Issued: 1993 - 1993
Varieties: Also called God Loves Me, LL3. LL10, LL17; Please, LL33, LL34

Model No.	U.S. $	Price Can. $	U.K. £	Aust. $
3336	125.00	175.00	75.00	150.00

LL25
(No Name)

Designer:	Warren Platt
Height:	4 ½", 11.9 cm
Colour:	White, pink and blue (gloss)
Issued:	1993 - 1993
Varieties:	Also called Just For You, LL4, LL11, LL18

Model No.		Price		
	U.S. $	Can. $	U.K. £	Aust. $
3361	95.00	125.00	65.00	125.00

LL26
(No Name)

Designer:	Amanda Hughes-Lubeck
Height:	4 ¼", 10.8 cm
Colour:	White, blue and purple (gloss)
Issued:	1993 - 1993
Varieties:	Also called To Mother, LL5, LL12, LL19;To Daddy, LL29

Model No.		Price		
	U.S. $	Can. $	U.K. £	Aust. $
3331	95.00	125.00	65.00	125.00

LL27
(No Name)

Designer:	Warren Platt
Height:	4 ½", 11.9 cm
Colour:	White, green and pink (gloss)
Issued:	1993 - 1993
Varieties:	Also called Congratulations, LL6, LL13, LL20

Model No.		Price		
	U.S. $	Can. $	U.K. £	Aust. $
3340	95.00	125.00	65.00	125.00

LL28
(No Name)

Designer: Amanda Hughes-Lubeck
Height: 3", 7.6 cm
Colour: White, lilac and pink (gloss)
Issued: 1993 - 1993
Varieties: Also called Passed, LL7, LL14, LL21

Model No.	Price			
	U.S. $	Can. $	U.K. £	Aust. $
3334	95.00	125.00	75.00	125.00

LL29
TO DADDY™

Designer: Amanda Hughes-Lubeck
Height: 4 ½", 11.9 cm
Colour: White, light blue and green (gloss)
Issued: 1994 - 1994
Varieties: Also called To Mother, LL5, LL12, LL19; also unnamed LL26

Model No.	Price			
	U.S. $	Can. $	U.K. £	Aust. $
3331	60.00	75.00	40.00	80.00

LL30
MERRY CHRISTMAS™

Designer: Amanda Hughes-Lubeck
Height: 4", 10.1 cm
Colour: White, red and green (gloss)
Issued: 1993 - 1994

Model No.	Price			
	U.S. $	Can. $	U.K. £	Aust. $
3389	95.00	125.00	50.00	125.00

LL31
GOOD LUCK™

Designer:	Amanda Hughes-Lubeck
Height:	4 ¼", 10.8 cm
Colour:	White, pink and green (gloss)
Issued:	1993 - 1994

(mark shown: BESWICK B ENGLAND LL 31)

Model No.		Price		
	U.S. $	Can. $	U.K. £	Aust. $
3388	80.00	125.00	50.00	125.00

LL32
GET WELL SOON™

Designer:	Amanda Hughes-Lubeck
Height:	4 ¼", 10.8 cm
Colour:	White, green and purple (gloss)
Issued:	1994 - 1994

(mark shown: BESWICK B ENGLAND LL 32)

Model No.		Price		
	U.S. $	Can. $	U.K. £	Aust. $
3390	80.00	125.00	50.00	125.00

(figurine: GET WELL SOON)

LL33
PLEASE™

Designer:	Amanda Hughes-Lubeck
Height:	3 ¾", 9.5 cm
Colour:	White, green and blue (gloss)
Issued:	1993 - 1994
Varieties:	LL34; also called God Loves Me, LL3, LL10, LL17; also unnamed LL24

(mark shown: BESWICK B ENGLAND LL 33)

Model No.		Price		
	U.S. $	Can. $	U.K. £	Aust. $
3336	60.00	75.00	35.00	75.00

LL34
PLEASE™

Designer:	Amanda Hughes-Lubeck
Height:	3 ¾", 9.5 cm
Colour:	White, gold and light blue (gloss)
Issued:	1993 - 1994
Varieties:	LL33; also called God Loves Me, LL3, LL10, LL17; also unnamed LL24

Model		Price		
No.	*U.S. $*	*Can. $*	*U.K. £*	*Aust. $*
3336	60.00	75.00	35.00	80.00

LL35 is the prototype for "I Love Beswick." Colourway not issued.

LL36
I LOVE BESWICK™

Designer:	Amanda Hughes-Lubeck
Height:	4 ½", 11.9 cm
Colour:	White, green and pink (gloss)
Issued:	1995 - 1995
Varieties:	Also called I Love You, LL2, LL9, LL16; also unamed LL23

Model		Price		
No.	*U.S. $*	*Can. $*	*U.K. £*	*Aust. $*
3320	225.00	300.00	125.00	275.00

Note: This piece was specially commissioned for the 10th Anniversary of the Beswick Collectors Circle.

NORMAN THELWELL

EARTHENWARE SERIES

RESIN STUDIO SCULPTURES

NORMAN THELWELL

EARTHENWARE SERIES 1981-1989

2704A
AN ANGEL ON HORSEBACK™
First Variation

Designer:	Harry Sales
Modeller:	David Lyttleton
Height:	4 ½", 11.4 cm
Colour:	Grey horse, rider wears brown jumper, yellow jodhpurs
Issued:	1981 - 1989
Varieties:	2704B

Beswick Number	Price			
	U.S. $	Can. $	U.K. £	Aust. $
2704A	250.00	450.00	150.00	400.00

2704B
AN ANGEL ON HORSEBACK™
Second Variation

Designer:	Harry Sales
Modeller:	David Lyttleton
Height:	4 ½", 11.4 cm
Colour:	Bay horse, rider wears red jumper, yellow jodhpurs
Issued:	1981 - 1989
Varieties:	2704A

Beswick Number	Price			
	U.S. $	Can. $	U.K. £	Aust. $
2704B	225.00	400.00	125.00	400.00

2769A
KICK-START™
First Variation

Designer:	Harry Sales
Modeller:	David Lyttleton
Height:	3 ½", 8.9 cm
Colour:	Grey horse, rider wears red jersey and yellow pants
Issued:	1982 - 1989
Varieties:	2769B

Beswick Number	Price			
	U.S. $	Can. $	U.K. £	Aust. $
2769A	250.00	450.00	150.00	425.00

2769B
KICK-START™
Second Variation

Designer:	Harry Sales
Modeller:	David Lyttleton
Height:	3 ½", 8.9 cm
Colour:	Bay horse, rider wears red jersey and yellow pants
Issued:	1982 - 1989
Varieties:	2769B

Beswick Number	Price			
	U.S. $	Can. $	U.K. £	Aust. $
2769B	225.00	400.00	125.00	375.00

2789A
PONY EXPRESS™
First Variation

Designer:	Harry Sales
Modeller:	David Lyttleton
Height:	4 ½", 11.4 cm
Colour:	Grey horse, rider wears green jersey and yellow trousers
Issued:	1982 - 1989
Varieties:	2789B

Beswick Number	Price			
	U.S. $	Can. $	U.K. £	Aust. $
2789A	250.00	450.00	150.00	425.00

2789B
PONY EXPRESS™
Second Variation

Designer:	Harry Sales
Modeller:	David Lyttleton
Height:	4 ½", 11.4 cm
Colour:	Bay horse, rider wears red jersey and yellow pants
Issued:	1982 - 1989
Varieties:	2789A

Beswick Number	Price			
	U.S. $	Can. $	U.K. £	Aust. $
2789B	225.00	400.00	125.00	425.00

NORMAN THEWELL

RESIN STUDIO SCULPTURES — 1985-1985

SS7A
I FORGIVE YOU™
First Variation

Designer:	Harry Sales
Modeller:	David Lyttleton
Height:	4", 10.1 cm
Colour:	Grey horse, rider wears red jacket and yellow pants
Issued:	1985 - 1985
Series:	Studio Sculptures
Varieties:	SS7B

Beswick	Price			
Number	U.S. $	Can. $	U.K. £	Aust. $
SS7A	225.00	400.00	135.00	350.00

SS7B
I FORGIVE YOU™
Second Variation

Designer:	Harry Sales
Modeller:	David Lyttleton
Height:	4", 10.1 cm
Colour:	Bay horse, rider wears red jacket and yellow pants
Issued:	1985 - 1985
Series:	Studio Sculptures
Varieties:	SS7A

Beswick	Price			
Number	U.S. $	Can. $	U.K. £	Aust. $
SS7B	225.00	400.00	135.00	350.00

SS12A
EARLY BATH™
First Variation

Designer:	Harry Sales
Modeller:	David Lyttleton
Height:	4 ¾", 12.1 cm
Colour:	Grey horse, rider wears red jacket and yellow pants
Issued:	1985 - 1985
Series:	Studio Sculptures
Varieties:	SS12B

Beswick	Price			
Number	U.S. $	Can. $	U.K. £	Aust. $
SS12A	225.00	400.00	150.00	375.00

SS12B
EARLY BATH™
Second Variation

Designer: Harry Sales
Height: 4 ¾", 12.1 cm
Colour: Bay horse, rider wears red jacket and yellow pants
Issued: 1985 - 1985
Series: Studio Sculptures
Varieties: SS12A

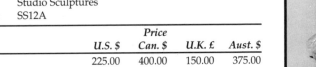

Beswick		Price		
Number	U.S. $	Can. $	U.K. £	Aust. $
SS12B	225.00	400.00	150.00	375.00

PADDINGTON BEAR CO. LTD.

PB1
PADDINGTON AT THE STATION™

Designer:	Zoe Annand
Height:	4 ¼", 11.0 cm
Colour:	Brown bear, blue coat, yellow hat, brown cobbled base
Issued:	1996 - 1998

Doulton Number		U.S. $	Price Can. $	U.K. £	Aust. $
PB1		25.00	35.00	15.00	35.00

Royal Doulton
Paddington ™
"At the Station"
PB1
© Paddington & Co. Ltd. 1996
Licensed by ©OPYRIGHTS

PB2
PADDINGTON BAKES A CAKE™

Designer:	Zoe Annand
Height:	4 ¼", 10.1 cm
Colour:	Red jacket, black hat, multi-coloured cake, blue and white striped bowl
Issued:	1996 - 1998

Doulton Number	U.S. $	Price Can. $	U.K. £	Aust. $
PB2	25.00	35.00	15.00	35.00

Royal Doulton
Paddington ™
"Bakes a Cake"
PB2
© Paddington & Co. Ltd. 1996
Licensed by ©OPYRIGHTS

PB3
PADDINGTON DECORATING™

Designer:	Zoe Annand
Height:	4 ¾", 12.0 cm
Colour:	Blue coat, red hat, silver bucket, cream paint
Issued:	1996 - 1998

Doulton Number		U.S. $	Price Can. $	U.K. £	Aust. $
PB3		25.00	35.00	15.00	35.00

Royal Doulton
Paddington ™
"Decorating"
PB3
© Paddington & Co. Ltd. 1996
Licensed by ©OPYRIGHTS

PB4
PADDINGTON SURFING™

Designer:	Zoe Annand
Height:	4", 10.1 cm
Colour:	Multi-coloured shorts, blue hat, yellow surfboard, red rubber ring, brown suitcase
Issued:	1996 - 1998

Royal Doulton
Paddington ™
"Surfing"
PB4
© Paddington & Co. Ltd. 1996
Licensed by ©OPYRIGHTS

Doulton Number		U.S. $	Price Can. $	U.K. £	Aust. $
PB4		25.00	35.00	15.00	35.00

PB5
PADDINGTON GARDENING™

Designer:	Zoe Annand
Height:	4", 10.1 cm
Colour:	Blue jacket, red hat, green watering can, yellow and red bucket and spade
Issued:	1996 - 1998

Royal Doulton
Paddington ™
"Gardening"
PB5
© Paddington & Co. Ltd. 1996
Licensed by ©OPYRIGHTS

Doulton Number		U.S. $	Price Can. $	U.K. £	Aust. $
PB5		25.00	35.00	15.00	35.00

PB6
PADDINGTON BATHTIME™

Designer:	Zoe Annand
Height:	3 ¼", 8.5 cm
Colour:	Blue coat, yellow hat, brown scrubbing brush, yellow duck, pink soap
Issued:	1996 - 1998

Royal Doulton
Paddington ™
"Bathtime"
PB6
© Paddington & Co. Ltd. 1996
Licensed by ©OPYRIGHTS

Doulton Number	Price U.S. $	Can. $	U.K. £	Aust. $
PB6	25.00	35.00	15.00	35.00

PB7
PADDINGTON THE GOLFER™

Designer:	Zoe Annand
Height:	3 ¾", 9.5 cm
Colour:	White top, red and yellow sweater, red hat, green trousers, white shoes
Issued:	1996 - 1998

Royal Doulton
Paddington ™
"The Golfer"
PB7
© Paddington & Co. Ltd. 1996
Licensed by ©OPYRIGHTS

Doulton Number	Price			
	U.S. $	Can. $	U.K. £	Aust. $
PB7	25.00	35.00	15.00	35.00

PB8
PADDINGTON THE MUSICIAN™

Designer:	Zoe Annand
Height:	3 ¾", 9.5 cm
Colour:	Black jacket, red waistcoat, brown trousers, brown violin, brass trumpet
Issued:	1996 - 1998

Royal Doulton
Paddington ™
"The Musician"
PB8
© Paddington & Co. Ltd. 1996
Licensed by ©OPYRIGHTS

Doulton Number	Price			
	U.S. $	Can. $	U.K. £	Aust. $
PB8	25.00	35.00	15.00	35.00

PB9
PADDINGTON AT CHRISTMAS TIME™

Designer:	Zoe Annand
Height:	3 ½", 8.9 cm
Colour:	Red coat, blue boots, yellow sleigh
Issued:	1996 - 1998

Royal Doulton
Paddington ™
"At Christmas Time"
PB9
© Paddington & Co. Ltd. 1996
Licensed by ©OPYRIGHTS

Doulton	Price			
	U.S. $	Can. $	U.K. £	Aust. $
PB9	25.00	35.00	15.00	35.00

PB10
PADDINGTON MARMALADE SANDWICH™

Designer:	Zoe Annand
Height:	3 ½", 8.9 cm
Colour:	Dark blue coat, yellow hat, green book, orange and white sandwiches
Issued:	1997 - 1998

Doulton Number	Price			
	U.S. $	Can. $	U.K. £	Aust. $
PB10	25.00	35.00	15.00	35.00

PB11
PADDINGTON GOING TO BED™

Designer:	Zoe Annand
Height:	3 ¾", 9.5 cm
Colour:	Turquoise, red and yellow pyjamas, red hat
Issued:	1997 - 1998

Doulton Number	Price			
	U.S. $	Can. $	U.K. £	Aust. $
PB11	25.00	35.00	15.00	35.00

PB12
PADDINGTON THE FISHERMAN™

Designer:	Zoe Annand
Modeller:	Andrew Hull
Height:	3 ½", 8.9 cm
Colour:	Dark blue hat and wellingtons, red jacket with yellow buttons
Issued:	1997 - 1998

Doulton Number	Price			
	U.S. $	Can. $	U.K. £	Aust. $
PB12	25.00	35.00	15.00	35.00

THE PIG PROMENADE

THE PIG PROMENADE BACKSTAMPS

BK-1. **BESWICK WARE SCRIPT**
1993 to mid 1994

BK-2. **BESWICK CREST**
mid 1994 to present

PP 1
JOHN THE CONDUCTOR™
(Vietnamese Pot Bellied Pig)

Designer:	Martyn Alcock
Height:	4 ¾", 12.1 cm
Colour:	Black jacket, black bowtie
Issued:	1993 - 1996

Beswick
Ware
JOHN
PP 1

Back Stamp	Price			
	U.S. $	Can. $	U.K. £	Aust. $
PPBS 1	100.00	150.00	50.00	160.00
PPBS 2	90.00	125.00	35.00	125.00

PP 2
MATTHEW THE TRUMPET PLAYER™
(Large White Pig)

Designer:	Amanda Hughes-Lubeck
Height:	5", 12.7 cm
Colour:	Light red waistcoat, black bowtie
Issued:	1993 - 1996

Beswick
Ware
MATTHEW
PP 2

Back Stamp	Price			
	U.S. $	Can. $	U.K. £	Aust. $
PPBS-1	100.00	150.00	50.00	160.00
PPBS-2	90.00	125.00	35.00	125.00

PP 3
DAVID THE FLUTE PLAYER™
(Tamworth Pig)

Designer:	Amanda Hughes-Lubeck
Height:	5 ¼", 13.3 cm
Colour:	Dark green waistcoat, black bowtie
Issued:	1993 - 1996

Beswick
Ware
DAVID
PP 3

Back Stamp	Price			
	U.S. $	Can. $	U.K. £	Aust. $
PPBS-1	100.00	150.00	50.00	160.00
PPBS-2	90.00	125.00	35.00	125.00

PP 4
ANDREW THE CYMBAL PLAYER™
(Gloucester Old Spotted Pig)

Designer:	Martyn Alcock
Height:	4 ¾", 12.1 cm
Colour:	Blue waistcoat, yellow cymbals, black bowtie
Issued:	1993 - 1996
Varieties:	Also called George, PP10

Beswick Ware
ANDREW
PP 4

Back Stamp	Price U.S. $	Can. $	U.K. £	Aust. $
PPBS-1	100.00	150.00	50.00	160.00
PPBS-2	90.00	125.00	35.00	125.00

PP 5
DANIEL THE VIOLINIST™
(Saddleback Pig)

Designer:	Amanda Hughes-Lubeck
Height:	5 ¼", 13.3 cm
Colour:	Pale blue waistcoat, brown violin
Issued:	1993 - 1996

Beswick Ware
DANIEL
PP 5

Back Stamp	Price U.S. $	Can. $	U.K. £	Aust. $
PPBS-1	100.00	150.00	50.00	160.00
PPBS-2	90.00	125.00	35.00	125.00

PP 6
MICHAEL THE BASS DRUM PLAYER™
(Large Black Pig)

Designer:	Martyn Alcock
Height:	4 ¾", 12.1 cm
Colour:	Yellow waistcoat, red and white drum
Issued:	1993 - 1996

Beswick Ware
MICHAEL
PP 6

Back Stamp	Price U.S. $	Can. $	U.K. £	Aust. $
PPBS-1	100.00	150.00	50.00	160.00
PPBS-2	90.00	125.00	35.00	125.00

PP 7
JAMES THE TRIANGLE PLAYER™
(Tamworth Piglet)

Designer:	Warren Platt
Height:	4", 10.1 cm
Colour:	Tan, purple waistcoat; black bowtie
Issued:	1995 - 1996

Back Stamp	U.S. $	Can. $	U.K. £	Aust. $
			Price	
PPBS-2	100.00	150.00	45.00	125.00

PP 8
RICHARD THE FRENCH HORN PLAYER™

Designer:	Shane Ridge
Height:	5", 12.7 cm
Colour:	Pale pink with dark grey spots, tan and beige waistcoat
Issued:	1996 - 1996
Varieties:	Also called Benjamin, PP12

Back Stamp	U.S. $	Can. $	U.K. £	Aust. $
			Price	
PPBS-2	100.00	150.00	35.00	125.00

PP 9
CHRISTOPHER THE GUITAR PLAYER™

Designer:	Warren Platt
Height:	5 ½", 13.3 cm
Colour:	Dark grey, yellow and cream waistcoat, black bowtie
Issued:	1996 - 1996
Varieties:	Also called Thomas, PP11

Back Stamp	U.S.$	Can. $	U.K. £	Aust. $
			Price	
PPBS-2	100.00	150.00	35.00	125.00

PP 10
GEORGE™

Designer:	Martyn Alcock
Height:	4 ¾", 12.1 cm
Colour:	Dark green waistcoat, yellow cymbals, black bowtie
Issued:	1996 in a limited edition of 2,000
Varieties:	Also called Andrew, PP4

Back Stamp		U.S.$	Can. $	Price U.K. £	Aust. $
PPBS-2		100.00	150.00	50.00	125.00

PP 11
THOMAS™

Designer:	Warren Platt
Height:	5", 12.7 cm
Colour:	Black pig with green jacket, yellow bowtie, white guitar
Issued:	1997 in a limited edition of 2,000
Varieties:	Also called Christopher the Guitar Player, PP9

Back Stamp		U.S.$	Can. $	Price U.K. £	Aust. $
PPBS-2		125.00	175.00	50.00	150.00

PP 12
BENJAMIN™

Designer:	Shane Ridge
Height:	5", 12.7 cm
Colour:	White and black pig, orange bowtie, gold french horn
Issued:	1997 in a limited edition of 2,000
Varieties:	Also called Richard the French Horn Player, PP8

Back Stamp		U.S.$	Can. $	Price U.K. £	Aust. $
PPBS-2		125.00	175.00	50.00	150.00

ST. TIGGYWINKLES

TW1
HENRY HEDGEHOG™
(Standing)

Designer:	Unknown
Modeller:	Amanda Hughes-Lubeck
Height:	3 ½", 8.5 cm
Colour:	Light and dark brown hedgehog wearing a purple shirt
Issued:	1997 to the present
Series:	The Wildlife Hospital Trust

Doulton Number		U.S. $	Price Can. $	U.K. £	Aust. $
TW1		25.00	35.00	14.00	35.00

TW2
HARRY HEDGEHOG™
(Sitting)

Designer:	Unknown
Modeller:	Amanda Hughes-Lubeck
Height:	3 ½", 8.9 cm
Colour:	Light and dark brown hedgehog wearing a purple shirt and red cap
Issued:	1997 to the present
Series:	The Wildlife Hospital Trust

Royal Doulton
St. Tiggywinkles
Harry Hedgehog
TW2/ *1269*
© St.Tiggywinkles 1996
Made in Thailand

Doulton Number		U.S. $	Price Can. $	U.K. £	Aust. $
TW2		25.00	35.00	14.00	35.00

TW3
FRED FOX™

Designer:	Unknown
Modeller:	Warren Platt
Height:	4", 10.1 cm
Colour:	Light brown fox wearing light blue overalls, pink shirt, white bandage around his head and tail
Issued:	1997 - 1998
Series:	The Wildlife Hospital Trust

Royal Doulton
St. Tiggywinkles
Fred Fox
TW3/ *1094*
© St.Tiggywinkles 1996
Made in Thailand

Doulton Number		U.S. $	Price Can. $	U.K. £	Aust. $
TW3		25.00	35.00	14.00	35.00

TW4
BOB BADGER™

Designer:	Unknown
Modeller:	Amanda Hughes-Lubeck
Height:	3 ¾", 9.5 cm
Colour:	Brown, black and white badger wearing a yellow jumper and brown scarf, beige crutch
Issued:	1997 to the present
Series:	The Wildlife Hospital Trust

Royal Doulton
St. Tiggywinkles
Bob Badger
TW4/ 1698
© St.Tiggywinkles 1996
Made in Thailand

Doulton Number	Price			
	U.S. $	Can. $	U.K. £	Aust. $
TW4	25.00	35.00	14.00	35.00

TW5
ROSIE RABBIT™

Designer:	Unknown
Modeller:	Amanda Hughes-Lubeck
Height:	3 ½", 8.9 cm
Colour:	Grey rabbit wearing a light blue dress and rose pinafore
Issued:	1997 to the present
Series:	The Wildlife Hospital Trust

Royal Doulton
St. Tiggywinkles
Rosie Rabbit
TW5/ 1456
© St.Tiggywinkles 1996
Made in Thailand

Doulton Number	Price			
	U.S. $	Can. $	U.K. £	Aust. $
TW5	25.00	35.00	14.00	35.00

TW6
SARAH SQUIRREL™

Designer:	Unknown
Modeller:	Amanda Hughes-Lubeck
Height:	3 ¼", 8.3 cm
Colour:	Brown squirrel wearing a pink and white dress
Issued:	1997 - 1998
Series:	The Wildlife Hospital Trust

Royal Doulton
St. Tiggywinkles
Sarah Squirrel
TW6/ 0122
© St.Tiggywinkles 1996
Made in Thailand

Doulton Number	Price			
	U.S. $	Can. $	U.K. £	Aust. $
TW6	25.00	35.00	14.00	35.00

TW7
DANIEL DUCK™

Designer:	Unknown
Modeller:	Shane Ridge
Height:	3 ½", 8.5 cm
Colour:	Yellow duck, white and red bandage, brown satchel
Issued:	1997 to the present
Series:	The Wildlife Hospital Trust

Royal Doulton
St. Tiggywinkles®
Daniel Duck
TW7/ 1925
© St.Tiggywinkles 1996
Made in Thailand

Doulton Number		Price		
	U.S. $	Can. $	U.K. £	Aust. $
TW7	25.00	35.00	14.00	35.00

TW8
OLIVER OWL™

Designer:	Unknown
Modeller:	Warren Platt
Height:	4", 10.1 cm
Colour:	Dark and light brown owl, white arm sling, red book
Issued:	1997 to the present
Series:	The Wildlife Hospital Trust

Royal Doulton
St. Tiggywinkles
Oliver Owl
TW8/ 1703
© St.Tiggywinkles 1996
Made in Thailand

Doulton Number		Price		
	U.S. $	Can. $	U.K. £	Aust. $
TW8	25.00	35.00	14.00	35.00

TW9
FRIENDS™

Designer:	Unknown
Modeller:	Amanda Hughes-Lubeck
Height:	4", 10.1 cm
Colour:	Brown hedgehog with green and yellow jacket, red hat, yellow ducks with blue scarf, white bandages
Issued:	1997 to the present
Series	The Wildlife Hospital Trust

Royal Doulton
St. Tiggywinkles®
Friends
TW9/ 1430
© St.Tiggywinkles 1996
Made in Thailand

Doulton Number		Price		
	U.S. $	Can. $	U.K. £	Aust. $
TW9	35.00	50.00	20.00	50.00

TW10
A HELPING HAND™

Designer:	Unknown
Modeller:	Amanda Hughes-Lubeck
Height:	4", 10.1 cm
Colour:	Light and dark brown hedgehogs, white and grey rabbits, blue, yellow, pink and red clothing
Issued:	1997 to the present
Series:	The Wildlife Hospital Trust

Royal Doulton
St. Tiggywinkles®
A Helping Hand
TW10/ 0303
© St.Tiggywinkles 1996
Made in Thailand

Doulton Number	Price			
	U.S. $	Can. $	U.K. £	Aust. $
TW10	50.00	75.00	30.00	75.00

TW11
DEBORAH DORMOUSE

Designer:	Unknown
Modeller:	Rob Simpson
Height:	3 ¼", 8.3 cm
Colour:	Brown dormouse wearing a pink dress, white apron, carrying a brown basket
Issued:	1998 to the present
Series:	The Wildlife Hospital Trust

Royal Doulton
St. Tiggywinkles®
Deborah Dormouse
TW11/458
© St.Tiggywinkles 1998
Made in Thailand

Doulton Number	Price			
	U.S. $	Can. $	U.K. £	Aust. $
TW11	25.00	35.00	14.00	35.00

TW12
MONTY MOLE

Designer:	Unknown
Modeller:	Rob Simpson
Height:	3 ½", 8.5 cm
Colour:	Dark brown mole wearing a blue jacket, yellow hat, white arm sling
Issued:	1998 to the present
Series:	The Wildlife Hospital Trust

Doulton Number	Price			
	U.S. $	Can. $	U.K. £	Aust. $
TW12	25.00	35.00	14.00	35.00

TW13
FRANCHESCA FAWN

Designer:	Unknown
Modeller:	Rob Simpson
Height:	3", 7.6 cm
Colour:	Pale brown fawn, white bandages
Issued:	1998 to the present
Series:	The Wildlife Hospital Trust

Royal Doulton
St. Tiggywinkles
Franchesca Fawn
TW13/ 48
© St. Tiggywinkles 1998
Made in Thailand

Doulton Number	Price			
	U.S. $	Can. $	U.K. £	Aust. $
TW13	25.00	35.00	14.00	35.00

THE SNOWMAN
GIFT COLLECTION

DS1
JAMES™
Style One

Designer: Harry Sales
Modeller: David Lyttleton
Height: 3 ¾", 9.5 cm
Colour: Blue and white striped pyjamas, brown dressing gown
Issued: 1985 - 1993

Doulton Number	Price			
	U.S. $	*Can. $*	*U.K. £*	*Aust. $*
DS1	175.00	250.00	75.00	200.00

DS2
THE SNOWMAN™
Style One

Designer: Harry Sales
Modeller: David Lyttleton
Height: 5", 12.7 cm
Colour: White snowman wearing a green hat and scarf
Issued: 1985 - 1994

Doulton Number	Price			
	U.S. $	*Can. $*	*U.K. £*	*Aust. $*
DS2	150.00	225.00	50.00	200.00

DS3
STYLISH SNOWMAN™

Designer: Harry Sales
Modeller: David Lyttleton
Height: 5", 12.7 cm
Colour: White snowman wearing blue trousers, lilac braces, grey hat, yellow tie with red stripes
Issued: 1985 - 1993

Doulton Number	Price			
	U.S. $	*Can. $*	*U.K. £*	*Aust. $*
DS3	175.00	250.00	100.00	225.00

DS4
THANK YOU SNOWMAN™

Designer:	Harry Sales
Modeller:	David Lyttleton
Height:	5", 12.7 cm
Colour:	Snowman - green hat and scarf
	James - brown dressing gown
Issued:	1985 - 1994

Royal Doulton®
THE SNOWMAN™
GIFT COLLECTION
THANK YOU SNOWMAN
DS 4
© 1985 ROYAL DOULTON (UK)
© S. ENT 1985

| Doulton | | Price | | |
Number	U.S. $	Can. $	U.K. £	Aust. $
DS4	125.00	175.00	60.00	185.00

DS5
SNOWMAN MAGIC MUSIC BOX™

Designer:	Harry Sales
Modeller:	David Lyttleton
Height:	8", 20.3 cm
Colour:	White snowman wearing a green hat
	and scarf, cream music box with blue,
	green and pink balloon design
Issued:	1985 - 1994
Tune:	Walking in the Air

| Doulton | | Price | | |
Number	U.S. $	Can. $	U.K. £	Aust. $
DS5	175.00	275.00	100.00	250.00

DS6
COWBOY SNOWMAN™

Designer:	Harry Sales
Modeller:	David Lyttleton
Height:	5", 12.7 cm
Colour:	White snowman wearing a
	brown hat and holster belt
Issued:	1986 - 1992

Royal Doulton®
THE SNOWMAN™
GIFT COLLECTION
COWBOY SNOWMAN
DS 6
© 1986 ROYAL DOULTON (UK)
© S. ENT 1985

| Doulton | | Price | | |
Number	U.S. $	Can. $	U.K. £	Aust. $
DS6	225.00	350.00	125.00	325.00

DS7
HIGHLAND SNOWMAN™

Designer:	Harry Sales
Modeller:	David Lyttleton
Height:	5 ¼", 13.3 cm
Colour:	White snowman wearing a red, blue and white kilt
Issued:	1987 - 1993

Doulton		Price		
Number	U.S. $	Can. $	U.K. £	Aust. $
DS7	275.00	375.00	150.00	350.00

DS8
LADY SNOWMAN™

Designer:	Harry Sales
Modeller:	David Lyttleton
Height:	5", 12.7 cm
Colour:	White snowman wearing a pink apron and blue hat
Issued:	1987 - 1992

Doulton		Price		
Number	U.S. $	Can. $	U.K. £	Aust. $
DS8	450.00	550.00	200.00	500.00

DS9
BASS DRUMMER SNOWMAN™

Designer:	Graham Tongue
Modeller:	Warren Platt
Height:	5 ¼", 13.3 cm
Colour:	White snowman with pale blue hat; pink and yellow drum, pale brown straps
Issued:	1987 - 1993

Doulton		Price		
Number	U.S. $	Can. $	U.K. £	Aust. $
DS9	450.00	500.00	150.00	475.00

DS10
FLAUTIST SNOWMAN™

Designer:	Graham Tongue
Modeller:	Warren Platt
Height:	5 ½", 14.0 cm
Colour:	White snowman wearing a yellow and red cap and a brown tie
Issued:	1987 - 1993

Doulton Number	Price			
	U.S. $	Can. $	U.K. £	Aust. $
DS10	225.00	400.00	150.00	350.00

DS11
VIOLINIST SNOWMAN™

Designer:	Graham Tongue
Modeller:	Warren Platt
Height:	5 ¼", 13.3 cm
Colour:	White snowman wearing a green waistcoat with yellow collar, blue bowtie, brown cap, playing a violin
Issued:	1987 - 1994

Doulton Number	Price			
	U.S. $	Can. $	U.K. £	Aust. $
DS11	100.00	150.00	50.00	150.00

DS12
PIANIST SNOWMAN™

Designer:	Graham Tongue
Modeller:	Warren Platt
Height:	5", 12.7 cm
Colour:	White snowman wearing a blue crown and orange tie
Issued:	1987 - 1994

Doulton Number	Price			
	U.S. $	Can. $	U.K. £	Aust. $
DS12	10.00	150.00	50.00	165.00

DS13
SNOWMAN'S PIANO™

Designer:	Graham Tongue
Modeller:	Warren Platt
Height:	5¼", 13.3 cm
Colour:	White piano
Issued:	1987 - 1994

Doulton		Price		
Number	U.S. $	Can. $	U.K. £	Aust. $
DS13	60.00	100.00	30.00	125.00

DS14
CYMBAL PLAYER SNOWMAN™

Designer:	Graham Tongue
Modeller:	Warren Platt
Height:	5 ¼", 13.3 cm
Colour:	White snowman wearing a brown waistcoat, green cap and bowtie, playing yellow cymbals
Issued:	1988 - 1993

Doulton		Price		
Number	U.S. $	Can. $	U.K. £	Aust. $
DS14	300.00	400.00	150.00	375.00

DS15
DRUMMER SNOWMAN™

Designer:	Graham Tongue
Modeller:	Warren Platt
Height:	5 ¾", 14.6 cm
Colour:	White snowman wearing a red and black hat, purple bowtie, playing pink and yellow drum
Issued:	1988 - 1994

Doulton		Price		
Number	U.S. $	Can. $	U.K. £	Aust. $
DS15	150.00	200.00	55.00	200.00

DS16
TRUMPETER SNOWMAN™

Designer:	Graham Tongue
Modeller:	Warren Platt
Height:	5", 12.7 cm
Colour:	White snowman wearing a pink hat playing a yellow trumpet
Issued:	1988 - 1993

Doulton		Price		
Number	U.S. $	Can. $	U.K. £	Aust. $
DS16	300.00	400.00	165.00	375.00

DS17
CELLIST SNOWMAN™

Designer:	Graham Tongue
Modeller:	Warren Platt
Height:	5 ¼", 13.3 cm
Colour:	White snowman wearing a green waistcoat with yellow collar, blue bowtie, playing a brown cello
Issued:	1988 - 1993

Doulton		Price		
Number	U.S. $	Can. $	U.K. £	Aust. $
DS17	150.00	175.00	60.00	175.00

DS18
SNOWMAN MUSICAL BOX™

Designer:	Unknown
Height:	8", 22.5 cm
Colour:	White snowman wearing a red, blue and white kilt; green, pink and blue balloons on box
Issued:	1988 - 1990
Tune:	Blue Bells of Scotland

Doulton		Price		
Numbers	U.S. $	Can. $	U.K. £	Aust. $
DS18	275.00	350.00	125.00	300.00

DS19
SNOWMAN MONEY BOX™

Designer:	Graham Tongue
Modeller:	Warren Platt
Height:	8 ½", 21.6 cm
Colour:	White snowman wearing a green hat with grey band and green scarf
Issued:	1990 - 1994

Doulton Number	Price U.S. $	Can. $	U.K. £	Aust. $
DS19	200.00	300.00	100.00	275.00

DS20
THE SNOWMAN TOBOGGANING™

Designer:	Graham Tongue
Modeller:	Warren Platt
Height:	5", 12.7 cm
Colour:	White snowman wearing a green hat and scarf, rose-pink toboggan
Issued:	1990 - 1994

Royal Doulton®
THE SNOWMAN™
GIFT COLLECTION
THE SNOWMAN
TOBOGGANING
DS 20
© 1990 ROYAL DOULTON
© S ENT 1990

Doulton Number	Price U.S. $	Can. $	U.K. £	Aust. $
DS20	150.00	250.00	50.00	250.00

DS21
THE SNOWMAN SKIING™

Designer:	Graham Tongue
Modeller:	Warren Platt
Height:	5", 12.7 cm
Colour:	White snowman wearing a green hat and scarf, yellow and black goggles
Issued:	1990 - 1992

Royal Doulton®
THE SNOWMAN™
GIFT COLLECTION
THE SNOWMAN
SKIING
DS 21
© 1990 ROYAL DOULTON
© S ENT 1990

Doulton Number	Price U.S. $	Can. $	U.K. £	Aust. $
DS21	850.00	1,350.00	500.00	1,250.00

DS22
THE SNOWMAN SNOWBALLING™

Designer:	Graham Tongue
Modeller:	Warren Platt
Height:	5", 12.7 cm
Colour:	White snowman wearing a green hat and scarf, brown tree stump
Issued:	1990 - 1994

Doulton		*Price*		
Number	*U.S. $*	*Can. $*	*U.K. £*	*Aust. $*
DS22	150.00	250.00	60.00	225.00

DS23
BUILDING THE SNOWMAN™

Designer:	Graham Tongue
Modeller:	Warren Platt
Height:	4", 10.1 cm
Colour:	White snowman wearing a green hat and scarf
Issued:	1990 - 1994

Doulton		*Price*		
Number	*U.S. $*	*Can. $*	*U.K. £*	*Aust. $*
DS23	150.00	250.00	60.00	250.00

D6972
SNOWMAN MINIATURE
CHARACTER JUG™

Designer:	Graham Tongue
Modeller:	Martyn Alcock
Height:	2 ¾", 7.0 cm
Colour:	White snowman wearing a black hat, green scarf forms the handle
Issued:	1994 - 1994

Doulton		*Price*		
Number	*U.S. $*	*Can. $*	*U.K. £*	*Aust. $*
D6972	150.00	200.00	60.00	225.00

THUNDERBIRDS

3337
LADY PENELOPE™

Designer:	William K. Harper
Height:	4", 10.1 cm
Colour:	Pink hat and coat, blonde hair
Issued:	1992 in a limited edition of 2,500

| Beswick | | Price | | |
Number	U.S. $	Can. $	U.K. £	Aust. $
3337	175.00	250.00	100.00	265.00
Complete set of 6 figures	800.00	1,200.00	475.00	1,300.00

3339
BRAINS™

Designer:	William K. Harper
Height:	4", 10.1 cm
Colour:	Black and blue uniform, blue glasses, black hair
Issued:	1992 in a limited edition of 2,500

| Beswick | | Price | | |
Number	U.S. $	Can. $	U.K. £	Aust. $
3339	150.00	225.00	90.00	235.00

3344
SCOTT TRACY™

Designer:	William K. Harper
Height:	4", 10.1 cm
Colour:	Blue uniform, light blue band
Issued:	1992 in a limited edition of 2,500

| Beswick | | Price | | |
Number	U.S. $	Can. $	U.K. £	Aust. $
3344	175.00	250.00	100.00	265.00

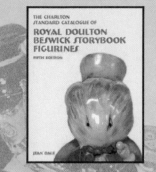

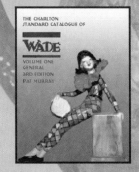

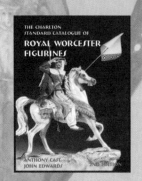

3345
VIRGIL TRACY™

Designer:	William K. Harper
Height:	4", 10.1 cm
Colour:	Blue uniform, yellow band
Issued:	1992 in a limited edition of 2,500

Beswick Number	Price			
	U.S. $	*Can. $*	*U.K. £*	*Aust. $*
3345	150.00	225.00	90.00	235.00

3346
PARKER™

Designer:	William K. Harper
Height:	4", 10.1 cm
Colour:	Blue-grey uniform
Issued:	1992 in a limited edition of 2,500

Beswick Number	Price			
	U.S. $	*Can. $*	*U.K. £*	*Aust. $*
3346	125.00	200.00	80.00	225.00

3348
THE HOOD™

Designer:	William K. Harper
Height:	4", 10.1 cm
Colour:	Browns
Issued:	1992 in a limited edition of 2,500

Beswick Number	Price			
	U.S. $	*Can. $*	*U.K. £*	*Aust. $*
3348	125.00	200.00	80.00	225.00

TURNER ENTERTAINMENT

3547
DROOPY™

Designer:	Simon Ward
Height:	4 ½", 11.4 cm
Colour:	White dog with black ears, red cap
Issued:	1995 in a special edition of 2,000

Beswick		*Price*		
Number	*U.S. $*	*Can. $*	*U.K. £*	*Aust. $*
3547	75.00	125.00	40.00	125.00

3549
JERRY™

Designer:	Simon Ward
Height:	3", 7.6 cm
Colour	Red-brown and cream mouse, white base
Issued:	1995 in special edition of 2,000

Beswick		*Price*		
Number	*U.S. $*	*Can. $*	*U.K. £*	*Aust. $*
3549	75.00	125.00	40.00	125.00

3552
TOM™

Designer:	Simon Ward
Height:	4 ½", 11.4 cm
Colour:	Grey-blue and pink cat, white base
Issued:	1995 in a special edition of 2,000

Beswick		*Price*		
Number	*U.S. $*	*Can. $*	*U.K. £*	*Aust. $*
3552	75.00	125.00	40.00	130.00

THE WIZARD OF OZ

3709
SCARECROW™

Designer:	Andy Moss
Height:	6 ½", 16.5 cm
Colour:	Black hat and shirt, brown pants and shoes
Issued:	1998 in a special edition of 1,500
Series:	The Wizard of Oz

Doulton Number	U.S. $	Price Can. $	U.K. £	Aust. $
3709	175.00	250.00	125.00	275.00
Set of 4 figures	675.00	800.00	400.00	850.00

3731
LION™

Designer:	Andy Moss
Height:	6", 15.0 cm
Colour:	Light and dark brown
Issued:	1998 in a special edition of 1,500
Series:	The Wizard of Oz

Doulton Number	U.S. $	Price Can. $	U.K. £	Aust. $
3731	175.00	250.00	125.00	275.00

3732
DOROTHY™

Designer:	Andy Moss
Height:	5", 12.7 cm
Colour:	Blue and white dress, red shoes, black dog
Issued:	1998 in a special edition of 1,500
Series:	The Wizard of Oz

Doulton Number	U.S. $	Price Can. $	U.K. £	Aust. $
3732	175.00	250.00	125.00	275.00

3738
TINMAN™

Designer:	Andy Moss
Height:	7", 17.8 cm
Colour:	Grey
Issued:	1998 in a special edition of 1,500
Series:	The Wizard of Oz

Doulton Number	U.S. $	Price Can. $	U.K. £	Aust. $
3738	175.00	250.00	125.00	275.00

WALT DISNEY

101 DALMATIANS

1997 to the present

DM 1
CRUELLA De VIL™
Style One

Designer:	Martyn Alcock
Height:	6 ¼", 15.9 cm
Colour:	Black dress, pale yellow coat with red lining and gloves
Issued:	1997 to the present
Series:	101 Dalmatians Collection

Royal Doulton®
DISNEY'S
101 DALMATIANS
CRUELLA DE VIL
DM 1
© Disney

Doulton	Price			
Number	U.S. $	Can. $	U.K. £	Aust. $
DM 1	150.00	225.00	85.00	225.00

DM 2
PENNY™

Designer:	Unknown
Modeller:	Shane Ridge
Height:	2 ¾", 7.0 cm
Colour:	White and black dalmatian, red collar
Issued:	1997 to the present
Series:	101 Dalmatians Collection

Royal Doulton®
DISNEY'S
101 DALMATIANS
PENNY
DM 2
© Disney

Doulton	Price			
Number	U.S. $	Can. $	U.K. £	Aust. $
DM 2	40.00	50.00	20.00	45.00

DM 3
PENNY™ AND FRECKLES™

Designer:	Unknown
Modeller:	Martyn Alcock
Height:	2 ¼", 5.5 cm
Colour:	Two white and black dalmatians with red collars
Issued:	1997 to the presemt
Series:	101 Dalmatians Collections

Royal Doulton®
DISNEY'S
101 DALMATIANS
PENNY AND FRECKLES
DM 3
© Disney

Doulton	Price			
Number	U.S. $	Can. $	U.K. £	Aust. $
DM 3	45.00	65.00	24.50	60.00

DM 4
ROLLY™

Designer:	Unknown
Modeller:	Shane Ridge
Height:	2 ¾", 7.0 cm
Colour:	White and black dalmatian, red collar, black base
Issued:	1997 to the present
Series:	101 Dalmatians Collections

Doulton Number	Price			
	U.S. $	Can. $	UK. £	Aust. $
DM 4	40.00	50.00	20.00	45.00

DM 5
PATCH™, ROLLY™ AND FRECKLES™

Designer:	Unknown
Modeller:	Shane Ridge
Height:	3 ¾", 9.5 cm
Length:	7 ½", 19 cm
Colour:	Three white and black dalmatians wearing red collars
Issued:	1997 in a limited edition of 3,500
Series:	1. 101 Dalmatians Collection
	2. Tableau

Doulton Number	Price			
	U.S. $	Can. $	U.K. £	Aust. $
DM 5	300.00	450.00	175.00	450.00

DM 6
PONGO™

Designer:	Unknown
Modeller:	Martyn Alcock
Height:	4 ½", 11.9 cm
Colour:	White and black dalmatian, red collar
Issued:	1997 - 1998
Series:	101 Dalmatians Collection

Doulton Number	Price			
	U.S. $	Can. $	U.K. £	Aust. $
DM 6	50.00	90.00	26.00	90.00

DM 7
PERDITA™

Designer:	Unknown
Modeller:	Martyn Alcock
Height:	2 ½", 6.4 cm
Colour:	White and black dalmatian dark turquoise collar and blanket
Issued:	1997 to the present
Series:	101 Dalmatians Collections

Royal Doulton®
DISNEY'S
101 DALMATIANS
PERDITA
DM 7
© Disney

Doulton Number	Price			
	U.S. $	Can. $	U.K. £	Aust. $
DM 7	45.00	65.00	24.50	60.00

DM 8
LUCKY™

Designer:	Unknown
Modeller:	Martyn Alcock
Height:	2 ¾", 7.0 cm
Colour:	White and black dalmatian, red collar
Issued:	1997 to the present
Series:	101 Dalmatians Collections

Royal Doulton®
DISNEY'S
101 DALMATIANS
LUCKY DM 8
© Disney

Doulton Number	Price			
	U.S. $	Can. $	U.K. £	Aust. $
DM 8	40.00	50.00	20.00	45.00

DM 9
PATCH™ IN BASKET

Designer:	Unknown
Modeller:	Graham Tongue
Height:	2 ¼", 5.7 cm
Colour:	White and black dalmatian, beige basket
Issued:	1998 to the present
Series:	101 Dalmatians Collections

DISNEY'S
101 DALMATIANS
PATCH IN BASKET
DM 9
Royal Doulton® © Disney

Doulton Number	Price			
	U.S. $	Can. $	U.K. £	Aust. $
DM 9	40.00	60.00	22.00	60.00

DM 10
LUCKY™ AND FRECKLES™ ON ICE

Designer:	Unknown
Modeller:	Warren Platt
Height:	2 ½", 6.4 cm
Colour:	White and black dalmatians
Issued:	1998 to the present
Series:	101 Dalmatians Collections

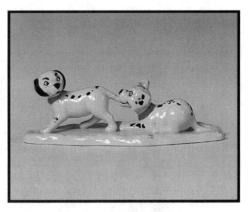

Doulton	Price			
Number	U.S. $	Can. $	U.K. £	Aust. $
DM 10	125.00	200.00	75.00	200.00

DM 11
PUPS IN THE CHAIR

Designer:	Unknown
Modeller:	Martyn Alcock
Height:	4", 10.1 cm
Colour:	White and black dalmatians, yellow chair
Issued:	February 1st to May 12th, 1999 (101 days)
Series:	101 Dalmatians Collections

Doulton	Price			
Number	U.S. $	Can. $	U.K. £	Aust. $
DM 11	125.00	200.00	75.00	200.00

DISNEY CHARACTERS

1952-1965

1278
MICKEY MOUSE™
Style One

Designer:	Jan Granoska
Height:	4", 10.1 cm
Colour:	Black, white and red
Issued:	1952 - 1965

Back Stamp	Beswick Number	Price U.S. $	Can. $	U.K.£	Aust. $
Beswick Gold	1278	1,000.00	1,200.00	425.00	1,000.00

1279
JIMINY CRICKET™

Designer:	Jan Granoska
Height:	4", 10.1 cm
Colour:	Black, white, beige and blue
Issued:	1952 - 1965

Back Stamp	Beswick Number	Price U.S. $	Can. $	U.K. £	Aust. $
Beswick Gold	1279	675.00	800.00	375.00	850.00

1280
PLUTO™
Style One

Designer:	Jan Granoska
Height:	3 ½", 8.9 cm
Colour:	Brown dog with red collar
Issued:	1953 - 1965

Back Stamp	Beswick Number	Price U.S. $	Can. $	U.K. £	Aust. $
Beswick Gold	1280	675.00	800.00	375.00	850.00

1281
GOOFY™
Style One

Designer:	Jan Granoska
Height:	4 ¼", 10.8 cm
Colour:	Red jersey, blue trousers, black suspenders, white gloves, brown and black hat, brown boots
Issued:	1953 - 1965

Back Stamp	Beswick Number	Price U.S. $	Can. $	U.K. £	Aust. $
Beswick Gold	1281	675.00	900.00	375.00	1,000.00

1282
PINOCCHIO™

Designer:	Jan Granoska
Height:	4", 10.1 cm
Colour:	White and yellow jacket, red trousers, blue bowtie and shoes, brown cap
Issued:	1953 - 1965

Back Stamp	Beswick Number	Price U.S. $	Can. $	U.K. £	Aust. $
Beswick Gold	1282	775.00	1,000.00	450.00	1,100.00

1283
DONALD DUCK™
Style One

Designer:	Jan Granoska
Height:	4", 10.1 cm
Colour:	White duck, blue sailors jacket, red bow, blue and black hat
Issued:	1953 - 1965

Back Stamp	Beswick Number	Price U.S. $	Can. $	U.K. £	Aust. $
Beswick Gold	1283	775.00	1,000.00	425.00	1,100.00

1289
MINNIE MOUSE™
Style One

Designer:	Jan Granoska
Height:	4", 10.1 cm
Colour:	Black and white mouse wearing a yellow top and red skirt with white spots, white gloves and hair bow, brown shoes
Issued:	1953 - 1965

Back Stamp	Beswick Number	U.S. $	Price Can. $	U.K. £	Aust. $
Beswick Gold	1289	750.00	1,000.00	425.00	1,100.00

1291
THUMPER™

Designer:	Jan Granoska
Height:	3 ¾", 9.5 cm
Colour:	Grey and white rabbit, yellow, red and pink flowers on brown base
Issued:	1953 - 1965

Back Stamp	Beswick Number	U.S. $	Price Can. $	U.K. £	Aust. $
Beswick Gold	1291	500.00	650.00	250.00	600.00

THE DISNEY PRINCESS COLLECTION

1995-1996

HN 3677
CINDERELLA™

Designer:	Pauline Parsons
Height:	8", 20.3 cm
Colour:	Blue and white dress, yellow hair
Issued:	1995 in a limited edition of 2,000
Series:	The Disney Princess Collection

Back Stamp	Doulton Number	U.S. $	Can. $	U.K.£	Aust. $
Doulton	HN 3677	400.00	600.00	200.00	550.00

HN 3678
SNOW WHITE™
Style Two

Designer:	Pauline Parsons
Height:	8 ¼", 21.0 cm
Colour:	Yellow, blue and white dress, royal blue and red cape, black hair
Issued:	1995 in a limited edition of 2,000
Series:	The Disney Princess Collection

Back Stamp	Doulton Number	U.S. $	Can. $	U.K. £	Aust. $
Doulton	HN 3678	500.00	750.00	325.00	800.00

HN 3830
BELLE™

Designer:	Pauline Parsons
Height:	8", 20.3 cm
Colour:	Yellow dress and gloves, brown hair
Issued:	1996 in a limited edition of 2,000
Series:	The Disney Princess Collection

Back Stamp	Doulton Number	U.S. $	Can. $	U.K. £	Aust. $
Doulton	HN3830	400.00	600.00	200.00	600.00

HN 3831
ARIEL™

Designer: Pauline Parsons
Height: 8 ¼", 21.0 cm
Colour: White dress and veil, red hair
Issued: 1996 in a limited edition of 2,000
Series: The Disney Princess Collection

Back Stamp	Doulton Number	Price			
		U.S. $	Can. $	U.K. £	Aust. $
Doulton	HN 3831	400.00	600.00	200.00	650.00

HN3832
JASMINE™

Designer: Pauline Parsons
Height: 7 ½", 19.1 cm
Colour: Lilac dress
Issued: 1996 in a limited edition of 2,000
Series: The Disney Princess Collection

Back Stamp	Doulton Number	Price			
		U.S. $	Can. $	U.K. £	Aust. $
Doulton	HN 3832	400.00	600.00	200.00	650.00

HN3833
AURORA™

Designer: Pauline Parsons
Height: 7 ½", 19.1 cm
Colour: Light and dark blue dress with white trim
Issued: 1996 in a limited edition of 2,000
Series: The Disney Princess Collection

Back Stamp	Doulton Number	Price			
		U.S. $	Can. $	U.K. £	Aust. $
Doulton	HN 3833	350.00	500.00	175.00	525.00

DISNEY VILLAINS COLLECTION

1997 - 1998

HN3839
CRUELLA De VIL™
Style Two

Designer:	Pauline Parsons
Height:	8", 20.3 cm
Colour:	Black dress, white fur coat, red gloves
Issued:	1997 in a limited edition of 2,000
Series:	The Disney Villains Collection

Back Stamp	Doulton Number	U.S. $	Price Can. $	U.K. £	Aust. $
Doulton	HN 3839	300.00	450.00	175.00	475.00

HN3840
MALEFICENT™

Designer:	Pauline Parsons
Height:	8", 20.3 cm
Colour:	Black and purple
Issued:	1997 in a limited edition of 2,000
Series:	The Disney Villains Collection

Back Stamp	Doulton Number	U.S. $	Price Can. $	U.K. £	Aust. $
Doulton	HN 3840	300.00	450.00	175.00	475.00

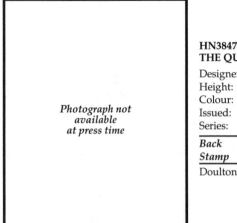

Photograph not available at press time

HN3847
THE QUEEN™

Designer:	Pauline Parson
Height:	8", 20.3 cm
Colour:	Purple gown, black cloak
Issued:	1998 in a limited edition of 2,000
Series:	The Disney Villains Collection

Back Stamp	Doulton Number	U.S. $	Price Can. $	U.K. £	Aust. $
Doulton	HN3847	300.00	450.00	175.00	475.00

HN3848
THE WITCH™

Designer:	Pauline Parsons
Height:	8", 20.3 cm
Colour:	Black robes, red apple
Issued:	1998 in a limited edition of 2,000
Series:	The Disney Villains Collection

Back Stamp	Doulton Number	U.S. $	Price Can. $	U.K. £	Aust. $
Doulton	HN 3848	300.00	450.00	175.00	475.00

MICKEY MOUSE COLLECTION

1998 to the present

MM1
MICKEY MOUSE™
Style Two

Designer:	Walt Disney
Modeller:	Warren Platt
Height:	4 ¾", 12.1 cm
Colour:	Black, red and light brown
Issued:	1998 to the present
Series:	Mickey Mouse Collection

Back Stamp	Doulton Number	Price			
		U.S. $	Can. $	U.K. £	Aust. $
BK-1 / 70th Anniv.	MM1	125.00	175.00	70.00	175.00
BK-2	MM1	100.00	150.00	60.00	150.00

MM2
MINNIE MOUSE™
Style Two

Designer:	Walt Disney
Modeller:	Warren Platt
Height:	5 ½", 14.0 cm
Colour:	Black, blue and red
Issued:	1998 to the present
Series:	Mickey Mouse Collection

Back Stamp	Doulton Number	Price			
		U.S. $	Can. $	U.K. £	Aust. $
BK-1 / 70th Anniv.	MM2	125.00	175.00	70.00	175.00
BK-2	MM2	100.00	150.00	60.00	150.00

MM3
DONALD DUCK™
Style Two

Designer:	Walt Disney
Modeller:	Shane Ridge
Height:	4 ¾", 12.1 cm
Colour:	Blue, white and red
Issued:	1998 to the present
Series:	Mickey Mouse Collection

Back Stamp	Doulton Number	Price			
		U.S. $	Can. $	U.K. £	Aust. $
BK-1 / 70 Anniv.	MM3	125.00	175.00	70.00	175.00
BK-2	MM3	100.00	150.00	60.00	150.00

MM4
DAISY DUCK™

Designer:	Walt Disney
Modeller:	Shane Ridge
Height:	5 ½", 14.0 cm
Colour:	Blue, white and pink
Issued:	1998 to the present
Series:	Mickey Mouse Collection

Back Stamp	Doulton Number	Price U.S. $	Can. $	U.K. £	Aust. $
BK-1 / 70th Anniv.	MM4	125.00	175.00	70.00	175.00
BK-2	MM4	100.00	150.00	60.00	150.00

MM5
GOOFY™
Style Two

Designer:	Walt Disney
Modeller:	Graham Tongue
Height:	5", 12.7 cm
Colour:	Red, blue and black
Issued:	1998 to the present
Series:	Mickey Mouse Collection

Back Stamp	Doulton Number	Price U.S. $	Can. $	U.K. £	Aust. $
BK-1 / 70th Anniv.	MM5	125.00	175.00	70.00	175.00
BK-2	MM5	100.00	150.00	60.00	150.00

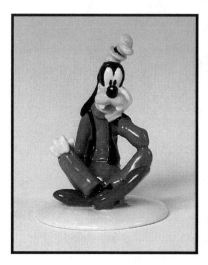

MM6
PLUTO™
Style Two

Designer:	Walt Disney
Modeller:	Graham Tongue
Height:	4 ½", 12.1 cm
Colour:	Light brown
Issued:	1998 to the present
Series:	Mickey Mouse Collection

Back Stamp	Doulton Number	Price U.S. $	Can. $	U.K. £	Aust. $
BK-1 / 70th Anniv.	MM6	125.00	175.00	70.00	175.00
BK-2	MM6	100.00	150.00	60.00	150.00

PETER PAN

1953-1965

1301
NANA™

Designer:	Jan Granoska
Height:	3 ¼", 8.3 cm
Colour:	Brown dog, white frilled cap with blue ribbon
Issued:	1953 - 1965
Series:	Peter Pan

Back Stamp	Beswick Number	U.S. $	Price Can. $	U.K. £	Aust. $
Beswick Gold	1301	750.00	900.00	425.00	950.00

1302
SMEE™

Designer:	Jan Granoska
Height:	4 ¼", 10.8 cm
Colour:	Blue and white shirt, blue pants, red cap, green bottle
Issued:	1953 - 1965
Series:	Peter Pan

Back Stamp	Beswick Number	U.S. $	Price Can. $	U.K. £	Aust. $
Beswick Gold	1302	700.00	850.00	375.00	900.00

1307
PETER PAN™

Designer: Jan Granoska
Height: 5", 12.7 cm
Colour: Light green tunic, dark green pants, brown shoes, red and green cap
Issued: 1953 - 1965
Series: Peter Pan

Back Stamp	Beswick Number	Price			
		U.S. $	Can. $	U.K. £	Aust. $
Beswick Gold	1307	1,000.00	1,300.00	550.00	1,350.00

1312
TINKER BELL™

Designer: Jan Granoska
Height: 5", 12.7 cm
Colour: Light green dress, dark green wings and shoes
Issued: 1953 - 1965
Series: Peter Pan

Back Stamp	Beswick Number	Price			
		U.S. $	Can. $	U.K. £	Aust. $
Beswick Gold	1312	900.00	1,200.00	500.00	1,200.00

SNOW WHITE AND THE SEVEN DWARFS

BESWICK SERIES 1954-1967

1325
DOPEY™
Style One

Designer:	Arthur Gredington
Height:	3 ½", 8.9 cm
Colour:	Green coat, maroon cap, grey shoes
Issued:	1954 - 1967
Series:	Snow White and the Seven Dwarfs (Style One)

Back Stamp	Beswick Number	Price			
		U.S. $	Can. $	U.K. £	Aust. $
Beswick Gold	1325	425.00	550.00	175.00	350.00

1326
HAPPY™
Style One

Designer:	Arthur Gredington
Height:	3 ½", 8.9 cm
Colour:	Purple tunic, light blue trousers, light brown cap, brown shoes
Issued:	1954 - 1967
Series:	Snow White and the Seven Dwarfs (Style One)

Back Stamp	Beswick Number	Price			
		U.S. $	Can. $	U.K. £	Aust. $
Beswick Gold	1326	425.00	550.00	175.00	350.00

1327
BASHFUL™
Style One

Designer:	Arthur Gredington
Height:	3 ½", 8.9 cm
Colour:	Brown tunic, purple trousers, grey cap, brown shoes
Issued:	1954 - 1967
Series:	Snow White and the Seven Dwarfs (Style One)

Back Stamp	Beswick Number	Price			
		U.S. $	Can. $	U.K. £	Aust. $
Beswick Gold	1327	425.00	550.00	175.00	350.00

1328
SNEEZY™
Style One

Designer:	Arthur Gredington
Height:	3 ½", 8.9 cm
Colour:	Green tunic, purple trousers, brown cap and shoes
Issued:	1954 - 1967
Series:	Snow White and the Seven Dwarfs (Style One)

Back Stamp	Beswick Number	U.S. $	Price Can. $	U.K. £	Aust. $
Beswick Gold	1328	425.00	550.00	175.00	350.00

1329
DOC™
Style One

Designer:	Arthur Gredington
Height:	3 ½", 8.9 cm
Colour:	Brown tunic, blue trousers, yellow cap, brown shoes
Issued:	1954 - 1967
Series:	Snow White and the Seven Dwarfs (Style One)

Back Stamp	Beswick Number	U.S. $	Price Can. $	U.K. £	Aust. $
Beswick Gold	1329	425.00	550.00	200.00	400.00

1330
GRUMPY™
Style One

Designer:	Arthur Gredington
Height:	3 ¾", 9.5 cm
Colour:	Purple tunic, red trousers, blue cap, brown shoes
Issued:	1954 - 1967
Series:	Snow White and the Seven Dwarfs (Style One)

Back Stamp	Beswick Number	U.S. $	Price Can. $	U.K. £	Aust. $
Beswick Gold	1330	425.00	550.00	175.00	300.00

1331
SLEEPY™
Style One

Designer: Arthur Gredington
Height: 3 ½", 8.9 cm
Colour: Tan tunic, red trousers, green hat, grey shoes
Issued: 1954 - 1967
Series: Snow White and the Seven Dwarfs (Style One)

Back Stamp	Beswick Number	U.S. $	Price Can. $	U.K. £	Aust. $
Beswick Gold	1331	425.00	550.00	175.00	375.00

1332A
SNOW WHITE™
Style One
First Version (Hair in Flounces)

Designer: Arthur Gredington
Height: 5 ½", 14.0 cm
Colour: Yellow and purple dress, red cape, white collar
Issued: 1954 - 1955

Back Stamp	Beswick Number	U.S. $	Price Can. $	U.K. £	Aust. $
Beswick Gold	1332A		Extremely rare		

Note: Snow White (Style One) was remodelled February 1955.

1332B
SNOW WHITE™
Style One
Second Version (Hair Flat to Head)

Designer: Arthur Gredington
Height: 5 ½", 14.0 cm
Colour: Yellow and purple dress, red cape, white collar
Issued: 1955 - 1967
Series: Snow White and the Seven Dwarfs (Style One)

Back Stamp	Beswick Number	U.S. $	Price Can. $	U.K. £	Aust. $
Beswick Gold	1332B	800.00	975.00	400.00	550.00

SNOW WHITE AND THE SEVEN DWARFS

ROYAL DOULTON SERIES 1997 to the present

SW1 - SW9
SNOW WHITE™
Style Three

Designer:	Amanda Hughes-Lubeck
Height:	5 ¾", 14.6 cm
Colour:	Yellow and blue dress, red cape, white collar
Issued:	SW1 1997 in a limited edition of 2,000
	SW9 1998 to the present
Series:	Snow White and the Seven Dwarfs (Style Two)

Back Stamp	Beswick Number	Price			
		U.S. $	Can. $	U.K. £	Aust. $
Doulton/Disney 60th	SW 1	300.00	400.00	150.00	425.00
Doulton/Disney	SW 9	150.00	225.00	85.00	225.00

SW2 - SW10
DOC™
Style Two

Designer:	Amanda Hughes-Lubeck
Height:	3 ¼", 8.3 cm
Colour:	Red jacket, brown trousers, yellow hat, green book
Issued:	SW2 1997 in a limited edition of 2,000
	SW10 1998 to the present
Series:	Snow White and the Seven Dwarfs (Style Two)

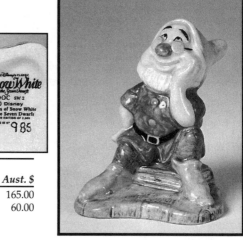

Back Stamp	Beswick Number	Price			
		U.S. $	Can. $	U.K. £	Aust. $
Doulton/Disney 60th	SW 2	100.00	150.00	50.00	165.00
Doulton/Disney	SW 10	40.00	60.00	24.00	60.00

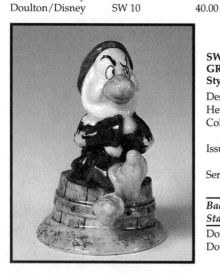

SW3 - SW11
GRUMPY™
Style Two

Designer:	Shane Ridge
Height:	3 ½", 8.9 cm
Colour:	Dark rust coat and trousers, brown hat, light brown basket
Issued:	SW3 1997 in a limited edition of 2,000
	SW11 1998 to the present
Series:	Snow White and the Seven Dwarfs (Style Two)

Back Stamp	Beswick Number	Price			
		U.S. $	Can. $	U.K. £	Aust. $
Doulton/Disney 60th	SW 3	100.00	150.00	50.00	165.00
Doulton/Disney	SW 11	40.00	60.00	24.00	60.00

SW4 - SW12
HAPPY™
Style Two

Designer:	Amanda Hughes-Lubeck
Height:	3 ½", 8.9 cm
Colour:	Brown vest, orange shirt, light blue trousers with black belt and a yellow hat
Issued:	SW4 1997 in a limited edition of 2,000
	SW12 1998 to the present
Series:	Snow White and the Seven Dwarfs (Style Two)

Back Stamp	Beswick Number	Price U.S. $	Can. $	U.K. £	Aust. $
Doulton/Disney 60th	SW 4	100.00	150.00	50.00	165.00
Doulton/Disney	SW 12	40.00	60.00	24.00	60.00

SW5 - SW13
DOPEY™
Style Two

Designer:	Shane Ridge
Height:	3 ½", 8.9 cm
Colour:	Yellow shirt and trousers, purple hat, black belt
Issued:	SW5 1997 in a limited edition of 2,000
	SW13 1998 to the present
Series:	Snow White and the Seven Dwarfs (Style Two)

Back Stamp	Beswick Number	Price U.S. $	Can. $	U.K. £	Aust. $
Doulton/Disney 60th	SW 5	100.00	150.00	50.00	165.00
Doulton/Disney	SW 13	40.00	60.00	24.00	60.00

SW6/SW14
SNEEZY™
Style Two

Designer:	Warren Platt
Height:	3 ½", 8.9 cm
Colour:	Light brown jacket, dark brown trousers, black belt
Issued:	SW6 1997 in a limited edition of 2,000
	SW14 1998 to the present
Series:	Snow White and the Seven Dwarfs (Style Two)

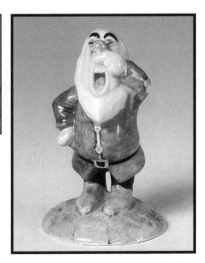

Back Stamp	Beswick Number	Price U.S. $	Can. $	U.K. £	Aust. $
Doulton/Disney 60th	SW 6	100.00	150.00	50.00	165.00
Doulton/Disney	SW 14	40.00	60.00	24.00	60.00

SW7 - SW15
SLEEPY™
Style Two

Deisgner:	Warren Platt
Height:	3 ½", 8.9 cm
Colour:	Beige jacket, dark brown trousers, green hat and a yellow bottle
Issued:	SW7 1997 in a limited edition of 2,000
	SW15 1998 to the present
Series:	Snow White and the Seven Dwarfs (Style Two)

Back Stamp	Beswick Number	Price U.S. $	Can. $	U.K. £	Aust. $
Doulton/Disney 60th	SW 7	100.00	300.00	50.00	165.00
Doulton/Disney	SW 15	40.00	60.00	24.00	60.00

SW8 - SW16
BASHFUL™
Style Two

Designer:	Amanda Hughes-Lubeck
Height:	3 ½", 8.9 cm
Colour:	Dark yellow jacket, light brown trousers, green hat
Issued:	SW8 1997 in a limited edition of 2,000
	SW16 1998 to the present
Series:	Snow White and the Seven Dwarfs (Style Two)

Back Stamp	Beswick Number	Price U.S. $	Can. $	U.K. £	Aust. $
Doulton/Disney 60th	SW 8	100.00	150.00	50.00	165.00
Doulton/Disney	SW 16	40.00	60.00	24.00	60.00

SW 17
DOPEY™ BY CANDLELIGHT

Designer:	Shane Ridge
Height:	3 ½", 8.9 cm
Colour:	Green
Issued:	1998 to the present
Series:	Snow White and the Seven Dwarfs

Back Stamp	Beswick Number	Price U.S. $	Can. $	U.K. £	Aust. $
Doulton/Disney	SW 17	40.00	75.00	30.00	75.00

SW 18
BASHFUL'S™ MELODY

Designer:	Walt Disney
Modeller:	Graham Tongue
Height:	3 ½", 8.9 cm
Colour:	Blue
Issued:	1998 to the present
Series:	Snow White and the Seven Dwarfs

Back Stamp	Beswick Number	U.S. $	Price Can. $	U.K. £	Aust. $
Doulton/Disney	SW 18	45.00	65.00	26.00	65.00

SW 19
DOC™ WITH THE LANTERN

Designer:	Walt Disney
Modeller:	Warren Platt
Height:	3 ½", 8.9 cm
Colour:	Red and yellow
Issued:	1999 to the present
Series:	Snow White and the Seven Dwarfs

Back Stamp	Beswick Number	U.S. $	Price Can. $	U.K. £	Aust. $
Doulton/Disney	SW 19	45.00	65.00	26.00	65.00

SW 20
GRUMPY'S™ BATHTIME

Designer:	Walt Disney
Modeller:	Shane Ridge
Height:	3 ½", 8.9 cm
Colour:	White, brown, red and yellow
Issued:	1999 to the present (serial numbered)
Series:	Snow White and the Seven Dwarfs

Back Stamp	Beswick Number	U.S. $	Price Can. $	U.K. £	Aust. $
Doulton/Disney	SW 20	50.00	75.00	30.00	75.00

WINNIE THE POOH

BESWICK SERIES 1968-1990

2193
WINNIE THE POOH™

Designer:	Albert Hallam
Height:	2 ½", 6.4 cm
Colour:	Golden brown and red
Issued:	1968 - 1990
Series:	Winnie The Pooh

Back Stamp	Beswick Number	Price U.S. $	Can. $	U.K. £	Aust. $
Beswick Gold	2193	200.00	300.00	100.00	250.00
Beswick Brown	2193	150.00	225.00	75.00	225.00

2196
EEYORE™

Designer:	Albert Hallam
Height:	2" 5.0 cm
Colour:	Grey with black markings
Issued:	1968 - 1990
Series:	Winnie The Pooh

Back Stamp	Beswick Number	Price U.S. $	Can. $	U.K. £	Aust. $
Beswick Gold	2196	200.00	300.00	100.00	250.00
Beswick Brown	2196	150.00	225.00	75.00	225.00

2214
PIGLET™

Designer:	Albert Hallam
Height:	2 ¾", 7.0 cm
Colour:	Pink and red
Issued:	1968 - 1990
Series:	Winnie The Pooh

Back Stamp	Beswick Number	Price U.S. $	Can. $	U.K. £	Aust. $
Beswick Gold	2214	200.00	300.00	100.00	250.00
Beswick Brown	2214	150.00	225.00	75.00	225.00

2215
RABBIT™

Designer:	Albert Hallam
Height:	3 ¼", 8.3 cm
Colour:	Brown and beige
Issued:	1968 - 1990
Series:	Winnie The Pooh

Back Stamp	Beswick Number	U.S. $	Price Can. $	U.K. £	Aust. $
Beswick Gold	2215	200.00	300.00	100.00	250.00
Beswick Brown	2215	150.00	200.00	75.00	225.00

2216
OWL™

Designer:	Albert Hallam
Height:	3", 7.6 cm
Colour:	Brown, white and black
Issued:	1968 - 1990
Series:	Winnie The Pooh

Back Stamp	Beswick Number	U.S. $	Price Can. $	U.K. £	Aust. $
Beswick Gold	2216	200.00	300.00	100.00	250.00
Beswick Brown	2216	150.00	200.00	75.00	225.00

2217
KANGA™

Designer:	Albert Hallam
Height:	3 ¼", 8.3 cm
Colour:	Dark and light brown
Issued:	1968 - 1990
Series:	Winnie The Pooh

Back Stamp	Beswick Number	U.S. $	Price Can. $	U.K. £	Aust. $
Beswick Gold	2217	200.00	300.00	100.00	250.00
Beswick Brown	2217	150.00	200.00	75.00	225.00

2394
TIGGER™

Designer:	Graham Tongue
Height:	3", 7.6 cm
Colour:	Yellow with black stripes
Issued:	1971 - 1990
Series:	Winnie The Pooh

Back Stamp	Beswick Number	U.S. $	Price Can. $	U.K. £	Aust. $
Beswick Gold	2394	275.00	400.00	150.00	375.00
Beswick Brown	2394	225.00	300.00	115.00	325.00

2395
CHRISTOPHER ROBIN™
Style One

Designer:	Graham Tongue
Height:	4 ¾", 12.1 cm
Colour:	Yellow, blue and white
Issued:	1971 - 1990
Series:	Winnie The Pooh

Back Stamp	Beswick Number	U.S. $	Price Can. $	U.K. £	Aust. $
Beswick Gold	2395	350.00	500.00	165.00	450.00
Beswick Brown	2395	300.00	400.00	150.00	400.00

WINNIE THE POOH

ROYAL DOULTON SERIES 1996 to the present

WP 1
WINNIE THE POOH™ AND THE HONEY POT

Designer:	Warren Platt
Height:	2 ½", 6.5 cm
Colour:	Yellow bear, red jersey, red-brown honey pot
Issued:	1996 to the present
Series:	Winnie the Pooh and Friends from the One Hundred Acre Wood

Back Stamp	Doulton Number	U.S. $	Can. $	U.K. £	Aust. $
BK-1	WP 1 / 70th	100.00	150.00	60.00	150.00
BK-2	WP 1	40.00	70.00	23.00	70.00

WP 2
POOH™ AND PIGLET™ THE WINDY DAY

Designer:	Martyn Alcock
Height:	3 ¼", 8 cm
Colour:	Yellow bear, pink piglet with green suit, light brown base
Issued:	1996 to the present
Series:	Winnie the Pooh and Friends from the One Hundred Acre Wood

Back Stamp	Doulton Number	U.S. $	Can. $	U.K. £	Aust. $
BK-1	WP 2 / 70th	85.00	125.00	50.00	125.00
BK-2	WP 2	50.00	75.00	30.00	75.00

WP 3
WINNIE THE POOH™ AND THE PAW-MARKS

Designer:	Warren Platt
Height:	2 ¾", 7.0 cm
Colour:	Yellow bear, red jersey
Issued:	1996 - 1997
Series:	Winnie the Pooh and Friends from the One Hundred Acre Wood

Back Stamp	Doulton Number	U.S. $	Can. $	U.K. £	Aust. $
BK-1	WP 3 / 70th	85.00	125.00	50.00	125.00
BK-2	WP 3	50.00	75.00	30.00	75.00

WP 4
WINNIE THE POOH™ IN THE ARMCHAIR

Designer:	Shane Ridge
Height:	3 ¼", 8 cm
Colour:	Yellow bear, pink armchair
Issued:	1996 - 1998
Series:	Winnie the Pooh and Friends from the One Hundred Acre Wood

Back Stamp	Doulton Number	Price U.S. $	Can. $	U.K. £	Aust. $
BK-1	WP 4 / 70th	85.00	125.00	50.00	125.00
BK-2	WP 4	35.00	70.00	20.00	75.00

WP 5
PIGLET™ AND THE BALLOON

Designer:	Warren Platt
Height:	2 ¾", 7.0 cm
Colour:	Pink piglet, green suit, blue balloon, light brown base
Issued:	1996 - 1998
Series:	Winnie the Pooh and Friends from the One Hundred Acre Wood

Back Stamp	Doulton Number	Price U.S. $	Can. $	U.K. £	Aust. $
BK-1	WP 5 / 70th	75.00	110.00	45.00	110.00
BK-2	WP 5	40.00	65.00	25.00	65.00

WP 6
TIGGER™ SIGNS THE RISSOLUTION

Designer:	Martyn Alcock
Height:	1 ¾", 4.5 cm
Colour:	Yellow tiger with black stripes
Issued:	1996 to the present
Series:	Winnie the Pooh and Friends from the One Hundred Acre Wood

Back Stamp	Doulton Number	Price U.S. $	Can. $	U.K. £	Aust. $
BK-1	WP 6 / 70th	75.00	110.00	45.00	110.00
BK-2	WP 6	35.00	70.00	20.00	70.00

WP 7
EEYORE'S™ TAIL

Designer:	Shane Ridge
Height:	3 ½", 8.9 cm
Colour:	Grey donkey with black markings, pink bow
Issued:	1996 to the present
Series:	Winnie the Pooh and Friends from the One Hundred Acre Wood

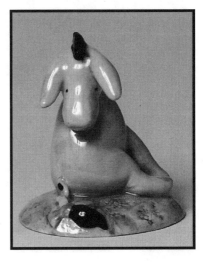

Back Stamp	Doulton Number	Price			
		U.S. $	Can. $	U.K. £	Aust. $
BK-1	WP 7 / 70th	75.00	110.00	45.00	110.00
BK-2	WP 7	35.00	70.00	22.00	70.00

WP 8
KANGA™ AND ROO™

Designer:	Martyn Alcock
Height:	3 ½", 8.9 cm
Colour:	Dark and light brown kangaroos
Issued:	1996 - 1998
Series:	Winnie the Pooh and Friends from the One Hundred Acre Wood

Back Stamp	Doulton Number	Price			
		U.S. $	Can. $	U.K. £	Aust. $
BK-1	WP 8 / 70th	75.00	110.00	45.00	110.00
BK-2	WP 8	45.00	70.00	25.00	70.00

WP 9
CHRISTOPHER ROBIN™
Style Two

Designer:	Shane Ridge
Height:	5 ½", 14.0 cm
Colour:	White and blue checkered shirt, blue shorts, black wellingtons, red-brown hair
Issued:	1996 to the present
Series:	Winnie the Pooh and Friends from the One Hundred Acre Wood

Back Stamp	Doulton Number	Price			
		U.S. $	Can. $	U.K. £	Aust. $
BK-1	WP 9 / 70th	100.00	150.00	60.00	150.00
BK-2	WP 9	45.00	95.00	25.00	100.00

WP 10
CHRISTOPHER ROBIN™ AND POOH™

Designer:	Shane Ridge
Height:	3 ¼", 8.5 cm
Colour:	Light blue shirt and shorts, black boots, reddish brown hair, yellow bear
Issued:	1996 - 1997
Series:	Winnie the Pooh and Friends from the One Hundred Acre Wood

Royal Doulton®
THE
WINNIE THE POOH
COLLECTION
CHRISTOPHER ROBIN AND POOH
WP 10
© Disney
70 YEARS OF
CLASSIC WINNIE THE POOH

Back Stamp	Doulton Number	Price			
		U.S.$	Can. $	U.K. £	Aust. $
BK-1	WP 10 / 70th	150.00	225.00	90.00	225.00
BK-2	WP 10	85.00	125.00	50.00	125.00

WP 11
POOH™ LIGHTS THE CANDLE

Designer:	Graham Tongue
Height:	3 ½", 8.9 cm
Colour:	Yellow bear with white candle and hat
Issued:	1997 - 1998
Series:	Winnie the Pooh and friends from the One Hundred Acre Wood

Royal Doulton®
THE
WINNIE THE POOH
COLLECTION
POOH LIGHTS
THE CANDLE
WP 11
© Disney

Back Stamp	Doulton Number	Price			
		U.S.$	Can. $	U.K. £	Aust. $
BK-2	WP 11	45.00	70.00	25.00	80.00

WP 12
POOH™ COUNTING THE HONEYPOTS

Designer:	Martyn Alcock
Height:	3 ½", 8.9 cm
Colour:	Yellow bear, brown honeypots
Issued:	1997 to the present
Series:	Winnie the Pooh and friends from the One Hundred Acre Wood

Royal Doulton®
THE
WINNIE THE POOH
COLLECTION
POOH COUNTING
THE HONEYPOTS
WP 12
© Disney

Back Stamp	Doulton Number	Price			
		U.S.$	Can. $	U.K. £	Aust. $
BK-2	WP 12	35.00	70.00	22.00	80.00

WP 13
PIGLET™ PICKING THE VIOLETS

Designer: Graham Tongue
Height: 2 ½", 6.4 cm
Colour: Pink, light and dark greens
Issued: 1997 to the present
Series: Winnie the Pooh and Friends
           from the One Hundred Acre Wood

Back Stamp	Doulton Number	Price			
		U.S. $	*Can. $*	*U.K. £*	*Aust.*
BK-2	WP 13	35.00	70.00	22.00	80.00

WP 14
EEYORE'S™ BIRTHDAY

Designer: Martyn Alcock
Height: 2 ¾", 7.0 cm
Colour: Grey and black
Issued: 1997 to the present
Series: Winnie the Pooh and Friends
           from the One Hundred Acre Wood

Back Stamp	Doulton Number	Price			
		U.S. $	*Can. $*	*U.K. £*	*Aust. $*
BK-2	WP 14	35.00	70.00	22.00	80.00

WP 15
EEYORE™ LOSES A TAIL

Designer: Martyn Alcock
Height: 4", 10.1 cm
Colour: Pink, yellow, grey,
           green and brown
Issued: 1997 in a limited edition of 5,000
Series: 1. Tableau
           2. Winnie the Pooh and Friends
              from the One Hundred Acre Wood

Back Stamp	Doulton Number	Price			
		U.S. $	*Can. $*	*U.K. £*	*Aust. $*
Doulton	WP 15	300.00	450.00	175.00	475.00

WP 16
POOH'S™ BLUE BALLOON MONEY BOX

Designer:	Shane Ridge
Height:	4 ¼", 10.8 cm
Colour:	Yellow bear, pink pig wearing green jumper, white balloon with dark blue rope
Issued:	1997 to the present
Series:	Winnie the Pooh and Friends from the One Hundred Acre Wood

Back Stamp	Doulton Number	Price			
		U.S. $	Can. $	U.K. £	Aust. $
Doulton	WP16	60.00	85.00	35.00	85.00

WP 17
WOL™ SIGNS THE RISSOLUTION

Designer:	Martyn Alcock
Height:	3 ¾", 9.5 cm
Colour:	Grey and black
Issued:	1998 in a limited edition of 2,500
Series:	Winnie the Pooh and Friends from the One Hundred Acre Wood

Back Stamp	Doulton Number	Price			
		U.S. $	Can. $	U.K. £	Aust. $
Doulton	WP 17	225.00	300.00	125.00	300.00

WP 18
WINNIE THE POOH™ AND THE PRESENT

Designer:	Graham Tongue
Height:	3 ¾", 9.5 cm
Colour:	Yellow and brown
Issued:	1999 to the present
Series:	Winnie the Pooh and Friends from the One Hundred Acre Wood

Back Stamp	Doulton Number	Price			
		U.S. $	Can. $	U.K. £	Aust. $
Doulton	WP 18	35.00	70.00	22.00	80.00

WP 19
WINNIE THE POOH™ AND THE FAIR SIZED BASKET

Designer:	Graham Tongue
Height:	2 ¾", 7.0 cm
Colour:	Yellow and brown
Issued:	1999 to the present
Series:	Winnie the Pooh and Friends from the One Hundred Acre Wood

Back Stamp	Doulton Number	Price			
		U.S. $	Can. $	U.K. £	Aust. $
Doulton	WP 19	50.00	95.00	30.00	95.00

WP 20
THE MORE IT SNOWS, TIDDLYPOM

Designer:	Shane Ridge
Height:	3 ¼", 8.3 cm
Colour:	Yellow and red
Issued:	1999 to the present
Series:	Winnie the Pooh and Friends from the One Hundred Acre Wood

Back Stamp	Doulton Number	Price			
		U.S. $	Can. $	U.K. £	Aust. $
Doulton	WP 20	50.00	95.00	30.00	95.00

WP 21
SUMMER'S DAY PICNIC

Designer:	Warren Platt
Length:	2 ½", 5.7 cm
Colour:	Blue , yellow and green
Issued:	1998 in a limited edition of 5,000
Series:	1. Tableau
	2. Winnie the Pooh and Friends from the One Hundred Acre Wood

Back Stamp	Doulton Number	Price			
		U.S. $	Can. $	U.K. £	Aust. $
Doulton	WP 21	250.00	375.00	150.00	350.00

WP 22
I'VE FOUND SOMEBODY JUST LIKE ME

Designer:	Martyn Alcock
Length:	5 ¼", 13.3 cm
Colour:	Yellow, black, blue and white
Issued:	1999 in a limited edition of 5,000
Series:	1. Tableau
	2. Winnie the Pooh and Friends from the One Hundred Acre Wood

Back Stamp	Doulton Number	Price			
		U.S. $	Can. $	U.K. £	Aust. $
Doulton	WP 22	175.00	250.00	100.00	275.00

WIND IN THE WILLOWS

AW1
TOAD™

Designer:	Harry Sales
Modeller:	David Lyttleton
Height:	3 ½", 8.9 cm
Colour:	Green toad, yellow waistcoat and trousers, white shirt, red bowtie
Issued:	1987 - 1989

Back Stamp	Beswick Number	Price			
		U.S. $	Can. $	U.K. £	Aust. $
AW1	2942	100.00	150.00	60.00	125.00

AW2
BADGER™

Designer:	Harry Sales
Modeller:	David Lyttleton
Height:	3", 7.6 cm
Colour:	Black and white badger, salmon dressing gown
Issued:	1987 - 1989

Back Stamp	Beswick Number	Price			
		U.S. $	Can. $	U.K. £	Aust. $
AW2	2940	80.00	125.00	50.00	125.00

AW3
RATTY™

Designer:	Harry Sales
Modeller:	David Lyttleton
Height:	3 ½", 8.9 cm
Colour:	Blue dungarees, white shirt
Issued:	1987 - 1989

Back Stamp	Beswick Number	Price			
		U.S. $	Can. $	U.K. £	Aust. $
AW3	2941	85.00	150.00	50.00	125.00

AW4
MOLE™

Designer:	Harry Sales
Modeller:	David Lyttleton
Height:	3", 7.6 cm
Colour:	Dark grey mole, brown dressing gown
Issued:	1987 - 1989

Back Stamp	Beswick Number	Price U.S. $	Can. $	U.K. £	Aust. $
AW4	2939	100.00	150.00	60.00	125.00

AW5
PORTLY™
(Otter)

Designer:	Unknown
Modeller:	Alan Maslankowski
Height:	2 ¾", 7.0 cm
Colour:	Brown otter, blue dungarees, green and yellow jumper, green shoes
Issued:	1988 - 1989

Back Stamp	Beswick Number	Price U.S. $	Can. $	U.K. £	Aust. $
AW5	3065	200.00	300.00	125.00	250.00

AW6
WEASEL GAMEKEEPER™

Designer:	Unknown
Modeller:	Alan Maslankowski
Height:	4", 10.1 cm
Colour:	Brown weasel, green jacket, trousers and cap, yellow waistcoat
Issued:	1988 - 1989

Back Stamp	Beswick Number	Price U.S. $	Can. $	U.K. £	Aust. $
AW6	3076	200.00	300.00	125.00	250.00

INDICES

ALPHABETICAL INDEX

MODEL NUMBER INDEX

3200	Gentleman Mouse Made a Bow
3219	Foxy Reading Country News
3220	Lady Mouse Made a Curtsey
3234	Benjamin Wakes Up
3242	Peter and the Red Pocket Handkerchief, First Version, First Variation
3251	Miss Dormouse
3252	Pigling Eats His Porridge
3257	Christmas Stocking
3278	Mrs Rabbit Cooking
3280	Ribby and the Patty Pan
3288	Hunca Munca Spills the Beads
3317	Benjamin Ate a Lettuce Leaf
3319	And This Pig Had None
3325	No More Twist
3356	Peter Rabbit, Second Version, First Variation
3372	Mr. Jeremy Fisher, Second Version, First Variation
3373	Jemima Puddle-Duck, Second Version, First Variation
3398	Mrs Rabbit, Third Version
3403	Benjamin Bunny, Fourth Version, First Variation
3405	Tom Kitten, Second Version, First Variation
3437	Mrs Tiggy-Winkle, Second Version, First Variation
3449	Tailor of Gloucester, Second Version, Second Variation
3450	Foxy Whiskered Gentleman, Second Version
3473	Peter in Bed
3506	Mr. McGregor, First Version
3506/2	Mr. McGregor, Second Version
3533	Peter Ate a Radish
3591	Peter With Postbag
3592	Peter and the Red Pocket Handkerchief, Second Version
3597	Peter With Daffodil
3646	Mrs Rabbit and Peter
3672	Mrs Rabbit and the Four Bunnies
3719	Tom Kitten in the Rockery
3739	Peter Rabbit Gardening
3766	Hiding from the Cat
3786	Jemima and Her Ducklings
3789	Mrs. Tiggy-Winkle Washing
3790	Ginger and Pickles
3792	Mittens, Tom Kitten and Moppet
3867	Mrs. Tiggy-Winkle and Lucie
3888	Sweet Peter Rabbit
PG1092	Jemima Puddle-Duck, First Version, Second Variation
PG1098	Peter Rabbit, First Version, Third Variation
PG1100	Tom Kitten, First Version, Third Variation
PG1105	Benjamin Bunny, Third Version, Second Variation
PG1107	Mrs Tiggy-Winkle, First Version, Third Variation
PG2584	Hunca Munca Sweeping, First Version, Second Variation
PG —	Hunca Munca Sweeping, Second Version
PG3373	Jemima Puddle-Duck, Second Version, Second Variation
PG3398	Mrs. Rabbit, Third Version, Second Variation
PG3242	Peter and the Red Pocket Handkerchief, First Version, Second Variation
PG3356	Peter Rabbit, Second Version, Second Variation
PG3403	Benjamin Bunny, Fourth Version, Second Variation
PG3437	Mrs Tiggy-Winkle, Second Version, Second Variation
PG3450	Foxy Whiskered Gentleman, Second Version, Second Variation
PG3592	Peter and the Red Pocket Handkerchief, Second Version, Second Variation
PG5190	Peter and the Red Pocket Handkerchief, First Version, Second Variation

Jugs

3088	Jemima Puddle-Duck
2960	Mr.Jeremy Fisher
3102	Mrs. Tiggy-Winkle
2959	Old Mr. Brown
3006	Peter Rabbit
3103	Tom Kitten

Plaques

2082	Jemima Puddle-Duck
2594	Jemima Puddle-Duck with Foxy Whiskered Gentleman
2685	Mrs. Tittlemouse
2083	Peter Rabbit, First Version
2650	Peter Rabbit, Second Version
2085	Tom Kitten

Stands

2295	Display stand
1531	Tree Lamp Base

Studio Sculptures

SS1	Timmy Willie
SS2	Flopsy Bunnies
SS3	Mr. Jeremy Fisher
SS4	Peter Rabbit
SS11	Mrs. Tiggy Winkle
SS26	Yock Yock (In the Tub)
SS27	Peter Rabbit (In the Watering Can)

BEDTIME CHORUS

1801	Pianist
1802	Piano
1803	Cat - Singing
1804	Boy without Spectacles
1805	Boy with Spectacles
1824	Dog - Singing
1825	Boy with Guitar
1826	Girl with Harp

BESWICK BEARS

BB001	William
BB002	Billy
BB003	Harry
BB004	Bobby
BB005	James
BB006	Susie
BB007	Angela
BB008	Charlotte
BB009	Sam
BB010	Lizzy
BB011	Emily
BB012	Sarah

BRAMBLY HEDGE

DBH1	Poppy Eyebright
DBH2	Mr Apple
DBH3	Mrs. Apple
DBH4	Lord Woodmouse
DBH5	Lady Woodmouse
DBH6	Dusty Dogwood
DBH7	Wilfred Toadflax
DBH8	Primrose Woodmouse
DBH9	Old Mrs Eyebright
DBH10A	Mr. Toadflax, First Version
DBH10B	Mr. Toadflex, Second Version
DBH10C	Mr. Toadflex, Third Version
DBH11	Mrs. Toadflax
DBH12	Catkin
DBH13	Old Vole
DBH14	Basil
DBH15	Mrs. Crustybread
DBH16	Clover
DBH17	Teasel
DBH18	Store Stump Money Box
DBH19	Lily Weaver
DBH20	Flax Weaver
DBH21	Conker
DBH22	Primrose Entertains
DBH23	Wilfred Entertains
DBH24	Mr. Saltapple
DBH25	Mrs. Saltapple
DBH26	Dusty and Baby

THE CAT'S CHORUS

CC1	Purrfect Pitch
CC2	Calypso Kitten
CC3	One Cool Cat
CC4	Ratcatcher Bilk
CC5	Trad Jazz Tom
CC6	Catwalking Bass
CC7	Feline Flamenco
CC8	Bravura Brass
CC9	Fat Cat
CC10	Glam Guitar

COMPTON & WOODHOUSE

—	Archie
—	Benjamin
—	Bertie
—	Henry

COUNTRY COUSINS

PM2101	Sweet Suzie "Thank You"
PM2102	Peter "Once Upon A Time"
PM2103	Harry "A New Home for Fred"
PM2104	Michael "Happily Ever After"
PM2105	Bertram "Ten Out of Ten"
PM2106	Leonardo "Practice Makes Perfect"
PM2107	Lily "Flowers Picked Just For You"
PM2108	Patrick "This Ways Best"
PM2109	Jamie "Hurrying Home"
PM2111	Mum and Lizzie "Let's Get Busy"
PM2112	Molly and Timmy "Picnic Time"
PM2113	Polly and Sarah "Good News!"
PM2114	Bill and Ted "Working Together"
PM2115	Jack and Daisy "How Does Your Garden Grow"
PM2116	Alison and Debbie "Friendship is Fun"
PM2119	Robert and Rosie "Perfect Partners"
PM2120	Sammy "Treasure Hunting"

DAVID HAND'S ANIMALAND

1148	Dinkum Platypus
1150	Zimmy Lion
1151	Felia
1152	Ginger Nutt
1153	Hazel Nutt
1154	Oscar Ostrich
1155	Dusty Mole
1156	Loopy Hare

ENGLISH COUNTRY FOLK

ECF 1	Huntsman Fox
ECF 2	Fisherman Otter
ECF 3	Gardener Rabbit, First Variation
ECF 4	Gentleman Pig, First Variation
ECF 5	Shepherd Sheepdog
ECF 6	Hiker Badger, First Variation
ECF 7	Mrs Rabbit Baking, First Variation
ECF 8	The Lady Pig, First Variation
ECF 9	Hiker Badger, Second Variation
ECF 10	Gentleman Pig, Second Variation
ECF 11	The Lady Pig, Second Variation
ECF 12	Gardener Rabbit, Second Variation
ECF 13	Mrs. Rabbit Baking, Second Variation

ENID BLYTON

Noddy Collection

3676	Big Ears
3678	Noddy
3679	Mr. Plod
3770	Tessie Bear

EXPRESS NEWSPAPERS PLC

Rupert Bear

2694	Rupert Bear, Style One
2710	Algy Pug
2711	Pong Ping
2720	Bill Badger
2779	Rupert Bear Snowballing
—	Rupert Bear, Style Two
—	Podgy Pug

HANNA-BARBERA

The Flintstones

3577	Pebbles
3579	Bamm Bamm
3581	Top Cat
3583	Wilma Flintstone
3584	Betty Rubble
3586	Choo-Choo
3587	Barney Rubble
3588	Fred Flintstone
3590	Dino

Top Cat

3624	Fancy Fancy
3627	Benny
3671	Officer Dibble
3673	Spook
3674	Brain

JANE HISSEY

Old Bear

OB4601	Old Bear
OB4602	Time For Bed
OB4603	Bramwell Brown Had A Good Idea
OB4604	Don't Worry Rabbit
OB4605	The Long Red Scarf
OB4606	Waiting For Snow
OB4607	The Snowflake Biscuits
OB4608	Welcome Home, Old Bear
OB4609	Ruff's Prize
OB4610	Time For A Hug Me Tight
OB4611	Don't Forget Old Bear
OB4612	Hold on Tight
OB4613	Resting with Cat

JOAN WALSH ANGLUND

2272	Anglund Boy
2293	Anglund Girl with Doll
2317	Anglund Girl with Flowers

KITTY MACBRIDE

2526	A Family Mouse
2527	A Double Act
2528	The Racegoer
2529	A Good Read
2530	Lazybones
2531	A Snack
2532	Strained Relations
2533	Just Good Friends
2565	The Ring
2566	Guilty Sweethearts
2589	All I Do is Think of You

LITTLE LIKABLES

LL1	Family Gathering (Hen and Two Chicks)
LL2	Watching the World Go By (Frog)
LL3	Hide and Sleep (Pig and Two Piglets)
LL4	My Pony (Pony)
LL5	On Top of the World (Elephant)
LL6	Treat Me Gently (Fawn
LL7	Out at Last (Duckling)
LL8	Cats Chorus (Cats)

LITTLE LOVABLES

LL1	Happy Birthday
LL2	I Love You
LL3	God Loves Me
LL4	Just For You
LL5	To Mother
LL6	Congratulations
LL7	Passed
LL8	Happy Birthday
LL9	I Love You
LL10	God Loves Me
LL11	Just For You
LL12	To Mother
LL13	Congratulations
LL14	Passed
LL15	Happy Birthday
LL16	I Love You
LL17	God Loves Me
LL18	Just For You
LL19	To Mother
LL20	Congratulations
LL21	Passed
LL22	(No Name)
LL23	(No Name)
LL24	(No Name)
LL25	(No Name)
LL26	(No Name)
LL27	(No Name)
LL28	(No Name)
LL29	To Daddy
LL30	Merry Christmas
LL31	Good Luck
LL32	Get Well Soon
LL33	Please
LL34	Please
LL35	Prototype for I Love Beswick
LL36	I Love Beswick

NORMAN THELWELL

Earthenware Series, 1981-1989

2704A	An Angel on Horseback, First Variation
2704B	An Angel on Horseback, Second Variation
2769A	Kick-Start, First Variation
2769B	Kick-Start, Second Variation
2789A	Pony Express, First Variation
2789B	Pony Express, Second Variation

Resin Studio Sculptures, 1985-1985

SS7A	I Forgive You, First Variation
SS7B	I Forgive You, Second Variation
SS12A	Early Bath, First Variation
SS12B	Early Bath, Second Variation

PADDINGTON BEAR CO. LTD.

PB1	Paddington at the Station
PB2	Paddington Bakes a Cake
PB3	Paddington Decorating
PB4	Paddington Surfing
PB5	Paddington Gardening
PB6	Paddington Bathtime
PB7	Paddington the Golfer
PB8	Paddington the Musician
PB9	Paddington at Christmas Time
PB10	Paddington Marmalade Sandwich
PB11	Paddington Going to Bed
PB12	Paddington the Fisherman

THE PIG PROMENADE

PP1	John the Conductor (Vietnamese Pot Bellied Pig)
PP2	Matthew the Trumpet Player (Large White Pig)
PP3	David the Flute Player (Tamworth Pig)
PP4	Andrew the Cymbal Player (Gloucester Old Spotted Pig)
PP5	Daniel the Violinist (Saddleback Pig)
PP6	Michael the Bass Drum Player (Large Black Pig)
PP7	James The Triangle Player (Tamworth Piglet)
PP8	Richard the French Horn Player
PP9	Christopher the Guitar Player
PP10	George
PP11	Thomas
PP12	Benjamin

ST. TIGGYWINKLES

TW1	Henry Hedgehog (Standing)
TW2	Harry Hedgehog (Sitting)
TW3	Fred Fox
TW4	Bob Badger
TW5	Rosie Rabbit
TW6	Sarah Squirrel
TW7	Daniel Duck
TW8	Oliver Owl
TW9	Friends
TW10	A Helping Hand
TW11	Deborah Dormouse
TW12	Monty Mole
TW13	Franchesca Fawn

THE SNOWMAN GIFT COLLECTION

Figurines

DS1	James, Style One
DS2	The Snowman, Style One
DS3	Stylish Snowman
DS4	Thank You Snowman
DS5	Snowman Magic Music Box
DS6	Cowboy Snowman
DS7	Highland Snowman
DS8	Lady Snowman
DS9	Bass Drummer Snowman
DS10	Flautist Snowman
DS11	Violinist Snowman
DS12	Pianist Snowman
DS13	Snowman's Piano
DS14	Cymbal Player Snowman
DS15	Drummer Snowman
DS16	Trumpeter Snowman
DS17	Cellist Snowman
DS18	Snowman Musical Box
DS19	Snowman Money Box
DS20	The Snowman Tobogganing
DS21	The Snowman Skiing
DS22	The Snowman Snowballing
DS23	Building the Snowman
—	James, Style Two
—	The Snowman, Style Two
—	Dancing in the Snow

Character Jug

D6972	Snowman Miniature

THUNDERBIRDS

3337	Lady Penelope
3339	Brains
3344	Scott Tracy
3345	Virgil Tracy
3346	Parker
3348	The Hood

266

268

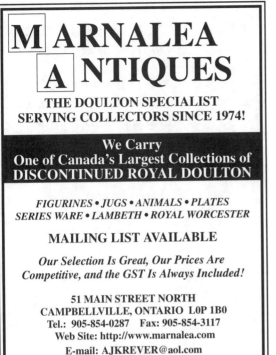

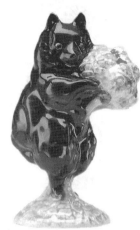

ROYAL DOULTON IS OUR SPECIALTY!

We Buy ♦ We Sell ♦ We Appraise

Colonial House Features the Largest Selection of Current and Discontinued Items in the Following Lines:

- ✦ OLD & NEW ROYAL DOULTON FIGURES & CHARACTER JUGS
- ✦ HUMMELS
- ✦ DAVID WINTER COTTAGES
- ✦ DEPT. 56 COTTAGES AND SNOWBABIES

- ✦ ROYAL WORCESTER
- ✦ WEE FOREST FOLK
- ✦ WALT DISNEY CLASSICS
- ✦ SWAROVSKI CRYSTAL
- ✦ LLADRÓ
- ✦ LILLIPUT LANE

Send for our latest product catalogue!

Colonial House of Collectibles

We Carry Current and Discontinued Beanie Babies!

WE DO MAIL ORDER

Monday to Saturday
10 a.m. to 5 p.m.
or by appointment

182 Front Street,
Berea, OH 44017
Tel.: (440) 826-4169 or
(800) 344-9299
Fax: (440) 826-0839
E-mail: yworrey@aol.com